A DESERT FEAST

The Southwest Center Series

Joseph C. Wilder, Editor

CELEBRATING TUCSON'S CULINARY HERITAGE

A DESERT FEAST

CAROLYN NIETHAMMER
FOREWORD BY JONATHAN MABRY

THE UNIVERSITY OF
ARIZONA PRESS
TUCSON

TUCSON
CITY OF GASTRONOMY

The University of Arizona Press
www.uapress.arizona.edu

ISBN-13: 978-0-8165-3889-8 (paper)

Cover and interior design by Leigh McDonald
Typeset by Sara Thaxton in Arno Pro 11/15 (text) and Enlow WF and Payson WF (display)

Library of Congress Cataloging-in-Publication Data
Names: Niethammer, Carolyn J., author. | Mabry, Jonathan B., 1961– writer of foreword.
Title: A desert feast : celebrating Tucson's culinary heritage / Carolyn Niethammer ; foreword by Jonathan Mabry.
Other titles: Southwest Center series.
Description: Tucson : University of Arizona Press, 2020. | Series: Southwest Center series | Includes bibliographical references and index.
Identifiers: LCCN 2020015373 | ISBN 9780816538898 (paperback)
Subjects: LCSH: Gastronomy—Arizona—Tucson. | Cooking—Arizona—Tucson. | Natural foods—Arizona—Tucson. | Tucson
    (Ariz.)—Social life and customs.
Classification: LCC TX633 .N54 2020 | DDC 641.59791/776—dc23
LC record available at https://lccn.loc.gov/2020015373

Printed in the United States of America
♾ This paper meets the requirements of ANSI/NISO Z39.48-1992 (Permanence of Paper).

CONTENTS

Foreword by Jonathan Mabry   vii

Acknowledgments   xi

Introduction: Why Tucson Is a UNESCO City of Gastronomy   3

Prehistoric and Early History of Wild Foods: Eating Off the Land   7

Traditional Early Agriculture: 4,000 Years in the Fields of the Santa Cruz Basin   23

Europeans, Mexicans, and Chinese: Bringing New Foods and Traditions   41

Gardening in the Desert: Growing Your Own Vegetables, Tucson Style   65

Small-Scale Commercial Agriculture: Contracting Tucson's Foodshed   93

Tucson's Artisan Food Producers   135

Our Sonoran Culinary Heritage—It's a Tucson Thing!   157

Food Justice   185

Epilogue. In the Coronavirus Crisis: How Tucson United to Feed the City   205

Index   209

FOREWORD

IT IS USUALLY IN RETROSPECT that I have recognized evidence of watersheds in Tucson's long food history, revealed by archaeological investigations. In the year 2000, my team uncovered house depressions, hearths, and storage pits of an ancient Native American settlement buried in the Santa Cruz River floodplain just west of downtown Tucson. It was at the base of the hill known as Sentinel Peak, or "A" Mountain—a site long considered Tucson's birthplace. The findings were revealed in an older layer of the floodplain, after we had discovered and documented traces of more recent farming, irrigation, and habitation activities in that same area, and then kept digging deeper. When we uncovered the features, we suspected they were important, but in our line of work we don't always fully recognize the significance of physical finds until the digging is done and the analyses of the finds begin.

We did not know that we had found some of the oldest evidence of agriculture and canals in the United States until months later, when we saw the results of radiocarbon dating of tiny fragments of charred maize (corn) recovered from the deepest cultural features. And a few years earlier, when my team found fragments of undecorated ceramic vessels at another early settlement in the floodplain just northwest of downtown, we did not know they represented the first use of pottery for seed storage and cooking in this region—leaps forward in food technology—until we obtained radiocarbon dates centered on AD 150 on fragments of charred maize from the same contexts.

In contrast, we immediately recognized evidence of the introduction of Old World crops and livestock as soon as we started finding charred wheat seeds, peach pits, and bones of cattle, sheep, and goats in another area below Sentinel Peak, where we knew a Spanish colonial period mission community had once been, and in a corner of the Spanish colonial fort we found miraculously preserved beneath a downtown parking lot (later analyses also identified wheat seeds from these sites). And when we excavated a downtown block demolished for a new bus station, we quickly understood that the abundant metal cans and glass bottles, and rarer shells of pickled oysters and trash of other exotic foods, were evidence of dramatic changes in household eating and material consumption habits immediately after the 1880 arrival of the railroad in Tucson connected the formerly isolated and self-sufficient oasis community to national and international markets.

As a co-leader of the two-year effort for Tucson to be designated a United Nations Educational, Scientific, and Cultural Organization (UNESCO) City of Gastronomy, I also saw up close the most recent turning point in our food history. In 2015, when Tucson became the first UNESCO City of Gastronomy in the United States, it joined the UNESCO Creative Cities Network (UCCN). As of 2020 the network is comprised of 246 cities in more than eighty countries, including nine U.S. cities. Founded in 2004, the UCCN is an association of urban areas around the world designated in recognition of their exemplary efforts in using cultural heritage and creativity for sustainable development. A city may apply for recognition in one of seven categories: crafts and folk art, design, gastronomy, literature, film, media arts, and music. Creative Cities use their designations to create sustainable futures for their communities and to support the cultural producers of their internationally recognized heritage. They also exchange knowledge and best practices with other cities in the network.

UNESCO defines *gastronomy* more broadly than just the cooking style of a particular area, extending it to food traditions as living cultural heritage. This means that designation of Tucson and its Southern Arizona foodshed as a UNESCO City of Gastronomy acknowledges not only the international significance of the long agricultural history documented by archaeologists but also the "universal value" of the "intangible cultural heritage" of our traditional foods and the traditional food knowledge and cultural practices, or foodways, associated with them.

Tucson's application to UNESCO highlighted that we have the longest agricultural history of any city in the United States, extending back more than 4,000 years. It also described our 300-year tradition of orchards, vineyards, and livestock ranching, and noted that we have more foods listed in the international Slow Food Ark of Taste catalog growing within 100 miles than any other city in North America. Here, heritage ingredients are used in both traditional and contemporary dishes and food products, and they create a distinctive "desert terroir."

It explained how Tucson's cuisine developed through the layering and blending of prehistoric native wild foods and preparation techniques, ancient crops arriving from Mesoamerica, introductions of plants and livestock from the Old World during the Spanish colonial period, ingredients and dishes brought by a sequence of later-arriving cultural groups, and contemporary culinary innovations using local heritage ingredients. Within this culturally layered cuisine we have more than 120 heritage food ingredients, including 39 important wild-plant foods; 72 native, Mesoamerican, and Old World crops; 7 wild-animal foods; and 5 domesticated-animal foods.

In addition to our unparalleled food heritage and distinctive cuisine, the application described:

- The importance of the food sector of our local economy, in which food businesses employ 39,000 people and provide 14 percent of all jobs in the city, and 63 percent of the 2,500 restaurants and bars in the metro area are locally owned rather than national chains (compared to the national average of 41 percent).

- The important work of five seed banks conserving more than 2,000 varieties of desert-adapted seeds, and how much of this food biodiversity is freely accessible to everyone through our public library system's seed library, and free or discounted for food-insecure refugees, Native Americans, and low-income community members through fourteen local organizations.
- The University of Arizona's international leadership in food research and education through multiple degree programs and eight research centers focused on agriculture, food, and nutrition.
- The diversity of culinary training programs that provide higher-education degrees or free job training for people facing hiring barriers.
- The extensive network of programs for hunger relief that includes thirty-two food banks, pantries, soup kitchens, and mobile outlets, and the collaboration of the Community Food Bank of Southern Arizona with more than 300 nonprofits, agencies, and faith-based groups provides 65,000 meals per day and serves 190,000 individuals and families every year.
- How the Food Bank also provides education in nutrition, gardening, cooking, and food business development for 20,000 people annually.
- The grassroots food activism of more than twenty nonprofits and alliances that address food justice, hunger, and food insecurity issues in our community.
- Recent policies and revisions of regulations for urban agriculture and food service by city and county governments to make it easier to grow, sell, and serve food in the urban area.

The nonprofit Tucson City of Gastronomy is charged with managing the UNESCO designation. It raises awareness of the range of community food assets and the many grassroots organizations working for food justice, incubates policy recommendations and helps lead planning for a more sustainable and resilient urban food system, provides business training for heritage food entrepreneurs, and certifies restaurants that cook with locally sourced and heritage ingredients and use socially and environmentally responsible business practices, as well as other programs.

The economic impacts of the designation have been significant for Tucson. After a big media splash during the first year of designation, related media coverage has continued at a fast pace, promoting tourism to Tucson and southern Arizona and lauding our unique food heritage and vibrant food scene. Coverage highlighting the designation has included national media outlets such as the *New York Times*, the *Chicago Tribune*, NPR, *USA Today*, *National Geographic*, *Food & Wine*, and TripAdvisor. The regional tourism agency Visit Tucson credits the UNESCO designation as *the* major factor behind an increase in free media coverage of Tucson from $5 million per year prior to the designation to $30 million per year by 2018, a 30 percent growth in lodging occupancy rates between 2016 and 2018, and a 10 percent increase in tourist spending and creation of more than 2,000 new hospitality jobs in 2018 alone. That year, tourists spent $84 million in Tucson's restaurants.

Boosted by an increase in gastronomic tourism and restaurant spending by visitors and locals, Tucson's culinary economy is thriving, as reflected in an 8 percent increase in food service permits for restaurants in the first year following designation. Demand for new local food products and opportunities for new food businesses have has also risen since the UNESCO designation. A 2019 compilation of locally made artisanal foods listed more than 150 unique regional food products by more than 50 artisans. Approximately a quarter of them are new food products or new food businesses since the designation. Other economic impacts of the designation include a 30 percent increase in annual food and drink festivals and expansions of many long-running culinary festivals.

While the designation has become another reason for tourists to visit, a driver for business revenues and jobs, and a key talking point to lure high-wage-paying companies to locate here, the noneconomic impacts of the UNESCO designation are equally important. The designation has also become a point of pride for locals, broadening the community's notions of what aspects of heritage should be valued and preserved, shifting from the previous focus on historic buildings, neighborhoods, and other physical things and places to also include the community's food traditions. Tucson's heritage foods are newly perceived as shared patrimony, elements of identity, and economic assets all at once.

Whether you are a local or a visitor, this book written by an award-winning author and authority on cooking with wild desert foods is your guide to Tucson's food heritage, distinctive cuisine, and many other reasons why Tucson and its southern Arizona foodshed earned the first UNESCO City of Gastronomy designation in the United States. To learn more about this and other turning points in Tucson's deep history of food, and to find current information on places, events, tours, and volunteer opportunities to experience our international City of Gastronomy, visit tucson.cityofgastronomy.org.

Jonathan Mabry, Executive Director
Tucson City of Gastronomy

ACKNOWLEDGMENTS

P UTTING TOGETHER THE NOMINATION PETITION for the UNESCO City of Gastronomy designation was a community project, and this book, which tells the culinary history of Tucson over 10,000 years, has also had the enthusiastic help of many in the community. The book could not have been produced in its present form without their assistance. Tucsonans are excited by the honor Tucson received and the story behind it. Actually, make that stories, for the long food history of the Santa Cruz Valley is thousands of years of stories of how people managed to feed themselves in this corner of the Sonoran Desert.

Tucsonans sat for long interviews recalling past food- and history-related events, they recounted their archaeological projects, patiently led me around their farms, and invited me into their class-rooms. They demonstrated how they mix spices, brew beer, and cook heritage ingredients. Members of the community have been especially generous with top-quality photographs. You can see this by the large number of photo credits in the captions. Maribel Alvarez, Erin Brown, Martha A. Burgess, Mike Christy, Dena Cowan, Emily Derks, Tim Fuller, David Gilmore, Bill Hatch, Jeaninne Kaufer, Michelle Kilander, Steven Meckler, Chris Richards, Brian Schutmaat, Guy Shovlin, Marty Smith, Bill Steen, Helga Teiwes, Henry Wallace, and P. K. Weis (Southwest Photobank) were all in the right place at the right time and their photos often say what words cannot.

My friend Roger C. Wolf plunged enthusiastically in the new-to-him field of food photography guided by his neighbor, professional food photographer Scott Payne. Though Roger took the photo-graphs credited to him, they are both responsible for many of the delicious images. (Pictures without a photo credit were taken by me.)

Much of Tucson culinary history happened before photography was invented, but talented artist Robert Ciaccio has the ability to bring to life village and agricultural scenes that took place thousands of years ago.

Although I have written about the food of the Southwest for five decades, much of the information about Tucson's culinary history was new to me. I am indebted to Wendy Hodgson for her help on edible wild plants (and elucidating the difference between a spine and a thorn). Archaeologists Suzanne Fish, Homer Thiel, and Jonathan Mabry generously read the material on early agriculture, the Hohokam, and the early Spanish period, corrected mistakes, and made suggestions for further reading. Gary Nabhan has been collecting community data on food consumption and production and has published lists and papers to help us understand what is happening in the field.

My friend Martha A. Burgess, who has a decades-long history with wild and local foods, was always ready to answer the phone or email when I was stuck or trying to recall an obscure fact about something that happened thirty years ago.

The Tucson Chinese community provided background on their part in Tucson's history. I built on Dena Cowan's extensive research on the vegetables the early Chinese farmers grew for the market and for their own use. Frances Wong Tom shared family photos.

The help of the librarians at the Arizona Historical Society was essential in unearthing documents and photographs.

I thank Joe Wilder, former director of the University of Arizona Southwest Center, for enthusiastically agreeing to add the book to the distinguished Southwest Center Series, and Jeffrey Banister, the current director, for picking up the baton. Jonathan Mabry, chairman of Tucson's City of Gastronomy committee, supported the project through the four years it took to work out the issues and write the text.

Generous financial support came from the Southwestern Foundation for Education and Historical Preservation, the Marshall Foundation, and the University of Arizona Southwest Center. These funds were essential to producing the book in its current form. I thank Ann-Eve Pederson and Jane McCollum for their encouragement during the granting process.

I thank my editor, Kristen Buckles, and my copyeditor, Debra Makay, for being willing to embark on our second book together, and for going way beyond what might be expected. Thanks also to Stacey Wujcik, who brought calm whenever twenty-first-century technology threatened to overwhelm me. My thanks also to the whole production team. Leigh McDonald's vibrant design and Sara Thaxton's supporting typography elevated the book's story. The folks in the University of Arizona Press marketing department offered a level of help few authors get these days.

My husband, Ford, one of the most thorough editors I know, read the manuscript several times and did what thorough editors do. When I was running out of time, he also took on the entire beer section and had fun doing it. How lucky I am to have him as a creative and life partner.

A DESERT FEAST

Traditional Tucson food relies heavily on Sonoran-style dishes such as (from left) tacos, tamales, and chimichangas.

INTRODUCTION

WHY TUCSON IS A UNESCO CITY OF GASTRONOMY

T UCSON BOASTS THAT IT HAS the best 23 square miles of Mexican food north of the border. No one has doubted that claim. But are our plates of fish tacos and enchiladas swimming in spicy mole sauce enough to earn the designation of UNESCO City of Gastronomy?

The honor is about much more than gourmet food and white-tablecloth restaurants. It is about our complete food system—traditional and heritage agriculture, local food-based businesses, and the overall food economy from farm to table. Locals know it is about the creaminess of summer's first batch of green corn tamales and the sweetness of an orange picked in January and peeled and eaten right next to the tree. It's about children learning about nutrition by eating vegetables they grew in school gardens using the same varieties of seeds grown in our valley for hundreds of years. And in our low-income areas, it's about people joining to make sure hungry people have access to food.

As described by a UNESCO officer, gastronomy is one of the most universal cultural and creative practices around the world. It is not only an inseparable part of history and tradition and a strong contributor to social identity and inclusion but also an inherent carrier of cultural heritage, both tangible and intangible. By bringing farmers and food producers together, it is a link between urban and rural areas.

Jonathan Mabry, an archaeologist and the lead author of the UNESCO application, brings it all together succinctly: "Our city doesn't taste like anywhere else," he says. "It's a combination of recipes and ingredients from a long and complex culture."

The agricultural part of Tucson's culture stretches back four millennia to a time when early farmers dug irrigation ditches to bring water from the Santa Cruz River to the rich alluvial soils. Mabry found evidence of those canals during an archaeological dig at the base of "A" Mountain. These early agriculturalists grew corn, squash, and beans, the same foods that are grown today a few miles south at the San Xavier Co-op Farm and by many gardeners citywide. Residents and visitors can get a glimpse of Tucson's food history at the Mission Garden, a 4-acre living agricultural museum at the site of a Spanish colonial farm and orchard.

Typical modern Tucson cuisine was "fusion" food long before the word became nationally trendy. It relies heavily on the past, blending the influences of Native American, northern Mexican or Sonoran, mission-era Mediterranean, and American ranch-style cowboy food traditions. This is true in both home kitchens and restaurants.

In fact, independently owned restaurants and other local food businesses represent one of Tucson's largest and fastest-growing economic sectors. More than 1,200 restaurants and drinking establishments employ more than 30,000 people; when grocery stores are included, food businesses provide 14 percent of all jobs in the city. Of the total number of food businesses in the city, almost two-thirds are locally owned. Frequently, these are family businesses with funding obtained from family investment. They begin with a food truck or a taco cart before scaling up to a brick-and-mortar restaurant. While the grown children might work the front of the house, Mama and Nana are in the back making the sauces and cooking the family recipes that draw in customers looking for authentic flavor. And it's not only the women. In two longtime Tucson food businesses, it's the papas that hold and execute the secret formulas.

To support the local food industry, Pima Community College offers degrees in several food industry and culinary programs, with courses in recipe and menu planning, preparing and cooking foods, supervising and training kitchen assistants, managing food supplies and kitchen resources, food presentation, and a variety of cuisines and culinary techniques.

Responding to an interest from students in food-related careers, the University of Arizona in 2018 developed two new undergraduate degrees. Students seeking a bachelor's in food studies will learn about the social, political, economic, and environmental dimensions of food and will be prepared to help resolve complex food issues such as food insecurity, food deserts, and food and environmental sustainability. Those earning a degree in nutrition and food systems will deal specifically with regional food issues such as food production challenges in an arid desert region and incorporating the cultural influences that shape the local cuisine.

Taking advantage of Tucson's heritage ingredients and flavors, local entrepreneurs produce more than 150 distinctive food and beverage products including beer. Gary Paul Nabhan, who keeps track of such statistics, writes that "the Metro-Tucson food economy has more wild food plant products and desert-adapted heirlooms in it than any other American city of comparable size. . . . They help generate livelihoods with livable wages for Tucson residents of many cultures, races, educational levels, and skill sets."

Throughout the chapters, some names appear repeatedly. That is because the effort of food production and distribution in Tucson is so collaborative.

The Mission Garden orchard is planted with cuttings taken from fruit tree varieties brought to the area by Spanish missionaries and cloned by the Kino Heritage Fruit Trees Project initiated by the

Arizona-Sonora Desert Museum. Seeds for the vegetable gardens were obtained from Native Seeds/ SEARCH, a local nonprofit seed bank that for thirty years has been collecting, increasing, and distributing desert-adapted seed varieties passed down by generations of farmers.

The Community Food Bank of Southern Arizona built school gardens, the Tucson Unified School District and other school districts planned curricula around the gardens to use in teaching science and math among other subjects, and the University of Arizona sent student interns to help maintain them. The Food Bank serves as a conduit between local farms and those schools and hospitals wanting to use local produce. Erik Stanford of Pivot Produce connects farms with restaurants.

Schools and churches broaden the reach of the Food Bank by setting up pantries in their facilities, and churches open their doors to serve the community meals prepared at the Caridad Community Kitchen from ingredients donated by Tucson businesses and individuals.

Cheri Romanoski of Cheri's Desert Harvest manages to gather more prickly pear fruit than she needs for her jams and syrups, and thus she can provide pasteurized juice to several local beer brewers. The San Xavier Co-op Farm delivers mesquite meal and other desert foods to businesses that turn them into local products.

Tucson's several dozen craft breweries experiment with local ingredients such as White Sonora wheat, chile, and prickly pear. The breweries purchase their heritage White Sonora wheat from BKW Farms in Marana, which grows it especially for them and for Don Guerra of Barrio Bread, who sources more than half of his heritage grains locally. Guerra also incorporates the spent grain from several breweries into his breads.

Other locally produced alcohol includes Whiskey del Bac made with mesquite-smoked malt. The grain left over after fermentation is delivered to E & R Pork where it becomes food for their heritage pigs.

The cooperation across the spectrum of people involved with Tucson's food is enhanced by a grassroots volunteer group called Pima County Food Alliance. The group, ranging from fourteen to sixteen members, was organized in 2011. Members are farmers, educators, dietitians, business owners, and employees of nonprofits. All share a passion for creating a more resilient, healthy, and inclusive food system. They share information and goals for food justice and have educated the public on the important aspects of the federal farm bill, advocated for the expansion of Supplemental Nutrition Assistance Program (SNAP) benefits at farmers' markets, and worked on reforming regulations so children could eat the food they produced in their school gardens.

Tucsonans love food festivals and one can be found nearly every month. At those events, restaurants and ethnic affiliation groups and gardens share their food traditions with the community.

Unfortunately, festivals and restaurant dining, even in a casual spot, aren't a frequent option for a large segment of Tucson residents. Many struggle simply to afford to purchase enough calories. One-third of children are at risk for hunger.

To address this issue and to help children learn about nutrition so they can make good choices as they mature, the Tucson Unified School District, the Community Food Bank, and the University of

Arizona have partnered to make sure that children have healthy and filling meals at school, made with locally grown produce when possible. There are even after-school snacks and supper if needed. When school is out during the summer, locations all over town provide free breakfast, lunch, and snacks. Some libraries offer after-school snacks throughout the school year.

The City of Gastronomy designation reflects the fact that many programs are in place with committed people working to combat the pockets of hunger in Tucson by focusing on rebuilding and re-localizing the city's food system. Food security is enhanced when people can grow at least some of their own food and Tucson's benevolent winter climate promotes gardening. Thousands of households maintain home gardens. Those without appropriate backyard space can participate in one of the community gardens. Children learn the value of growing their own food in school gardens and in programs at Tucson Village Farm. The Community Food Bank helps its clients learn to garden.

Among Tucson's poor are many refugees from all over the world who have been resettled here. The people have brought with them a wealth of traditional knowledge for using fruits and vegetables. A nonprofit group called Iskashitaa Refugee Network organizes the newcomers and community volunteers to glean unused produce including citrus, pomegranates, and dates. They can take it home to feed their families or get together in work parties in commercial kitchens to turn the produce into products to sell at farmers' markets. Training in food production can be a step to restaurant employment. More than two dozen ethnic restaurants run by refugees have brought the world of food to Tucson.

A more complex look at what Tucson is doing to address hunger in the community is addressed in the last several chapters of this book.

The magnitude of the problem cannot be addressed by nonprofit organizations alone. That was why then Tucson mayor Jonathan Rothschild appointed a Commission on Food Security, Heritage, and Economy to break down the barriers to improving the health of the city's vulnerable residents. It will work with the University of Arizona Center for Regional Food Studies to integrate research, community outreach, private sector opportunities, local government support, and international connections with the goal of improving food supply chains impacting Arizona and the United States / Mexico borderlands.

The following pages will explore some of these events and programs more closely and introduce you to some of the engaging Tucsonans who are coming up with new and creative ideas to celebrate our culinary heritage and make sure their fellow citizens have access to enough healthy food to enable them to fully participate in this vibrant desert city.

The scope of Tucson's food scene is much too broad to be addressed in one book of reasonable length. Some topics were touched only lightly, others passed over. The city's vibrant international restaurants and markets were not discussed at all, due not to lack of importance but to lack of space.

I did, however, feel it was worth the space to include three poems by local poets as well as the lyrics to a song celebrating our local food—together they show how seriously Tucsonans take their food!

PREHISTORIC AND EARLY HISTORY OF WILD FOODS

EATING OFF THE LAND

TAKE AN IMAGINARY TRIP WITH me, zooming back a thousand years to a small village where Fort Lowell Park now stands. We're going to peek in on a family living there in a pit house, partially underground with a roof made of brush and mud. The mother is making a porridge from mesquite meal that she ground from the pods earlier in the day in a bedrock mortar. She sifted the rough meal through a loosely woven basket and is now cooking it over a fire. It is easy to imagine that later her children might beg for a sweet treat of dried saguaro or prickly pear fruit.

Jump forward on the calendar and just last week a Tucson family might have enjoyed a weekend breakfast of mesquite pancakes or waffles with prickly pear syrup. The breakfast cook could have purchased the mesquite meal already ground or gathered the pods and had them ground and sifted by a gas-powered hammermill. Same ingredients, still relished by desert dwellers separated by a thousand years.

Newcomers to the desert surrounding Tucson, seeing nothing but cactus, thorny scrub brush, and bush-like trees, might ponder how the original inhabitants of the Tucson basin managed to feed themselves and survive for millennia. In fact, for more than 10,000 years, the Sonoran Desert has supplied the original residents and those who passed through with hundreds of edible wild plants. The number of plants used for food climbs to more than 500 if you count all the species of similar plants, such as the various agaves.

There is evidence that Paleoindians roamed through the Tucson basin as far back as 11,500 years ago. They were hunter-gatherers, moving with the seasons, eating what they could find such as cactus fruits, wild grass seeds, and game. Then about 7500 BC, the climate became warmer and drier, closer to what we have today, and the people gradually adapted and learned to eat the different plants that appeared on the landscape.

Eating a balanced diet back then involved being intimately attuned to the land and the seasons. To live well in the Tucson basin wasn't easy, but families who were industrious could usually provide for themselves. Emphasis on *usually*. Their lives were at the whim of Mother Nature, as humans have been for most of our species' existence. When times of severe drought led to famine, people ate anything with food value, even things usually considered unpalatable such as insects and bitter plants. When even those didn't provide enough calories, the population shrank due to starvation and people migrated to find food.

During years of normal rainfall, the early desert dwellers were happy with the food that the land provided them. Most people, if they have enough to eat, consider their own diet superior to that of other groups. This was certainly the case with a Tohono O'odham woman named Maria Chona who told the anthropologist Ruth Underhill in the 1930s: "To the White Man the great spirit gave peaches and grapes and wheat, but to us he gave the wild seeds and the cactus. Those are the good foods."

Modern foragers in the Sonoran Desert follow the same calendar as did the native population. Spring comes as early as February in this area. The winter rains bring soft green plants like monkey flower and watercress that grow in the shade of rocks at the edges of streams trickling with water from springs, rain, or even snow higher in the mountains. The large leaves of wild rhubarb and sharp-tasting pods of peppergrass appear in the damp sand. The delicate leaves of miner's lettuce aren't far behind. These greens provide important vitamins, antioxidants, and phytochemicals in much higher proportions than our grocery-store greens. While these plants provide an enjoyable day of foraging for us in the twenty-first century, imagine how welcome these fresh foods must have been for earlier residents after months of dried, stored provisions, which by that time were nearly exhausted and probably moldy or insect infested.

The warmth of mid-March awakens the cactus, and the spiny branches of the cholla cactus swell with flower buds. Picked when the flower petals are still tightly furled, cholla buds provide a small amount of iron but are high in calcium. The early desert dwellers gathered cholla buds in great numbers. After getting rid of the numerous spines by rolling them in rough ground with switches of creosote, they frequently baked them in rock-lined earth ovens. Those not eaten right away were dried for storage.

In cases where the people couldn't find enough flower buds, they would pick the young joints of the cactus. Cholla buds that remain on the plant turn into fruits later in the year and some varieties were also baked and eaten, but weren't as prized, tasty, or nutritious as the flower buds.

Modern-day foragers can gather cholla buds with tongs and clean them by rolling them over a screen, which grabs and removes the spines. Cleaned and dried cholla buds are available in specialty stores and online, but the price reflects the labor involved in cleaning them.

Today, cooked cholla buds, which have a bright, slightly lemony flavor and taste a little like asparagus, appear in season on the menus of some Tucson restaurants specializing in southwestern regional dishes. You will frequently find them incorporated in salads.

As cholla bud season ends, the next arrivals in nature's progression of desert foods are the new pads of the prickly pear cactus, called *nopales* in Spanish. With spines scraped off, they can be eaten

The Tohono O'odham have relished tasty and nutritious cholla buds for untold centuries. Now they are appearing in salads on trendy restaurant menus as well.

After the spring harvest, the Native people dried their extra cholla buds for storage.

The juicy fruit of the saguaro cactus ripens in the heat of the summer. Its appearance marks the beginning of the year for the Tohono O'odham people. (Martha A. Burgess)

Two Tohono O'odham women in their saguaro camp process the saguaro fruit they have gathered into juice and dried cakes. (Southwest Photobank) raw, boiled, or grilled over coals. Nopales (called *nopalitos* when they are cut small) are a popular ingredient in Mexican dishes and may show up at dinner in Mexican homes and in the most authentic restaurants, often in a red chile sauce.

Spring is also the time that palo verde trees flower and fruit. Littleleaf palo verdes, which cover sunny hillsides, produce pods with seeds so sweet they can be gathered and cooked like peas. Dried, they can be ground into meal. Modern foragers like to sprout the seeds and use them in salads.

June brings dry and searing heat to the Sonoran Desert, but slender golden mesquite pods remain on the trees in abundance, ready for gathering. Mesquite is an ancient desert dweller. In the *Savor the Southwest* blog, ethnobotanist Martha A. Burgess writes: "Having evolved with large Pleistocene herbivores, mesquite's survival strategy is to over-produce quantities of tasty pods to entice mammoths or (extinct) ungulates to eat them and spread their seeds, scarified and delivered in ready-made fertilizer packages. In more recent centuries, cattle have provided a similar service to spread mesquite."

The time for collecting mesquite was the most important wild-food harvest of the year as sweet mesquite meal was the staple around which the Tohono O'odham and their ancestors formed their meals. Gatherers had their favorite plants and returned to harvest from them year after year. I'll discuss mesquite further toward the end of this chapter.

In the depths of summer, desert dwellers know that is the time to get up in the cool of dawn to gather the fruits of the saguaro cactus. Even within their range of Southern Arizona and the northern state of Sonora, Mexico, saguaros are finicky about where they grow. They seem to prefer rocky hillsides although many can be found on plains as well.

For the Tohono O'odham, the saguaro harvest was the beginning of the new year and they looked forward to the season with anticipation. Saguaro fruit is sweet and juicy, and they hadn't had much sweet food in months since by then the stored mesquite had been consumed. During the season, families moved from their villages to set up camp for two or three weeks in dense stands of saguaro to gather the fruit and to make wine for religious ceremonies to hasten the rain.

The saguaro fruit grows on the top of each arm or branch with an average mature saguaro reaching 18 to 30 feet tall. To reach the fruit, each family would fashion a gathering stick called a *kuibit* of two saguaro ribs (from dead saguaros) spliced together with a short traverse stick of creosote bush or cat's claw affixed on the end. The people would go out early in the morning to collect the fruit. At midday, when it was too hot to walk around gathering, they took their harvest back to camp where the pulp was soaked in water to loosen the minute black seeds, which were then sun-dried to be ground and used for bread or mush. They worked in the shade of ramadas built of mesquite and brush to form the pulp into cakes or patties, which they dried for storage. The liquid that had held the sweet pulp was boiled down in large pots over outdoor fires until it thickened into a syrup to be stored in sealed jars. Each family also contributed a portion of their gathered juice to large ceremonial jars overseen by an elder; the juice was fermented, usually for around three days, making a lightly alcoholic wine or cider. With no refrigeration, the wine spoiled quickly, so the ceremony was held immediately. It included prayers,

Barrel cactus fruit have no thorns and have a light lemon flavor. The seeds make a good addition to baked goods.

some light drunkenness (the only time of the year), and ritual songs. It was called "singing down the clouds," and anyone who has spent a summer in Tucson knows that by early July you are very anxious for the clouds to produce rain.

A small amount of saguaro syrup is commercially available today.

In good years, the dried saguaro seed and mesquite meal could be gathered in sufficient quantity to be stored and used as the basis of meals for months.

With the mesquite season tapering off over the summer and saguaro season over, a few weeks remain until late July when the fruits of prickly pear cactus turn to blazing magenta as they ripen. The early inhabitants were surrounded by hundreds of acres of prickly pear plants that in years of moderate rainfall produced an abundance of fruit. The tastiest come from the *Opuntia engelmannii*. Prickly pear plants proliferate throughout the city and adjacent rural areas, and anyone who has a desire to collect some has easy access.

The sweet fruit, with its slightly musky undernotes, can be dried or juiced, but it is prepared most frequently as jelly or as syrup used on pancakes or in margaritas. Preparing the juice and syrup is easy for the home cook, but several local businesses do the prep work for those lacking the time or inclination to gather, clean, boil, and strain.

Prickly pear fruit is a good entry point for anyone new to desert foraging. Even those hesitant about trying a strange wild food generally are game for a prickly pear margarita. Prickly pear sauces are often found on the menus of restaurants specializing in Southwest cuisine, and more recently, craft brewers and makers of spirits incorporate the juice.

Once the summer rains start, other wild greens appear. Amaranth provides both mild greens and nutritious seeds if left to mature, as does lamb's-quarter (goosefoot). Purslane, called *verdolaga* in Spanish, has fleshy leaves and stems that are high in vitamin C and omega-3 fatty acids.

Also easily recognized are the yellow barrel cactus fruits. Foragers can gather them effortlessly because they grow about knee high and their smooth skin is without thorns. The fruit has a lemony flavor and the abundant black seeds can be easily dislodged and dried.

Martha A. Burgess says that her Tohono O'odham friend and teacher Juanita Ahil told her that her people waited to collect the barrel cactus fruits until their other wild stores had been depleted. Barrel cactus fruits with their waxy outer skin stay fresh on the plant for months and serve as a sort of pantry for when extra food is needed.

So far, we've discussed about fifteen wild foods. What about the hundreds of others? There are also less common and tasty greens; *Yucca baccata* with its fleshy fruits; sotol, which is roasted like agave; roots of some wildflowers; mushrooms; and berries such as garnet-colored wolfberries and hackberries that appear like tiny orange gems in the fall. Sweet Emory acorns would require a foraging expedition to slightly higher elevations. Most numerous, though, are seeds of grasses, wild sunflower, ironwood trees, and devil's claw. Ethnobotanist Wendy Hodgson tells us that more than one hundred species in the northern Sonoran Desert produce edible and harvestable seeds, and more than seventy-five species produce leaves, which are tastiest shortly after they appear, when they are less apt to be bitter.

By the second half of the twentieth century, mesquite and prickly pear, among the basics for survival in earlier times, were nearly forgotten after the native elders who had relied on them were no longer around. Younger people found fast food more appealing.

Then, in the 1980s, a group of researchers, concerned about the growing problem of diabetes on the Tohono O'odham Reservation, did some tests on the plants and found that they and other traditional native foods contained healthy amounts of gums and fibers important in managing blood sugar spikes.

Add to that a growing interest among the general population in eating from the local foodshed. Attention to native wild foods continued to surge as we approached the millennium. Local chefs interested in the emerging "Southwest cuisine" competed to add items using local wild foods to their menus.

> Your *foodshed* refers to everything between where your food is produced and where it is consumed—the land it grows in, the routes it travels, the markets it goes through, the kitchens where it is cooked.

THE MODERN DESERT FORAGER

Adopting an all-wild-foods diet today is unrealistic. We are too many here and we can't devote all our time to food gathering and processing. But collecting a few wild plants, even just recognizing and maybe nibbling them on a hike, adds immensely to our feeling of integration into our natural surroundings. For some it can be a spiritual feeling of a relationship with Mother Nature. For others it is a connection to ancestors who had an elemental bond with wild foods. For these and many other reasons, foraging or dining on wild foods that others have collected has actually become quite trendy.

With the appearance of mesquite and prickly pear fruit in many homes and restaurants, they now rank among the most prevalent uses of wild foods today. And of course, we must include agave in the form of agave syrup; mescal, a spirit made from agave hearts; tequila, which is mescal from the Mexican state of Jalisco; and bacanora, which is a mescal made in Sonora. Mescal is the more common spelling, with *mezcal* used in Mexico.

FOR FURTHER READING

Desert Harvesters. *Eat Mesquite and More: A Cookbook for Sonoran Desert Foods and Living*. RainSource Press, 2018.

Hodgson, Wendy. *Food Plants of the Sonoran Desert*. University of Arizona Press, Tucson, 2001.

Nabhan, Gary Paul. *Gathering the Desert*. University of Arizona Press, Tucson, 1985.

Niethammer, Carolyn. *American Indian Cooking: Recipes from the Southwest*. University of Nebraska Press, Lincoln, 1999.

———. *Cooking the Wild Southwest*. University of Arizona Press, Tucson, 2011.

Slattery, John. *Southwest Foraging*. Timber Press, Portland, Oregon, 2016.

Underhill, Ruth. *Autobiography of a Papago Woman*. American Anthropological Association Memoir 48, 1937.

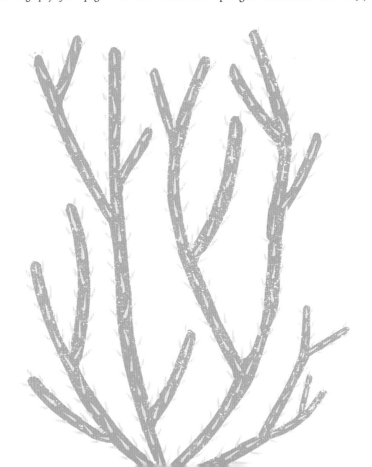

PRICKLY PEAR

Hundreds of acres of wild prickly pear surround the outskirts of Tucson. The fruits are 85 percent water, and thus are low in calories, at about 12 calories each, and high in vitamins A and C and other antioxidants and flavonoids. The fruits also contain calcium, magnesium, and potassium. Additionally, the unsweetened juice has proven helpful in lowering cholesterol and blood sugar, helping athletes with endurance, and even preventing a hangover.

Not only the fruits are used for food. The young pads, which appear in the spring, are also nutritious. Mexicans call them *nopales* and they are a common vegetable in Mexico. When the pads are cut into small pieces for combining with other foods, they are called *nopalitos*.

Prickly pear fruits and pads have sustained desert dwellers for 10,000 years.

While both prickly pear pads and fruits were a staple for early native and Mexican populations, for decades the fruits were used by Anglos only as a jelly ingredient. Then with the arrival of a new interest in Southwest flavors, top chefs began looking at the juice as an interesting novelty, including it on their menus as a sauce or drink ingredient.

The flavor, which depends on the variety and varies from plant to plant, was an easy sell. People have compared it to watermelon or honeydew melon. Others suggest the flavor is berry-like or similar to cucumbers. Most fruits have slightly musky notes. It is truly one of the major flavors of the Southwest.

Both the pads and fruits contain gums and fibers that are helpful in controlling blood sugar and cholesterol. The plant has been a folk remedy for generations in Mexico, but scientific studies have shown that just 100 grams a day of nopales (about two pads the size of a woman's hand) can control non-insulin-dependent (type 2) diabetes and help other diabetics reduce their need for insulin.

HOW TO PREPARE PRICKLY PEAR PADS

All very young prickly pear pads are edible, but those from the tall *Opuntia ficus-indica* are the tastiest and easiest to clean. The new pads must be gathered in the spring before they develop a woody interior structure. Wearing rubber gloves, scrape off the spines and trim off the edges. Rinse the pads and check under a strong light to make sure you have removed all the spines. The pads can then be grilled, fried whole, or cut into small pieces and sautéed or baked in the oven. Some people find the mucilaginous sap objectionable, but once the pads or pieces are cooked and a little dried out, the sap is less noticeable. Mexican grocery stores sell already-cleaned nopales.

If you'd like to try gathering prickly pear yourself, it's easy. Prickly pears ripen in late July through September and some late-ripening plants have fruit into October. Harvest from your own yard or a neighbor's (ask first, of course). Feel free to gather small amounts for personal use on Bureau of Land Management habitat, but you must get a $7 permit from the Arizona State Land Department to harvest prickly pears on state land.

To set out on your harvesting trip, you'll need tongs and a bucket. Sometimes a fruit will look deep red and ripe from the outside, but the inside will still be green, so cut one open to check before you harvest a bucketful. Stick a good pair of tweezers in your pocket. At some point, you are going to get a stray spine in your finger. It will happen. Use the tweezers; take it out. Get on with the job. About a dozen prickly pears will give you a cup of juice.

Once home, keep the tweezers handy and don some heavy-duty rubber gloves to wash the fruit. Place as many washed fruit as you wish to process in a pot, cover with water, bring to a boil, and simmer for about 5 minutes. (Skip this step if you are using the juice fresh right away or are going to put it into another cooked recipe. Just quarter the fruit.) Transfer the boiled fruit a few at a time to a blender and run until contents are smooth. If you are using fresh fruit, you will need to add a little water to get the process going. Blend the fruit until liquefied. Blend long enough to get the skins pulverized to get all those nutrients into the juice. Set a fine mesh strainer over a bowl and strain. If your strainer has large holes, you'll need to line it with cheesecloth or a piece of an old sheet.

Use the juice fresh, freeze it, or make it into syrup for longer storage. If you want the juice to be more concentrated, put it back in the pot and simmer for a while until it reaches the desired strength. Some greenish froth will rise to the top—just skim it off. Use your juice or syrup on pancakes or to flavor lemonade, mixed drinks, or ice cream, or as an ingredient in sauces for meats.

Prickly Pear Syrup

1 cup prickly pear juice
Juice of one lemon
1 cup sugar or sweetener of choice
1 teaspoon cornstarch (optional)

Combine 1 cup of prickly pear juice, the juice of one lemon, and 1 cup of sugar in a small saucepan over medium heat. Slowly bring ingredients to a simmer. Cook until it begins to thicken. If you want a thicker syrup, dissolve 1 teaspoon of cornstarch in a little cold water and slowly add to the juice, stirring as you do so. Stir with a wire whisk if necessary to get a smooth consistency. Cook until desired thickness. This will store in the refrigerator for weeks and in the freezer for a year.

MESQUITE: A REDISCOVERED STAPLE

For thousands of years, residents of the Santa Cruz Valley have eaten mesquite pods. They gathered them long before they lived in villages, long before the valley had a name. Then as now, the long thin pods turned from green to deep gold around the beginning of the hot summer rainy season. In their natural state, mesquite trees have a bush form, so the pods are low and easy to harvest. If the rains were good, a second crop appeared a few months later, providing a fresh supply of food. The taste of the pods, which was usually sweet, varied from tree to tree and each gatherer had her favorite trees that she returned to annually. In a normal year, the trees hung thick with the pods, but occasionally the harvest was meager, and the people needed to range over a wider area to satisfy their needs. The women went in groups for mutual protection from animals or the enemy.

Every industrious family built and filled a cylindrical granary bin to hold their mesquite harvest. The people, probably women, pounded the beans to meal in bedrock mortars, which over generations of use wore deep into the rock. The mortars are often found in multiples, suggesting that grinding was a communal activity. When I come upon these mortars, a scene flashes across my imagination of the women of a band or village discussing the gossip of the day or perhaps singing to pass the time. They pressed the sticky meal into cakes for storage.

Several early European explorers wrote about their experiences with mesquite. Álvar Núñez Cabeza de Vaca, who made the first overland crossing of North America between 1528 and 1536, wrote about being offered mesquite meal in great quantities. Pedro Castañeda, who kept notes for the Coronado expedition from 1540 to 1542 in what is now northern Mexico and the southwestern United States, described "bread of mesquite which like cheese keeps for a year."

When I began researching Native American use of wild foods in 1972, Molly Manuel and her elderly aunt, both Tohono O'odham elders who lived near San Xavier Mission, agreed to teach me some of the old ways. They instructed me to bring a supply of mesquite pods and saguaro seeds. We laughed through an afternoon of making mesquite gravy and mush and a gruel of ground saguaro seeds. Mesquite pods taste sweet and fruity and eating mesquite mush twice a day as a staple would not have been an unpleasant way to dine. Saguaro seeds have a slightly nutty flavor and are as tasty as many modern cooked cereals. My teachers recalled making these foods as children with their mothers and grandmothers. They hadn't eaten them in years and said that hardly anyone still gathered and ate the wild plants their ancestors had relied on.

We all had a light snack of what we had cooked, and as I packed up some of the leftovers to share with friends, Molly's aunt, rather quiet until then, had apparently been reminiscing about her earlier life. She looked off into the distance and said, "The Indians ate good food. They never sickened, and they got real old."

A few years later, Molly's aunt was proven right about the good food as university researchers found that the gums and fibers in mesquite control blood sugar. Returning to a more traditional diet can help the Tohono O'odham people avoid or control diabetes, which afflicts up to 70 percent of the

Mesquite pods mature in early summer and were a staple for the desert-dwelling Native Americans. They can be ground into a sweet meal delicious for baking.

population. The sweetness comes from fructose, which the body can process without insulin. In addition, soluble fibers, such as galactomannan gum, in the seeds and pods slow absorption of nutrients, resulting in a flattened blood sugar curve, unlike the peaks that follow consumption of wheat flour, corn meal, and other common staples.

While mesquite mush sustained desert inhabitants for thousands of years, modern desert dwellers would not consider that an acceptable dinner. Devising modern recipes to highlight mesquite's complex flavor was an intriguing challenge. But even more of a challenge was grinding the pods to a fine enough meal to use. The teeth of my Corona hand-cranked mill got gummed up, and pounding them in my metate was too laborious. The blender worked best, especially if the pods were frozen. The resulting product needed to be sifted and was still coarse.

Then over a few years, beginning around 1978, several creative individuals moved mesquite processing into the modern world.

Leading Sonoran Desert researcher Richard Felger was working at the Arizona-Sonora Desert Museum looking into forgotten or underutilized drought-hardy food crops when he discovered that the University of Arizona Environmental Research Lab out at the airport had a hammermill. He took some mesquite pods there to grind. In what I can only describe as modern-day magic, the hammermill ground and sifted the pods, producing a silky pale golden meal. What's more, the power of the hammermill managed to crush the rock-hard exterior of the true seed, making the meal much higher in protein. Hoping to start a trend, the docents at the Desert Museum gathered mesquite pods and sold the ground meal at their Desert Harvest Bazaar. I, along with many other mesquite harvesters, was delighted. Except—when that batch of meal was gone, it was gone.

But the market for mesquite meal was awakened. There is something about gathering and eating this centuries-old desert food that is compelling to anyone with even a bit of interest in foraging. It helps that most people love the sweet caramel-like flavor.

In 1996, Brad Lancaster, an expert in permaculture and rainwater harvesting, began promoting the planting of mesquite (as well as palo verde and ironwood) in the Dunbar/Spring neighborhood just north of downtown Tucson. In a few years, neighbors soon had access to bountiful crops of mesquite pods, but they were facing the same difficulties as I did in processing them. Lancaster had heard that David Omick, out in the San Pedro Valley, the next valley to the east, had done his own experimenting with a hammermill he had found in a local farmer's barn. He used the mesquite meal for the annual Cascabel Mesquite Milling and Pancake Breakfast.

Lancaster's excitement at seeing the beautiful flour so easily produced echoed my amazement. He writes in *Eat Mesquite and More*: "I was overjoyed. The process was so much quicker than any of my previous experiments and here I was now milling and eating mesquite in a great community of people!. . . . The experience inspired me and others to spark a homegrown, mesquite-harvesting food revolution, which became Desert Harvesters in Tucson."

Desert Harvesters, a nonprofit, grassroots organization, has done more to move mesquite into the diet of Tucsonans (or should we say *back* into the diet) than any other group. With a grant to acquire their first hammermill, Desert Harvesters held their first public milling in the fall of 2003 along with a mesquite pancake breakfast. The annual event attracted wild-food enthusiasts from miles around. By 2013 Desert Harvesters had acquired three hammermills to keep up with the demand. When the fall event opened for business at 8 o'clock, the line typically stretched for a half block with people toting one to sometimes five 5-gallon buckets of mesquite pods.

An additional benefit of grinding the pods with the hammermill is that the equipment breaks through (and sifts out) the stony exocarp and gets into the true seed which is 37.2 percent protein, making the resulting meal much more nutritious. The whole pod ground without the seed is only 14.7 percent protein.

The numerous Desert Harvesters volunteers published a cookbook in 2011 called *Eat Mesquite* and in 2018 revised it as *Eat Mesquite and More* to include other tree legumes, such as palo verde and ironwood, as well as additional wild foods, including acorn, saguaro, cholla, prickly pear, wild greens, and more.

As mesquite has begun to move back into the mainstream, more research has been done, and it appears that an invisible mold (*Aspergillus flavus*) that can produce aflatoxin B1 sometimes develops on the pods when they fall to the ground or get wet in the summer monsoon rains. Desert Harvesters has moved their grinding events to June to catch a short window between when the pods ripen and the rains can be expected to begin. More information on safe harvesting can be found on the Desert Harvesters website.

For those who are not able to gather their own pods and attend a grinding event but still would like to use mesquite meal, sources come and go. Most online commercial mesquite products are sourced out of South America as there are limited amounts of meal from the Sonoran Desert and production costs are higher here. Desert Harvesters sells mesquite meal only during their milling day. The Native Seeds/SEARCH retail and online stores carry several types of meal, changing suppliers when one vanishes and another appears.

Every year the Desert Harvesters organization fires up their hammermills. For a reasonable fee, mesquite pod foragers can have their pods ground into tasty meal ready for baking.

The store at the San Xavier Co-op Farm often carries mesquite meal from beans gathered and processed by the Tohono O'odham who live on that part of the reservation. After moving away from this traditional food for most of the twentieth century, Tohono O'odham health educators are reminding their people that this is the food that their desert DNA has adapted to over thousands of years and the food that will help to protect them from diabetes. Whether they sit down to a bowl of beans with a mesquite tortilla or enjoy a stack of mesquite pancakes, they are honoring their grandmothers and their grandmothers' grandmothers. That line stretches back many thousands of years—when they all relied on this sweet nutritious pod to feed their families in good times, when it was served with a side of venison, or in more desperate periods when it was the one thing that kept their children from hunger.

Desert Dry Rub

Desert Harvesters volunteers don't just talk about mesquite, they are also avid cooks. Here is a recipe from their cookbook *Eat Mesquite and More*. This versatile recipe was devised by Jill Lorenzini, an expert and inventive desert cook.

> 2 cups mesquite flour
> 1½ teaspoons salt
> 1 teaspoon ground black pepper
> 2 tablespoons ground barrel cactus seeds
> 1 teaspoon chile powder (your choice)
> 1 tablespoon ground, dried herbs (your choice of
>   juniper berry, marjoram, basil, rosemary, sage,
>   coriander)

In a small bowl, mix all ingredients. Store in a glass jar and use as a dry rub for vegetables, tofu, tempeh, meats, poultry, or fish.

Cinnamon Mesquite Waffles

Cinnamon Mesquite Waffles are a Tucson treat and a great use for mesquite meal. Delicious with prickly pear syrup. This is a modification of a recipe from Bodie Robins of Big Skye Bakers. Makes eight 6-inch waffles.

2 eggs, separated
1½ cups milk
¼ cup oil
1 cup all-purpose flour
½ cup whole-wheat flour
½ cup mesquite meal
1 tablespoon cinnamon
1 tablespoon baking powder
½ teaspoon salt
1 tablespoon sugar

Lightly oil and preheat waffle iron. Separate eggs, reserving the whites in a bowl, and set aside. In another bowl, mix egg yolks, milk, and oil.

Mix all dry ingredients together. Add liquids to dry ingredients. Gently mix until smooth.

Beat the egg whites until stiff. Fold the egg whites into the waffle mix.

Place ½ cup of batter onto hot waffle iron. Close lid. Bake until golden. Repeat with remaining batter, oiling again if necessary.

VELVET MESQUITE
PROSOPIS VELUTINA
By Eric Magrane

Down here
the layers of earth
are comforting
like blankets.

The soil I think of
as time. Below the caliche
I sift through sediment
from thousands of years.

Though the sharp desert light above
is another world, its pulse
courses through me.

When the mastodons
and ground sloths roamed,
its pulse coursed through me.

When the Hohokam
in the canyon
ground my pods
in the stone,
its pulse coursed through me.

When the new gatherers
of the desert
learn again how to live here,
its pulse will course through me.

And I say, I will be ready
if the drought comes.

And I say, go deep
into the Earth.

And I say, go deep
into yourself, go deep
and be ready.

From The Sonoran Desert: A Literary Field Guide
Used with permission

TRADITIONAL EARLY AGRICULTURE

4,000 YEARS IN THE FIELDS OF THE SANTA CRUZ BASIN

In the Southwest, throughout a thousand-mile circle of semiarid, subtropical country, are found the scattered relics of prehistoric agricultural tribes. The ruins of their houses and their ditches, their pottery, their implements of stone, their pictographs ... remain to us; but of greater value and interest than any of these are the descendants of these tribes, and some of their ancient crop plants, which yet endure.
–G. F. FREEMAN, *SOUTHWESTERN BEANS AND TEPARIES,* 1912

FOR UNTOLD THOUSANDS OF YEARS, small bands of hunter-gatherers roamed the Tucson basin, eating the plants in season, subsisting on seeds, and hunting small animals and the occasional mammoth, never staying anywhere long enough to build a permanent home or village. They lived so simply that they left little trace. According to Jonathan Mabry, around 5,000 years ago the people began to intensively collect edible weedy plants that favored damp alluvial soils. Many archaeologists think it is likely that they were protecting, encouraging, and manipulating these species in a form of "proto-agriculture." This made them culturally preadapted to the adoption of maize horticulture.

Then around 4,000 years (2100 BC) or more ago, corn, or maize, which had been domesticated in Mexico, made its way to the Santa Cruz River Valley and life began to change. Corn needs to be planted by people and once early inhabitants went to the trouble of putting in a field, it made sense to stay in one place, at least for a while, and oversee the growing of the crop and enjoy the harvest. The early corn was a popcorn variety and the cobs were very small.

Despite the new crop, the people needed to continue their reliance on the wild foods that had sustained their ancestors forever—cactus fruit and mesquite pods, amaranth and lamb's-quarter for both greens and seeds, and the wild grasses.

Advances in corn adoption didn't occur in a straight line where one year the entire population decided to adopt this new way of life. The best guess of the experts is that corn cultivation, and the whole idea of settled agriculture, arrived through several paths and was spaced throughout time—we're talking hundreds of years—in an on-again/off-again pattern. One can imagine that it would take only one bad year for a family group to decide that this new crop wasn't such a good idea, not worth the expenditure of time and effort, and that it was better to rely on the old time-tested ways of food gathering. Starvation is a potent persuader.

Nevertheless, there was more success than failure and as corn grew in importance over the next few hundred years, wild grass seeds became less important. It appears that corn arrived in the Santa Cruz River Valley at a particularly advantageous ecological period when heavy rainfall made for a wet floodplain, perfect for planting. This cooler, moister climate with predictable rains persisted for a millennium, creating a long span for many groups to give the new crop a try.

Archaeologists have found evidence of early agricultural settlements near the Santa Cruz River both in downtown Tucson and in Marana on the east bank of the Santa Cruz. Other settlements were scattered over the valley, where smaller streams made agriculture feasible.

It took another 500 years or so after corn arrived, to around 1500 BC, for the local inhabitants to build the first irrigation canals. The systems began small and became more elaborate over time. Now the farmers could use the river and sometimes even tributaries to water their corn rather than having to rely on rain. After another 500 years, around 1000 BC, people were relying on corn as an established and reliable part of their diet.

In our world, where we learn of new, startling, culture-changing innovations nearly every week, it is hard to understand the slow pace of change when time was measured in several thousands of years. The development of irrigation was a major achievement allowing more reliable food production. Cultural progress became more rapid after that. Farmers all over the Tucson basin moved into villages, dug pit houses to live in, and constructed increasingly sophisticated systems of canals to water their fields.

Evidence of early agriculture makes Tucson the U.S. city with the oldest continuous history of agriculture within its boundaries.

We don't know how many of these villages existed because evidence of their houses and fields is now often many feet underground or has been obliterated by modern land use. But occasionally, modern construction requires digging and both the National Historic Preservation Act of 1966 and state law require that archaeological finds be investigated before they are destroyed if a federal or state agency is conducting or approving the project. The City of Tucson and Pima County do it as a policy. That was the case when Pima County decided to expand the Tres Rios Water Reclamation Facility on Ina Road and conduct some improvements along I-10. Preliminary investigation suggested that an early village might be there. Indeed, underneath the future construction lay a substantial settlement with homes, fields,

This Early Agricultural period village, bordering a field system dating from about 875 to 800 BC, was uncovered at the Las Capas site during expansion of the modern Pima County Wastewater Treatment Facility in Tucson. In small, roughly square individual fields, crops like corn and beans would have been planted, enclosed by berms. Small canals brought in water to the mosaic of fields, allowing ancient farmers to periodically flood their crops. The farmers lived in small clusters of huts near their fields, allowing them to tend the crops and repair berms and canals. (Henry Wallace, photographer, courtesy Desert Archaeology, Inc.)

and irrigation canals, located in the very advantageous position of the confluence of the Santa Cruz River with the Rillito and the Cañada del Oro Wash. The archaeologists called the village Las Capas.

Thirty people from Desert Archaeology spent thirteen months over 1998 and 1999 investigating the site for an Arizona Department of Transportation improvement to the I-10 on-ramp. The investigators returned for further work from 2009 to 2013. Archaeologists estimate that most of the Las Capas fields date to the Early Agricultural period, from 1200 to 800 BC, and then sporadically through AD 50. Based on estimations of the size of the fields and the water flow available, Las Capas could have supported a community of up to 125 people.

Although the development of irrigation provided a more reliable corn crop, it also led to cultural changes as well. Digging and maintaining the canals and allocating the water required social organization so that farmers could collaborate and share labor. Some archaeologists see in these collective actions the beginning of village communities in the Southwest.

Since the farmers were putting so much of their time and energy into growing corn, it was vital that the crop thrived. As the centuries passed and the culture gained experience in agriculture, farmers became skilled agronomists. They looked at which wild plants grew where, assessed the soil, looked at the slopes, and watched the runoff patterns when it rained. They began planting in their fields some of the greens like amaranth, panic grass, and lamb's-quarter that they had gathered in the wild. Through selective breeding, they increased the size of the corn cobs providing a more reliable food supply.

Eventually the farmers also began growing gourds, which they used as containers. In good years, farming produced more food than what could be immediately consumed, and they began to save their produce for leaner times of the year. Corn was dried on the cob and stored in gourds, baskets, and leather pouches that they hung from the rafters of their pit houses or buried in in-ground storage pits.

The rise of farming had many sociological consequences. A stable source of food supported an increase in population, required socioeconomic cooperation, and led to an increased ecological footprint. According to the archaeologist J. Homer Thiel, the advance of maize agriculture and the storage of food appear to be associated with a rise in violence: "We have seen numerous cases of people, both men and women, with traumatic injuries to their heads and stone spear points imbedding in their skeletons or inside their rib cages," he says. "It is likely that some people during the Early Agricultural period raided communities for the stored maize."

The people also needed protein to round out the corn and wild vegetables in their diet. The tiny bones that archaeologists sifted from their excavations showed that jackrabbits made up most of the animal food the farmers consumed. Anthropologists speculate that it was the children who were tasked with hunting the jackrabbits, cottontails, and other rodents, with slingshots and snares. Rabbits coming to find dinner in the fields became dinner themselves.

The people of this time continued to do much of their cooking in underground pits. The pits were lined with stones that were heated with fire and then lined with weeds or prickly pear pads, which protected the food from the intense heat of the stones and provided steam for moisture once everything was covered with more stones and dirt. They toasted corn and small seeds by tossing them with coals in baskets.

Despite the advantages of being near reliable water, not all the people chose to live near the river. The groups who still inhabited areas to the west where there was no regular water continued to subsist mainly on wild plants. The small amount of corn that they were able to grow had to be produced during the monsoon rains, planted in the alluvial fans where rainwater ran off the sides of the hills. Gathering wild-plant foods was mainly a task for women, and little girls began their education as botanists when they went on gathering expeditions with their mothers and grandmothers. Their gathering range was generally confined to the distance they could travel round-trip in one day.

While we always think of early agriculture as including the New World triad of corn, squash, and beans, the three foods did not appear in the Tucson basin all at the same time.

If the people began using wild and domestic beans before they had ceramic pots suitable for cooking, the beans could have been toasted, then ground and mixed with water or roasted as small patties, leaving little trace.

What archaeologists are able to document is the appearance of common beans about 1,500 years ago (AD 500), not until 2,500 years after the earliest appearance of corn. This was about the same time as undecorated plainware pottery appeared in pots in shapes useful for cooking the beans. Cultivated tepary beans appeared in the next centuries after that. The farmers eventually added desert-adapted varieties of jack and lima beans and butternut and cushaw squash. Sunflowers were grown for the seeds and the oil from the seeds. All were varieties that were able to produce under the difficult conditions of heat and low humidity.

THE HOHOKAM

Around AD 450 the rate of change in cultural patterns and lifestyle accelerated in the Tucson basin. Brown local pottery with red designs and similar imported buff pottery became the hallmark of Tucson membership in a Hohokam tradition found in most of southern and central Arizona. Hohokam people were inventive farmers and elaborated on the earlier irrigation canals, using more substantial dams and weirs so that water could be directed to expanded areas with fields.

Where did the Hohokam come from? Nobody is sure. Anthropologists don't agree on their origins. It is possible that some migrated from the south bringing along cultural elements or perhaps it was simply a natural development with the previous culture incorporating elements from newcomers from

In a tour of ancient agave fields, anthropologist Suzanne Fish shows an agave group she planted on a slope to replicate the way the Hohokam structured their fields, surrounding each plant with rocks to conserve moisture.

An early farmer tends his irrigation ditch in this re-creation of a scene from a farm at the base of Sentinel Peak where Mission Garden is located today. Archaeologists have found evidence of habitation in this area from 800 BC to AD 1300. (Robert B. Ciaccio, courtesy Desert Archaeology, Inc.)

other areas. With no written records, scientists have to piece together the story from bits of pottery, remains of homes and fields, and trash piles. The distinct Hohokam culture persisted for more than one thousand years, until about 1500, during what archaeologists and Hohokam experts Paul and Suzanne Fish call "the Hohokam millennium."

As the centuries passed, many aspects of the Hohokam culture became more sophisticated as the people developed better farming techniques. They balanced the harvest times of grown and gathered crops, planting so that as one resource was exhausted, another became available. Among the crop improvements was corn closer in size to the modern ears than the tiny earliest specimens. Maize and beans ruled as produced foods, while mesquite pods and saguaro fruit were the top collected items. When they had an abundance, they stored beans and corn in pottery vessels. Squash was cut into long ribbons, dried, and hung from poles inside their dwellings.

The success of the Hohokam and earlier farmers is remarkable considering that everything was accomplished with hand labor. They had no draft animals, thus no manure for fertilization, no plows, not even any metal shovels. They dug with their hands and with wooden and stone implements. The soil in their fields was renewed from the silt that washed up from the river during periodic flooding. This is the same system used by the ancient Egyptians farming along the Nile; this type of farming disappeared when the Aswan High Dam, built between 1960 and 1970, stopped the floods.

Evidence of a Hohokam village was found in downtown Tucson during excavation for the YMCA at the northeast corner of Church and Alameda Streets. The village extended under the reconstructed Presidio. This area was always good for farming because the Santa Cruz River, much of which flows underground, is forced to the surface by the geology of the area. Experts surmise that there were probably a dozen other small settlements up and down this stretch of the river. The farmers excavated ditches leading from the river to their fields to irrigate crops of corn, beans, squash, tobacco, and cotton. They also spent time in the mountains where they would gather wild plants and hunt.

Here is how J. Homer Thiel and his associates described it: "A substantial Hohokam village once stood in the area near Church and Alameda streets between AD 450 and 1250. Before we began our Block 192 projects, archaeological excavations at the corner of Washington and Church in 1954 and at the northeast corner of Church and Alameda in 1989–1990 had located pithouses built by these early people. Our own excavations last year exposed other prehistoric pithouses, pits for storage, and a large, filled-in hole that we think was used prehistorically for mining caliche to mix with dirt and water for making adobe. In the courtyard of the old Pima County Courthouse, the deepest of our excavations went down almost 7 feet below the current ground surface, revealing the prehistoric occupation layers underneath Spanish colonial, Mexican, and Anglo-American materials that came later. Artifacts associated with the Hohokam features included parts of pottery bowls and jars, shell ornaments, chipped and ground stones used for manufacturing pottery and processing plant and animal resources, and polishing stones for putting the finish on pottery vessels. A ceramic figurine representing a woman was found in one abandoned storage feature."

As the Hohokam population began to outgrow its ability to produce food in their irrigated fields, they turned to farming agave. In Mexico, farmers had cultivated it for hundreds of years as a source of food and as a base for nondistilled alcoholic beverages. According to the ethnobotanist Wendy Hodgson, the Hohokam cultivated at least four kinds of domesticated agaves including *Agave murpheyi*, which originally came from northern Mexico. The Hohokam used agave for food and for fiber to weave into mats and baskets and were likely to ferment it for alcohol as well. The spines became sewing needles, and various parts were used as construction material.

Agave grows on rocky slopes unsuited for other agriculture. Once planted, it doesn't require any attention, sending out "pups" or clones to start new plants. The farmers ensured that the agave plants would take major advantage of the rains by planting them on slopes, then piling small rocks around the base of the plants to catch water and the debris that flowed down the incline. The rocks also protected the roots from small rodents.

In the mid-1980s, a team of archaeologists including Paul and Suzanne Fish, Charles Miksicek, John Madsen, and their graduate students found evidence of large-scale agave farming between 1100 and 1300. They discovered that the Hohokam cultivated agave on about 1,200 acres near Marana and in a smaller area near Tumamoc Hill near downtown Tucson. The researchers counted 42,000 rock piles in the Marana area leading them to estimate that 102,000 agave plants were under cultivation at one time. This would allow the farmers to harvest more than 10,000 agaves each year.

At harvest, the long leaves of the agave plants were cut off, leaving leaf bases and a less fibrous heart containing stored carbohydrates. To lessen the weight and exposure to sharp spines, the people probably cut off the leaves in the field using sharpened rock knives. Much of the harvest was cooked in large roasting pits in the fields. Some of the harvest was carried back to the village for roasting in smaller earthen pits. This was a convenient food preparation method for not only agave hearts but other foods as well.

Even after approximately AD 450 when ceramics that could be used for cooking began to appear in the Santa Cruz River Valley, pit cooking remained a popular method for bulky foodstuffs and resources that required extended cooking. The agave hearts were baked in huge earth ovens for up to 48 hours. The baked hearts and leaf bases were sweet and a desirable food. Today, baked agave leaves can still be found in Mexican markets.

For protein, the Hohokam weren't fussy, making use of nineteen different animals. Anthropologists have discovered the details by sifting the material left behind in their middens or trash piles. Using fine mesh screens, they find bones including tiny vertebrae that they can later identify. Like the earlier agriculturalists, the Hohokam mostly ate rabbits. But they also left behind evidence that they ate mule deer, bighorn sheep, lizards, snakes, and birds. Since they had pottery, they could cook the meat they hunted and the vegetables they grew into stews.

Despite their skill at farming, the Hohokam experienced lean years, a reality for all agricultural cultures, particularly those in arid areas. Voracious pests, drought, and flooding could not be controlled. Scientists have used tree-ring data to see which years were particularly wet or dry and try to correlate that with the movement of people and the size of populations.

Emil Haury, one of the foremost researchers of the Hohokam, wrote: "My own subjectively-derived explanation of their exceptional capacity to persist was the simpleness and uncomplicated nature of the social and political systems. Shifts in food dependencies could be made with no more than the temporary trauma of being hungry. Tribal cohesion was not threatened as long as people were willing to move down the food scale to the less desirable resources. Fortunately, those resources were always there."

About two hundred years before the arrival of the Spanish in the Santa Cruz Valley, the Hohokam culture disappeared.

Little is known about the time between the Hohokam and the Spanish. Generations of archaeologists and anthropologists have tried to figure out why a sophisticated culture would dissolve. A large group of archaeologists believe that this major change in Hohokam culture was the outcome of various natural processes such as a slow decline in population, the salination of the fields from hundreds of years of irrigation, a reduction of wild-plant resources leading to a diminished lack of nutrients, and a rise in disease from people clustered together along irrigation canals. Other processes are still being seriously considered, however, as differing ideas are tested and new information becomes available.

Anthropologist Michael Diehl speculates that the decrease in population might have been caused by the consumption of the seeds of the cotton that the Hohokam grew alongside their other crops. Gossypol, a substance found in cotton seeds, is a natural form of birth control, which works by reducing sperm count and function although the Hohokam had no way of knowing this.

At any rate, the people didn't disappear; over time they may have intermarried or may have broken up into smaller groups and reverted to a less complex way of life. Today's Tohono O'odham view the Hohokam as their ancestors.

FOR FURTHER READING

Archaeology Southwest, Volume 23, Number 1. Center for Desert Archaeology, Winter 2009. Includes 12 articles on early farming in the Santa Cruz River basin and the Southwest.

Archaeology Southwest, Volume 24, Numbers 1–2. Center for Desert Archaeology, Winter–Spring 2010. Includes 21 articles on Tucson archaeology and history. Expanded edition, "Tucson Underground: 4,000 Years of History," Volume 32, Number 4, Fall 2018.

Fish, Suzanne K., and Karen R. Adams. "Plants." In *The Oxford Handbook of Southwest Archaeology*. Edited by Barbara J. Mills and Severin Fowles. Oxford University Press, New York, 2017.

Fish, Suzanne K., and Paul R. Fish. *The Hohokam Millennium*. University of New Mexico Press, Albuquerque, 2008.

Fish, Suzanne K., and Gary P. Nabhan. "Desert as Context: The Hohokam Environment." In *Exploring the Hohokam: Prehistoric Desert Peoples of the American Southwest*. Edited by George Gumerman. University of New Mexico Press, Albuquerque, 1991.

Freeman, George F. "Southwestern Beans and Teparies." *University of Arizona Agricultural Experiment Station Bulletin*, Volume 68, 1912: 1–55.

Hanselka, J. Kevin. "A Pan-Regional Overview of Archaic Agriculture in the Southwest." In *The Archaic Southwest: Foragers in an Arid Land*. Edited by Bradley J. Vierra. University of Utah Press, Salt Lake City, 2018.

Haury, Emil W. *The Hohokam: Desert Farmers and Craftsmen—Excavations at Snaketown, 1964–1965*. University of Arizona Press, Tucson, 1976.

Mabry, J. B., editor. *Las Capas: Early Irrigation and Sedentism in a Southwestern Floodplain*. Anthropological Papers No. 28, Center for Desert Archaeology, 2006.

Nabhan, Gary Paul. "Tepary Bean Domestication: Ecological and Nutritional Changes during *Phaseolus acutifolius* Evolution," University of Arizona master's thesis, 1978.

Niethammer, Carolyn. *American Indian Cooking: Recipes from the Southwest*. University of Nebraska Press, Lincoln, 1999.

Thiel, Homer K., Michael K. Fought, and James M. Bayman. "Archaeology in the Heart of Downtown Tucson." In *Archaeology in Tucson* (Newsletter of the Center for Desert Archaeology), Volume 7, Number 3, 1993.

Thiel, J. Homer, and Jonathan B. Mabry, editors. *Río Nuevo Archaeology Program, 2000–2003: Investigations at the San Agustín Mission and Mission Gardens, Tucson Presidio, Tucson Pressed Brick Company, and Clearwater Site*. Technical Report No. 2004–11, Center for Desert Archaeology, Tucson, Arizona, 2006.

ANCIENT FOOTPRINTS FROZEN IN TIME

It was a wet day 2,500 years ago in a field north of Tucson, probably in the summer. The farmer crossed the muddy field to check on his crops, his child by his side and trailed by his dog.

Archaeologists have to infer so much about the people they study from fragments of daily life they left behind. But in 2016, scientists encountered what was close to a time machine in the form of a backhoe that took them back to a 2,500-year-old farm field north of Tucson. The area was due to be covered by construction for a new bridge and was being investigated to conform to the National Historic Preservation Act.

As the layers of soil were removed, there appeared to be what looked like a human footprint. Closer inspection showed more footprints were distributed across the 18-square-yard field that was uncovered.

The prints are distinct enough that the movements of specific individuals can be traced. People were in their field trying to divert the rain and river water to their thirsty plants.

The first print that was found appeared to be of a heavy adult male walking diagonally across the field. He stopped to do some work, perhaps to repair an earthen berm, then walked on. Much smaller footprints show that a child walked beside him. They were followed by their canine companion.

Another farmer was also accompanied by a child, then stopped to pick up the child. Maybe the little one had a splinter or was afraid of its feet being sucked into the mud. After being carried for a few steps, the child then walked alongside the adult again. It was such an intimate detail of family life from so long ago that some of the archaeologists were moved to tears.

The tracks were preserved in such pristine condition because of a sudden flood from a nearby creek, archaeologists said. The creek overran its banks soon after the prints were made, covering them in its uniquely mica-rich sandy sediment, forming a kind of mineralized cast.

Casts were made of the footprints for further study and they were then re-covered to preserve them under the new construction. Who knows who might want to look at them in the future?

Archaeologists investigating an area north of Tucson to be covered by a new bridge found a 2,500-year-old farm field with footprints of an early farmer, a child, and a dog. Amateur photographer Guy Shovlin outlined the hard-to-discern footprints with wire. (Guy Shovlin)

Rock Corral Canyon Wild **Santa Rosa White** **Yellow** **Yoeme Brown**

Domesticated tepary beans, grown in the Santa Cruz Valley since the early centuries AD, vary widely in color. Native Seeds/SEARCH sells sixteen varieties. (Courtesy Native Seeds/SEARCH)

TEPARY BEANS: AN EARLY DOMESTICATE

After the summer rains, wild tepary bean vines still sprout and wind their way over rocks and around tree trunks deep in some canyons surrounding the Tucson basin. Finding one is a cause for excitement for any desert-plant-loving person.

Fortunately, about 5,000 years ago in an unknown place, maybe in northern Mexico, early agriculturists began to domesticate the vines. The wild beans have fragile pods that shatter and scatter the seeds before they can be harvested by people or eaten by animals. The seeds are so small and dark that they disappear into the soil. In generations stretching over millennia, farmers bred tepary beans that had sturdier pods and fewer but larger beans in each pod. Domesticated pods also germinate more quickly when exposed to water.

By the first centuries AD, cultivated teparies appear to have reached the Tucson area. The Tohono O'odham called them *pawi*, which the Spanish corrupted to *tepary*. The early farmers embraced them because they could withstand the high summer temperatures and could grow with much less water than other crops. Farmers planted teparies in the alluvial fans where water rushed off the sides of the hills and could soak deep into the ground. The soil there was rich in nutrients and trace minerals that washed down from the hillsides. The farmers also constructed berms or piled up brush to channel as much water as possible into their fields. When rains began in the evening, the farmers would go out into the fields by torchlight to direct the flow where it would be most beneficial and sink into the soil rather than run off. And because the beans' long roots could access the deeper soil moisture, the plants could grow, flower, and set seed during the summer rainy season. While most crops needed the typical

33

HOW TO COOK TEPARY BEANS

Presoaking

Because teparies seem to dry out more completely than other beans, it is essential that they be presoaked before cooking. Beans that have been stored awhile should soak about 12 hours. Very fresh beans need less soaking and have even been known to start sprouting during a long soak. During the soaking, they will absorb quite a quantity of water. The more water they take up, the easier they will be to cook. You can figure that 2 cups of dried beans will swell to about 5 cups during soaking. Doug Levy, chef-owner of Feast restaurant, soaks tepary beans for two days in the refrigerator to ensure he will be able to cook them in a day and have nice soft beans to serve on the days he has teparies on his menu.

If you are using beans that have been stored for more than half a year, it will be helpful to add 1/8 teaspoon of baking soda to the water for each cup of beans to be soaked.

Cooking Hints

Although cooking times may fluctuate depending on freshness of the beans, location of the field, type of tepary, and other yet undiscovered factors, it can generally be assumed that teparies will take considerably longer to cook than other beans.

With a heavy cast-iron pot at a full boil, the beans may be done in a couple of hours. With an electric slow cooker, plan on 8 to 14 hours of cooking. A pressure cooker will complete the job in anywhere from a half hour to an hour and 15 minutes. Never fill a pressure cooker more than half full and use at least 2 quarts of water.

Some bean-cooking experts suggest bringing water to a boil in a pot and then adding the beans as a method of quickly softening the seed coat. If you find you must add water during cooking, it should be hot water because reduction in cooking temperature seems to have a toughening effect on the beans.

three to five heavy downpours to do well, teparies in prepared fields could produce on just two rains. The plants appear to stop flowering at 105 degrees Fahrenheit and even drop their leaves if it gets too dry, but they continue to live and resume growing and flowering when the temperatures abate a bit.

For the early farmers, teparies also filled a nutritional need. The corn that began to occupy a larger part of their diet is low in lysine while tepary beans provide the sulfur-based amino acids that corn lacks.

I once talked to an elderly Tohono O'odham woman who said that in the past, tepary beans had been a particularly good traveling food because human beings could be well nourished by eating these beans just once a day, whereas they would need two servings of another kind of bean to feel full. The Indians' preference for tepary beans was based on more than emotional factors. Since then, scientific analyses have shown us that teparies rank slightly higher than most other beans in protein, in niacin, iron, and other minerals, and quite a lot higher in calcium (beneficial for people whose diet lacks dairy products).

Teparies also have a low glycemic index that protects people who eat them from a dangerously rapid rise in blood glucose levels after meals. This is particularly important for the modern Native American populations who experience an extremely high rate of adult-onset diabetes (type 2 diabetes). Those who suffer from diabetes can reduce their need for insulin shots by eating plenty of teparies and other desert foods such as prickly pear that have gums and fibers useful in control of blood sugar.

The researchers at *Cook's Illustrated* are known for doing exhaustive research on the best cooking techniques. When they put their attention to tepary beans, this is what they reported on their website: "After testing different soaking and cooking methods, we determined that soaking the beans overnight in water with a little salt and baking soda before simmering reduced the cooking time and yielded especially tender, creamy beans. Both salt and baking soda work to weaken cell-wall structure; the alkalinity of baking soda helps dissolve hemicelluloses, and sodium displaces magnesium, which facilitates the dissolving of cell-wall pectins. However, the baking soda also weakens the cell-wall structure of the other vegetables in the soup. In order to maintain the texture of the vegetables, we sauté them separately and add them to the pot partway through cooking. In keeping with the Greek dish that inspired this recipe, the soup is finished with a healthy splash of red wine vinegar and some fresh parsley to brighten things up."

Whatever cooking method you prefer, you should also understand that a tepary bean that has finally become soft is not necessarily a fully cooked bean. You must continue cooking the teparies until they have lost the starchy, raw flavor, which, with conventional methods, may be as long as two additional hours.

It is at this point that the creativity starts. The recipe for poshol is a suggestion for a delicious use for teparies. A creative cook can come up with many more.

Remember, however, that as with other beans, teparies should be fully cooked before the addition of salt, molasses, brown sugar, tomatoes, tomato sauce, ketchup, or vinegar. When added during cooking, these ingredients tend to harden the beans. *Cook's Illustrated* suggests salt in the soaking water, which is then drained and replaced with fresh water for cooking.

It makes sense to cook three or four times as many beans as you will need for one day and divide the remainder into portions to be frozen for future fast-food meals.

The earliest written records of tepary cultivation come from the Spanish explorers and missionaries. Padre Luis Velarde noted in 1716 that the principal harvests of the Tohono O'odham living west of the Río Santa Cruz were tepary beans, which even outweighed corn in overall production.

Teparies were given their scientific name (*Phaseolus acutifolius var. latifolius*) in 1850 from a specimen collected in West Texas. They didn't receive much attention for the next sixty years—except of course from the people growing and eating them. In 1910, two researchers at the University of Arizona Agricultural Experiment Station, Robert Forbes and G. F. Freeman, became interested in teparies because of their drought hardiness. The two agronomists spent time in the summer months of July and August in several Tohono O'odham villages to the west of Tucson. In 1912, Freeman published a bulletin extolling the benefits of teparies and detailing forty-six separate varieties by color.

Freeman wrote: "By both irrigation and dry-farming methods of culture, these native grown beans yield excellent crops—from 450–700 pounds per acre by dry-farming to 800–1,500 pounds under irrigation. Under all conditions, however, teparies have out-yielded frijoles, and in nine experiments herein reported, where these two crops have been compared, have averaged four times the productiveness of frijole beans." (The frijoles he mentions were pintos.)

Perhaps because of Freeman's enthusiasm, Anglo-American farmers had a brief flirtation with tepary farming beginning around 1914. Farmers in Arizona and New Mexico began cultivating the little bean when they heard that teparies were a nutritious crop adapted over centuries to dry-land farming. In wet years, teparies achieved or surpassed the average bean yield without irrigation and in drought years teparies still produced a small crop when other crops failed completely. One report says that in 1919, the Tohono O'odham produced 300,000 pounds of corn, and 1.8 million pounds of beans although how that number was reached is unclear. At any rate, we can assume it was lots of beans.

Though the modern farmers were successful in growing the beans, that was before mass marketing and new-product introduction techniques had been developed to their present levels. Despite their advantages, teparies had to compete with the better-known pintos and were slow to be accepted by buyers. Then, before they really had a chance to catch on, gasoline-powered engines made it possible for farmers to suck up groundwater to irrigate their dry fields. Drought hardiness became an irrelevant issue, and when the farmers grew beans, they planted new hybrids instead.

Small-scale Mexican and Indian farmers began to turn to the hybrids as well, but many of them continued to grow small plots of teparies. The older farmers, particularly, were reluctant to give up something that had been so important to their grandfathers and their grandfathers before them. The beans were more than food, they were also culture. However, as the elderly population began to die, fewer and fewer farmers grew teparies. Despite their adaptation to the growing conditions of the area, their reliability, and their tastiness, teparies were almost lost to us with one scientist predicting in the 1960s that they would soon disappear.

Fortunately, several champions worked concurrently to save the beans. In the 1980s, ethnobotanist Martha A. Burgess was working for the Arizona-Sonora Desert Museum and looking for a source of tepary beans so she could introduce them to the museum members. There were small amounts of teparies available in trading posts on the reservation, usually grown by hobby farmers, but she was looking for a bigger source. Her search led her north of Tucson to Coolidge and an Anglo farmer named W. D. Hood. Hood needed a late-summer crop to use in a rotation cycle after his barley and winter wheat had been harvested. He learned about teparies and their low water requirements and found seed for white teparies in a long-stored unsold crop from another farmer and got some brown seed from Mexico. Then he had to modify some equipment to deal with his harvest. Hood found a ready market for his teparies among Native American populations throughout Arizona.

Interest began building among non-Indians who were interested in traditional and wild foods. In 1974, my book *American Indian Food and Lore* was published with a chapter on traditional beans, and in 1978 Gary Paul Nabhan submitted his University of Arizona master's thesis, which is an exhaustive treatise on all aspects of teparies. In 1982, a Meals for Millions group that was a precursor of the Native Seeds/SEARCH seed bank was offering six varieties of teparies as seed, including two from W. D. Hood, who that year stopped growing teparies.

With Hood out of business, teparies, never plentiful, disappeared from the commercial market for a few years. Fortunately, Ramona and Terry Button began growing teparies on farmland on the Gila River Indian Reservation near Sacaton left to Ramona by her mother and great-uncle. Ramona, whose father is Tohono O'odham and mother is Pima, found the seed her father had saved in a Mason jar in a trunk.

Today Ramona Farms has grown from the original 26-acre plot to 4,500 acres of commercial and heritage crops. Their nicely packaged white, brown, and black teparies are widely available in stores and by mail order. You can even find several other varieties in a number of online stores.

For those folks willing to grow their own beans, Native Seeds/SEARCH offers seed for sixteen varieties of domesticated teparies and four strains of wild teparies. Several varieties are also available free from the Pima County Public Library Seed Library.

Poshol

Phyllis Valenzuela works at the San Xavier Co-op Farm and cooks most of the prepared food for sale in the farm store. One windy, rainy winter day, when everyone was craving something warm, she made this soup for people working on the farm and anybody else who dropped in. It could well have been made by Valenzuela's Tohono O'odham many-times-great-grandmother as it includes only ingredients available before European contact. You'll need your largest soup pot. The first three ingredients are available at the San Xavier Co-op Farm store.

> 1 pound tepary beans
> 1 cup dried whole-kernel roasted 60-day corn
> 1 cup dried cholla buds
> 1 gallon water
> 1 tablespoon salt

Combine the beans, corn, and cholla buds in the pot and cover with the water. Bring to a full, rolling boil for 3 hours. Test beans. If still starchy, continue cooking until soft. Sprinkle in the salt to taste before serving.

PLACES YOU CAN VISIT

Fort Lowell Park—Hardy Archaeological Site

The bridge over the Rillito River on Craycroft Road just south of River Road marks the spot where the Tanque Verde and Pantano Washes join the Rillito. As in the areas at the San Xavier Mission and the base of "A" Mountain, a rocky underlayment forced the water to the surface. Both ancient and modern humans found it a great place to live. Archaeological excavations in 1997 uncovered portions of a large Hohokam site occupied from around AD 675 to 1150. There is no evidence remaining, but a series of metal signs provide good information on the history.

To get to the site you can enter the Loop Trail on the west side of Craycroft Road where it crosses the Rillito and walk about 20 minutes to the site. Or drive east on Glenn Street east of Craycroft until the second entrance to Fort Lowell Park on your left. After passing the tennis courts there are two stone pillars on the right. Drive through the gate to a parking lot. The Hardy site is a short walk down the hill toward the mountains.

Honeybee Village

Many generations of Hohokam called Honeybee Village home. Archaeologists tell us that it was inhabited continuously from about AD 500 to 1200. Over that time the people built about a dozen hornos (outdoor ovens) and hundreds of houses that incorporated wood from the Santa Catalina Mountains, as well as cemeteries to bury their dead. The Tohono O'odham Nation considers Honeybee Village an ancestral site. No pets other than service animals are allowed.

Honeybee Canyon Archaeological Preserve is located at 13800 North Rancho Vistoso Boulevard in Oro Valley.

Julian Wash Archaeological Park

It requires some imagination to transport yourself back 900 years at this small park dedicated to the very early farmers and later a small Hohokam village that existed here in the 1100s. There is a small parking lot on South 12th Avenue at 38th

These sculptures depict the type of pottery made by the people who lived in a Hohokam village around AD 1100. It's now the Julian Wash Archaeological Park.

Street. The park has natural desert landscaping and a path that leads you through a timeline describing the people who once made a life next to this waterway.

A panel says, "For thousands of years, the Santa Cruz River and Julian Wash have provided a reliable source of water, attracting both humans and animals to their banks. These waterways filled canals that irrigated the crops of Arizona's first farmers in the Early Agricultural Period (2100 BC to AD 50)."

Los Morteros Conservation Area

This 120-acre site near the northern end of the Tucson Mountains, once a Hohokam village, is now a Pima County natural and cultural resources park. The name *morteros* refers to several bedrock mortars where women ground mesquite pods, corn, and other seeds. The site was inhabited from AD 850 to 1300. Still visible are the remains of a ball court, a feature of Hohokam villages, and an irrigation canal system.

To the west along the volcanic hillsides are stone terraces or *trincheras* in a village, built between AD 1100 and 1300.

Some of these trincheras that have been excavated held pit houses with adjacent areas for outdoor activities. Others are too narrow to accommodate pit houses. The soil behind the stone terraces in these cases appears to have caught water running off slopes above them, providing extra moisture for small gardens. Archaeologists also theorize that trincheras villages might have been placed on hills for defense or as prominent elevated positions for conducting public events and ceremonies.

About four hundred years after the Hohokam left, the site became the camping grounds for the famous 1775–1776 expedition of the Spanish explorer Juan Bautista de Anza, who led more than 240 colonists from Nogales, Arizona, to the San Francisco Bay Area.

Bedrock mortars at Los Morteros Hohokam archaeological site are the result of many years of pounding and grinding mesquite pods and other foods.

Los Morteros is located in Marana on El Uno Minor Road. To get there, take Silverbell Road or Twin Peaks Road to Coachline Boulevard. Continue north on Coachline and turn left at West Oasis and left again at El Uno Minor. The sign with directions at the gate will be on your left.

Tumamoc Hill

The summit of Tumamoc Hill supported two villages. The first has been dated to around 300 BC, which was pre-pottery. It is defined by more than a mile of rock walls that archaeologists (with the help of graduate student labor) have determined would have taken about five years to build. So far, only two structures have been investigated, but since one of them was a community room with artifacts of a ritual nature, it's clear this was a village.

The second village arose about 800 years later, around AD 500, the start of the Hohokam sequence. This later village reused the community room of the earlier occupation although it was substantially remodeled. This time the inhabitants stayed for only one or two generations, then moved on.

It's a steep (and popular) walk up the 600-foot-high hill. Halfway up you'll pass the stone structures of the University of Arizona Desert Laboratory on Tumamoc Hill.

Access to the archaeological field is restricted and open only for official tours. However, you can do plenty of imagining of what it might have been like to live up there with a view of all the surrounding mountain ranges.

Vista del Río Cultural Resource Park

This almost 4-acre park is nestled in a residential area on Tucson's east side. The site, which extends beyond the borders of the park, was inhabited by Hohokam between AD 950 and 1150. The people drew water from Tanque Verde Creek to water their fields. The park area alone included perhaps as many as 70 houses grouped in clusters around a shared yard.

Excavation uncovered broken pottery, jewelry, arrow points, and metates.

Vista del Río Park is located at 7575 East Desert Arbors Street near the intersection of Tanque Verde and Sabino Canyon Roads.

EUROPEANS, MEXICANS, AND CHINESE

BRINGING NEW FOODS AND TRADITIONS

CHRISTIANITY ARRIVES WITH CATTLE AND WHEAT

The arrival of the Spanish in Mexico in 1519 bringing European customs and religion as well as food from all over the world profoundly changed the Americas. The Europeans also learned about New World crops and sometimes had to subsist on wild foods because they were months away from home.

It wasn't until 1692, 173 years after the first Spanish had landed, that the Italian Jesuit priest Father Eusebio Francisco Kino rode into an area about 9 miles south of present-day Tucson. There he found a village of about eight hundred Native Americans who called themselves the Tohono O'odham. They subsisted largely on wild plants they gathered from the desert, but since they lived near the Santa Cruz River, they had water to cultivate gardens of corn, squash, common beans, and a domesticated version of the native tepary bean. Father Kino discovered they were also growing watermelons, with both pink and yellow flesh. Watermelons were a European cultivar that originated on the African continent. They had been introduced by priests farther south years before, but their cooling, thirst-quenching sweetness had been so popular with the people they had been traded northward, hand to hand, traveling faster than the missionaries. The native people also ground the seeds of the watermelon to release their oil.

Father Kino established a mission at a place called Wa:k and called it San Xavier del Bac, as he had heard the pronunciation. *Wa:k* means "where the river appears in the sand," and the location was precisely where the waters of the frequently underground Santa Cruz flowed on the surface because the substratum was forcing the water upward, making gardening possible.

Over several trips, the missionary brought with him many vegetable seeds adapted to the European Mediterranean climate. Among his introductions were chickpeas, lentils, cabbages, lettuce, and the flavorings onions, leeks, garlic, cilantro, anise, and possibly mint. He also brought fruits—figs, quinces,

Father Eusebio Kino introduced many European plants as well as cattle to the Native Americans.

oranges, pomegranates, peaches, apricots, pears, and apples. And, of course, there were grapes to produce the wine that would be needed for Mass once the church was established.

The first fruit trees brought to the New World had a perilous journey. They boarded ship at Cádiz, Spain, transferred in Cuba, were off-loaded in Veracruz, and then transported to Mexico City. They then were loaded on burros and sent to the northern missions on journeys that took months. Before Father Kino came to the Tucson area, he had ranched for several years in Dolores, Mexico, and it is reasonable to assume that the cuttings he brought were from his trees there. Nevertheless, considering the time it took to travel and the primitive circumstances, it was a miracle any of the cuttings survived.

Father Kino also brought a New World plant, chile, which had been domesticated long before in Mexico. Interestingly, the progenitor of the long varieties of chiles we know today was a tiny, extremely spicy chile called a chiltepin, about the size of a small pea, that grew wild in an area near Tumacácori. Archaeologists haven't found much evidence that the native people made extensive use of this chile.

Father Kino firmly believed that the new foods he brought would improve nutrition for the desert inhabitants, but he faced a challenge in trying to promote them. It's hard for anybody to visualize what plant might grow from a tiny seed, and impossible for someone who had never seen, for example, a cabbage, to imagine what might emerge from the ground. To demonstrate to the Tohono O'odham what the seeds of all these new fruits and vegetables would produce, Kino took a delegation of Tohono O'odham down to his headquarters at Dolores (about 19 miles north of Cucurpe, Sonora) to observe a lush mature garden. There is some indication that Kino's Pima helpers (he called them his servants) from Dolores came up to Wa:k and planted the first gardens for their northern cousins.

The introduction of domestic animals to the Santa Cruz River basin is also credited to Father Kino. This wasn't just a few head, it was vast numbers. The anthropologist James Officer wrote: "Livestock operations at San Xavier and Tumacácori began in 1695 with animals driven up from Caborca. Two years later, Kino increased the San Xavier herd with cattle from his home mission of Dolores. By 1700, when he laid the foundation for a church at Bac, the cattle herd there numbered 300. Horses and more than forty sheep and goats were also grazing in the vicinity. A month after starting work on the church, Kino directed his cowboys at Dolores to drive another 700 head of cattle to San Xavier, swelling the herd to 1,000 animals."

It is interesting that Father Kino didn't just bring the livestock, he also brought cowboys he had trained at his ranch in Dolores to help the Tohono O'odham learn to care for the animals. These animals were the tough and wiry criollo cattle, more able to survive in the dry desert than other species of cows.

Perhaps the most important foods that Father Kino brought were grains: wheat and barley. Just as he needed wine for Communion, he also needed wafers, thus the wheat. This particular type of wheat, which grows in the winter, was perfect for filling in the gap in the Tohono O'odham diet. Spring was a time of scarcity for the Tohono O'odham and this soft wheat, which makes particularly good pastry when ripe, could also be roasted and eaten green in the spring when the people were really hungry. The rest of the crop was left to ripen in the field.

According to Jonathan Mabry, "Kino's introduction of wheat and cattle was transformative for the O'odham, vastly improving their food security by providing a spring harvest to complement their native summer crops, as well as year-round food on the hoof."

During a visit to W:ak in January 1697, five years after his first visit, Father Kino commented on the fields of wheat, and when he returned in November, he reported that he ate bread (probably tortillas) made from the wheat sown during his previous visit.

After that, San Xavier was left on its own for several decades. The first priest to arrive at the far-flung mission after the staffing gap was Father Philipp Segesser, who came from a wealthy Swiss family. He arrived at Bac in 1732, escorted by Captain Juan Bautista de Anza. Father Segesser reported that the Indians of Bac hadn't retained much of the religion they had been taught but were doing fine raising cattle and horses and had bountiful gardens of wheat, mulberries, and a variety of garden vegetables. He worked at San Xavier for a short time and then was transferred to Guevavi, a now-ruined mission located between Tubac and Tumacácori, and later to a few other missions in Sonora.

Father Segesser was a great correspondent, writing long letters to his family back in Switzerland. Fortunately for history, his family saved the letters, and they have been translated and published. Although we don't have such documentation of the experiences of other priests, we can assume that much of what he relates is typical of what happened to other European missionaries.

Father Segesser wrote that he arrived at San Xavier with barely more than his bedding, his clothing, and some chocolate. He even had to build a shack to live in. (The elegant mission we see today was not even begun until fifty-one years later and took fourteen years to build.) Fortunately, it appears that at that time the people of the village were growing enough food to share with him.

Coming from a wealthy family, he wasn't accustomed to doing any of the tasks that faced him. Chores had been done by servants or perhaps by his mother and sisters. But having taken a vow of obedience, he plunged ahead and tried to figure out how to make it work. He not only needed seeds, he also needed European food technology.

In a lengthy letter home, he asked for hoes to make a garden and scythes and sickles to harvest grass to feed the cows brought by earlier missionaries, hoping that would lead the cows to produce more milk, and he also wanted a butter churn for the milk. An additional list included knives, a soup ladle, a roasting spit, and "a grill big enough to roast the head of a goat." He also wanted wax to make candles. In terms of gardening, he requested seeds of hemp, flax, turnips, carrots, beets, fennel, sage, mint, anise, and caraway. He thought if they sent some dried cherries and plums with seeds intact, he could try to plant some trees.

It appears Father Segesser had an intense case of culture shock, which can often be relieved by familiar food. He wanted to know in detail how to make cheese and asked his mother and sisters to send recipes for pie crusts, almond cake, gingerbread, almond doughnuts, and sugar cookies. He even asked for a waffle iron. In later letters he responded that he hadn't received any letters from home for two years, so we can assume he never got the recipes although he did eventually after three years receive some of the goods he had requested. Unfortunately, one of the trunks had been opened and much of the contents stolen.

When the priests set up a mission, they expected the Native Americans to move near the mission and work the mission fields. They were then fed a gruel of corn or wheat and beef and probably not much of that because Father Segesser recounted a conversation with a Tohono O'odham helper who told him that people were complaining about being hungry. He admitted to being irritated when the Tohono O'odham left the mission and went in search of the wild foods they were used to and that were no doubt tastier and certainly healthier with a broader range of vitamins.

Segesser did eventually get used to a more local diet and claimed to enjoy it. In one letter, he acknowledged the use of wild prickly pear fruit. The letter was written in June 1735, three years after he arrived in Pimería Alta, and it appears he actually liked the flavor, for he wrote: "For me these fruits take the place of cherries, plums, sour cherries, and many pears. God sends and provides in every place that which refreshes man."

Father Segesser talked about eating the meal ground from mesquite pods in several of his letters. In a letter in 1737, five years into his mission, he discussed having been served a beverage of mesquite meal in water "both sweet and sour." He said it was often served to him on his travels to slake his thirst.

He also wrote about mescal (agave), writing "a fire is built in a trench and stones are heated in it. Mescal hearts are then spread upon the red-hot stones. When these hearts are roasted to a yellow color, they are ground between stones into a porridge which is as sweet as honey. I have enjoyed this often."

But the customs of the local people continued to confound him. Father Segesser complained to his family that the natives ate up whatever they had and didn't worry about tomorrow. But he also mentioned how generous they were, saying that if one was having a meal and someone else came by, the visitor would be offered half of whatever there was. He also related that he knew a farmer at Bac who had harvested 135 bushels of wheat but soon had none left having distributed it to people who had done him favors. The farmer seemed not concerned, and said he was going to gather mountain fruits.

The local priest was always expected to extend hospitality to any European passing through. In a letter to his family, Father Segesser complained that he had become "an innkeeper." No matter how remote the mission, the padre was expected to welcome the travelers. And that welcome was expected to involve a cup of hot chocolate. One priest wrote that the cost of chocolate and the requisite sugar was a big expense for his mission, while Father Segesser suggested economizing by being less liberal in offering chocolate and by providing chocolate of lesser quality for some visitors.

Father Segesser's death in 1762 at the mission in Ures, Sonora, was related to the attacks on his mission by Apaches and Seris.

SPANISH SOLDIERS ESTABLISH A PRESIDIO

Apache attacks were a continual threat to all the missions and settlers in Pimería Alta. On August 20, 1775, a red-haired Regular Spanish Army officer, Lieutenant Colonel Hugo O'Conor, who was of Irish descent, decided the presidio at Tubac should be relocated to the banks of the Santa Cruz in what is now Tucson to better protect travelers coming through the area on the way to California. The Apaches threatened the settled native population both at the missions and in their own villages, and travelers as well. Erecting the presidio in Tucson had a double purpose. Not only did it close off the northern frontier from Apache attacks, it also was intended to prevent other European powers from claiming the region. Colonel O'Conor named the fort the Presidio San Agustín del Tucson.

In October 1776, Spanish soldiers began arriving with their families and for protection lived inside the walls of the Presidio. At first, the fort was so small and poorly constructed it was barely better than nothing. Over the years the walls were strengthened, and more land was enclosed until it reached approximately 11 acres. The land enclosed in these walls is now the center of downtown Tucson, approximately within the confines of Church Avenue, Washington Street, Main Avenue, and Pennington Street. Among the largest of the frontier presidios, the fortress was manned by about a hundred soldiers; eventually an additional three hundred retired soldiers, civilians, and family members lived in the community. (A reconstruction of a small portion of the Presidio area can be visited downtown from the entrance at 196 North Court Avenue.)

It was the water provided by the Santa Cruz River that made the substantial settlement in the Tucson area possible. The desert areas away from the river could support only small bands or villages with few enough inhabitants to be sustained by a trickling spring or a waterhole filled by winter rain.

Because of the moisture from the meandering stream, the soldiers found thick forests (*bosques*) of mesquite for firewood and meadows of grass for their horses and sheep and for the king's cattle herd. A spring called El Ojito provided drinking water. However, the north-flowing Santa Cruz was not a perennial river and was dependent on seasonal rainfall in both winter and summer. After heavy winter or summer rains it could be a rushing torrent, but usually it was slow and shallow. For example, the available irrigation water in late April as Tucson moved into summer was only half of what was present in the river in the winter months. What water there was needed to be allocated carefully and shared.

The Presidio residents were far from any supply chain, 1,300 miles from Mexico City, and months from Spain. They had to become subsistence farmers like the O'odham who were already living and farming along both banks of the Santa Cruz River, growing irrigated fields planted with wheat, corn, beans, squash, and melons.

It was not an easy life. According to the archaeologist J. Homer Thiel, Presidio residents preferred wheat because it was European, while corn was considered Native American and thus was a lower-status food. The Presidio women ground wheat and corn on metates using stone manos. "Skeletal remains from the Presidio cemetery showed that the women tended to have arthritic joint damage

The Spanish soldiers and their families stationed at the Presidio San Agustín considered themselves Europeans and preferred bread made from wheat rather than the corn tortillas eaten by the local inhabitants. Bread was baked in hornos like this. (Roger C. Wolf)

Rachel Pollack and Daniel Maldonado portray a Presidio homemaker and her soldier husband during a Living History Day at the Presidio San Agustín de Tucson. (Roger C. Wolf)

As late as the 1920s, farm fields bordered the Santa Cruz River, which still ran even with its banks in some spots. (Arizona Historical Society)

from that work," Thiel writes. "By the mid-1840s, the donkey-powered grain mills probably made life a lot easier."

Despite the challenges, in 1804, twenty-eight years after its founding, the remote community was thriving. In addition to the vegetables they grew, Presidio residents had meat, primarily beef, but also mutton. They kept chickens to supply their eggs.

The historian Thomas Sheridan writes in his book *Los Tucsonenses*: "Presidial captain José de Zúñiga reported that Tucson's fields produced 600 bushels of corn and 2,800 bushels of wheat a year. Her herds of cattle numbered 3,500 with 2,600 sheep, 1,200 horses, 120 mules and 30 burros. These fields and herds supported a human population of 1,015 scattered among the presidio, the Piman village across the river, and Mission San Xavier del Bac. Tucson had evolved into a typical agrarian community of Northern Sonora, a self-sufficient settlement of rancher-farmers supporting a garrison of soldiers no different in most respects from many other pueblos scattered across New Spain's northern frontier."

Sheridan continues: "They relied on a mixed economy of both agriculture and stock raising to make a living. It was a way of life geared to subsistence rather than commercial exploitation and expansion.

Rooted in the land, Tucsonenses endured flood and drought, assault and devastation, surviving largely because they understood the limitations imposed by a harsh environment and learned to live with it."

Although the soldiers were at the Presidio to protect citizens from Apache depredations, a group of "tame" Apaches settled next to the Presidio in 1792. Thiel writes, "In exchange for peace, the Spaniards provided them with about two hundred head of beef a year, along with agricultural tools and cloth and sewing goods."

In 1821, forty-five years after the first Spanish soldiers occupied the Presidio, Mexico won its independence from Spain and Mexican soldiers took over staffing of the fort.

Many of the Spanish soldiers, released from duty, decided to stay in the Tucson area. Those that had been farming outside the walls continued to do so. When the newly arrived Mexican officials took over, they often tried to assign lands to their soldiers that were already part of fields that belonged to other farmers. Many disputes followed, and the ultimate adjudications weren't always fair.

As important as the division of land was the allocation of water, and the choice of crops that could be grown on the water available. Again, Sheridan gives us a good look at what was going on, writing: "Cropping patterns were perhaps the most important adaptation to the scarcity of water. When most people think of preindustrial agriculture in the Sonoran Desert, they think of maize, beans and squash. Yet the foremost cultigen in Tucson was wheat, as both the 1804 Zúñiga report and an 1885 court case attest. Unlike the New World crops, wheat was sown in December or January and harvested in May or June. Along the Santa Cruz, farmers usually had enough water in their acequias (canals) to give their wheat or barley two irrigations during the growing season—enough moisture barely to ripen the grain. By early summer, however, when canals were nearly dry, the acequia system almost shut down. Corn grows in the summer, and because of the decreased flow in the river that staple of southwestern Indians could rarely be brought to maturity. When maize was planted, it was often only for fodder, the stalks serving as forage for hungry livestock. The constraints of their semiarid environment limited Tucson farmers to one major crop a year. Interestingly, that crop was a winter one, imported from the Old World."

Travelers through the area who stopped at the Presidio frequently reported what they had been served for dinner. By 1849, the reports included quinces, apples, pears, peaches, grapes, saguaro fruit, green beans, pumpkins, squash, and peas along with the usual beans and corn. James G. Bell, who ate at the Presidio in 1854, reported a dinner that concluded with pudding with almonds and peach marmalade. By the next year, bottled, canned, and dried foods, including rice, were arriving in Tucson on freight wagons. Oysters, a popular food of the day, arrived in barrels of ice.

TUCSON BECOMES PART OF THE UNITED STATES

After the ratification of the Gadsden Purchase in 1854, Tucson became part of the United States. It took two years for the Americans to send staff to the Presidio and when the soldiers arrived, they found the

Mexicans still on duty. Like the Spanish soldiers, many of the Mexicans elected to stay in the area and continue farming the fields they had been working.

In 1876, the U.S. government commissioned a study of Tucson's fields in order to grant title to lands occupied before 1875. When the Spanish soldiers had arrived at the Presidio in 1776 and needed to begin providing for themselves and their families, they each found a piece of land that appeared unoccupied and began planting. With no deeds, just customary use, they passed the fields on to their children for generations. Of course, all these fields had originally belonged to the Tohono O'odham. Only some of the native inhabitants had received compensation.

By the later part of 1880, some of the largest landowners were not farming themselves, but rather renting out their fields to others, in some cases to Chinese truck farmers. There was a growing market for fresh vegetables in Tucson and the Chinese farmers, some of whom had been railroad workers, took advantage of it by industriously working the fields. However, their vegetables were thirstier than the wheat, which could go weeks without water. The Chinese wanted to water every day and that put too much pressure on the limited water and left nothing for the Mexican farmers north of Sisters Lane (now St. Mary's Road).

Here's the point where the story of early farming in Tucson changes from accommodation to competition. The finely tuned custom of sharing agricultural water so everyone had barely enough broke down when the powerful men of the town were able to divert the limited water for their own purposes. Since the Santa Cruz flows north, the fields to the south of what was Sisters Lane got access to the water first. Traditionally the distribution of water was controlled by a *zanjero*, who would also oversee disputes. Landowners Sam Hughes, Leopoldo Carrillo, and W. C. Davis, who held lands to the south, appointed themselves water commissioners and instructed the *zanjero* to let their fields have all the water they required and if there wasn't any left for the poorer Mexicans downstream to the north of Sisters Lane, well, that was unfortunate.

There was some local acrimony when the Chinese were accused by the Mexican farmers downstream of stealing water. It came to a head in a court case in 1885. Since the landlords of the Chinese were the most powerful men in town, it wasn't a surprise to anyone how the case would turn out. It hinged on an assertion that the fields to the south were the oldest and deserved to get water first. The upshot was that the Chinese got as much water as they needed for their thirsty vegetables. In the opinion of some, their lavish use of the Santa Cruz's limited surface waters contributed to the disastrous erosion of the Santa Cruz River banks.

Meanwhile, after 1882 Tucson's domestic water needs were taken care of by a new water company with wells south of town. The articles of incorporation said that they planned to provide water for private residences, irrigation, and distribution ditches. Family gardens probably were able to make use of this supply.

The overuse of the Santa Cruz water continued, and some ill-advised schemes to divert water led to erosion. Several drought years were followed by heavy floods. The riverbanks were weakened by the canals and overgrazing. The result was that the streambed was lowered so far that all the ditches coming off the river were useless. The farmland that had nourished people along the Santa Cruz River for thousands of years became a neighborhood of modest homes. Part of it was used as the city dump.

More than a decade before the issue with the Santa Cruz water, some of the Mexican families found farmland about 7 miles to the east of Tucson near where the Pantano and Tanque Verde Washes came together to form the Rillito. The land had hosted centuries of farmers. Several Hohokam villages existed there between AD 675 and 1450. It was rich land, perfect for farming, and after the Gadsden Purchase a few Euro-American farmers joined the Mexican families. They gardened, planted fruit trees, and harvested mesquite firewood to sell in town.

Then in 1873 Camp Lowell was moved from the east side of 6th Avenue, between 12th and 14th Streets, to the Tanque Verde area and named the Fort Lowell Military Reservation. The military claimed a huge piece of land, 6 by 13 miles, so it could include all the water supply in its domain. Soldiers diverted some of the large acequias the farmers had been using into the fort. The settlers were ordered to give up their claims to the grass, wood, and water, but they refused to leave. It was the classic Arizona battle over water resources.

The tension continued for years, but after Geronimo was captured in 1886, there was less need for the fort. In January 1891, the troops left and the wood fixtures of the adobe buildings that had housed the operations were auctioned off. Without doors and windows, the buildings began to deteriorate rapidly, but they were houses, and they and the nearby fertile fields were attractive. Some Mexican families who had been living in central Tucson moved out there to take up farming and fix up the buildings for homes. They were soon joined by relatives and families from northern Sonora. Gilbert Molina, whose family came from Sonora in 1910 and raised chiles in the area, said, "Anything you stuck in the ground would grow the soil was so rich. We never had to add manure or fertilizer."

The community was called El Fuerte, and it was largely self-sufficient. The farmers grew chile, corn, beans, squash, watermelon, and other produce along the Rillito. There were also dairy farms. Seasonal wild foods supplemented the farmers' diets—greens in the spring and summer, acorns in the fall. Residents recalled thick clusters of watercress in the river. Hunters found adequate sources of meat in the foothills.

What the families didn't consume themselves they transported to Tucson by wagon to exchange for goods they couldn't grow such as salt, sugar, coffee, flour, matches, lamp chimneys, and wicks.

People remember the chile ristras that would hang from the walls in the fall, decorating the homes in fiery red and scenting the air.

By 1889, at least one Chinese farmer had joined the Mexican farmers. The *Arizona Daily Star* reported that a man named Lin Kee rented 16 acres of rich land near the Tanque Verde Wash where he raised corn, potatoes, sweet potatoes, onions, and chiles. In May, he sent a load of vegetables to Tombstone for sale.

Also settling in the area were Mormons, members of the Church of Jesus Christ of Latter-day Saints. Brothers Nephi and Dan Bingham arrived first and found good land near the Rillito where Dodge Boulevard meets River Road. They attracted more Mormons, most of them becoming dairy farmers who also raised hay and corn for their cattle. They called their self-sufficient community Binghamton.

As more residents moved to Tucson and spread out over the valley, wells were dug and later drilled, and with each new wave of inhabitants, the water table sank even deeper. Erosion lowered the stream-beds of the Pantano, the Tanque Verde, and the Rillito as it had the Santa Cruz making the old acequias worthless. Today that rich, deep soil still exists along the banks of the rivers, but the few farmers who wish to take advantage of it must rely on increasingly deep wells for irrigation.

Today visitors can see re-creations of thousands of years of farming cultures at the Mission Garden run by Friends of Tucson's Birthplace. The 4-acre site next to the Santa Cruz River is an outdoor museum on the exact spot where successions of farmers grew the food that fed the residents of S-cuk Son, and later Tucson. Read more on page 84.

FOR FURTHER READING

Burns, Barney. "Spanish Additions to the Agriculture of the Sonoran Desert." *Seedhead News*, Native Seeds/SEARCH, Autumn Equinox 2008.

Dunmire, William W. *Gardens of New Spain: How Mediterranean Plants and Foods Changed America*. University of Texas Press, Austin, 2005.

Esther Tang Files, Arizona Historical Society, Tucson.

Ferin, Clara. Handwritten manuscript. Arizona Historical Society, Tucson.

Lister, Florence C., and Robert H. Lister. *The Chinese of Early Tucson*. University of Arizona Press, Tucson, 2015.

Mabry, Jonathan. "Changing Knowledge and Ideas about the First Farmers in Southeastern Arizona." In *The Late Archaic across the Borderlands: From Foraging to Farming*. Edited by Bradley J. Vierra. University of Texas Press, Austin, 2005, pp. 41–83.

Maria Urquides Files, Arizona Historical Society, Tucson.

Officer, James E. "Kino and Agriculture in the Pimería Alta." *Journal of Arizona History*, Volume 34, Number 3, 1993, Arizona Historical Society, Tucson.

Sheridan, Thomas. *Los Tucsonenses*. University of Arizona Press, Tucson, 1986.

Thiel, J. Homer, and Alison Cohen Diehl. *Archaeological Investigations of a Chinese Gardener's Household*. Technical Report No. 96–22, Center for Desert Archaeology, Tucson, 1997.

Thompson, Raymond H., editor. *A Jesuit Missionary in Eighteenth-Century Sonora: The Family Correspondence of Philipp Segesser*. Translated by Werner S. Zimmt and Robert E. Dahlquist. University of New Mexico Press, Albuquerque, 2014.

Turner, Teresa. *The People of Fort Lowell*. Privately printed, Tucson, 1982.

U.S. Territorial Papers, Interior Department, 1863–1913, Report of Acting Governor Gosper, 1881. National Archives and Records Service, 1963.

WHITE SONORA HERITAGE WHEAT

The local-food movement is built on flavor, nutrition, and freshness. But it is also built on story and a sense of place. The word *heritage* feeds our longing for a feeling of rootedness. White Sonora wheat has a great story and that has led to its charisma. Actually, throughout the country, grains have been slower to join the lineup of reintroduced foods than other heritage seeds because unlike a vegetable like a squash, which can be picked and eaten quickly, wheat involves additional processing to become food. The early agriculturalists were accustomed to grinding seeds and wild grain in bedrock or free-standing mortars. Modern Americans are not.

The introduction of spring wheat (also called winter wheat) by the Spanish missionaries was a most welcome addition to the food cycle of local native people. The wheat came from Andalucía in southern Spain, where the climate is similar to the Santa Cruz basin. We can assume the Spanish brought several kinds of wheat seeds, but it was the spring wheat that adapted to local conditions best and made the most impact. By March, the Tohono O'odham granaries of stored foods, such as mesquite, were empty, and the early populations were getting hungry awaiting the plants that would be available later in the spring. But the various varieties of wheat we now call White Sonora and Pima Club could be planted in the fall or winter in our mild climate and take advantage of the winter rains. Some of the crop was harvested green in the spring, just when the people needed food the most. They prepared the grain by roasting it over coals. The rest was ripe by May having by then turned into golden fields.

Although the introduction of spring wheat to the people of the Sonoran Desert is attributed to Father Kino, it may have arrived even earlier in Sonora between 1640 and 1650 when Padre Lorenzo de Cárdenas provided it to the Eudeve Indians near the rural village of Tuape, about 170 miles south of Tucson in what is now Mexico. At first the wheat crop didn't produce as well as the native corn, but over the next hundred years the farmers learned how to grow it more successfully and the White Sonora and Pima Club wheat yielded twice as much food as did the fields planted with corn.

If the rapid spread of watermelons outpacing the northern movement of the missions is any indication, perhaps the native farmers shared knowledge of the new grain as well, with the introduction moving north from village to village. At any rate, Father Kino introduced the spring wheats widely to people living in the Santa Cruz Valley upon his arrival here in 1692.

The easy and quick adoption of spring wheat can be attributed to the fact that it filled an important niche in the food cycle. And, as a new crop, it came without cultural baggage. Corn was traditionally planted and curated through its life cycle with ceremony and song; wheat, on the other hand, with no such requirements, was easier to grow.

We also must not overlook the fact that in some mission communities, the local people had no choice but were forced to grow wheat for the padres' sacramental wafers.

Wheat berry–tepary bean stew became a popular dish especially in the Hispanic and Native American communities because for that recipe, the wheat didn't need to be ground.

By the mid-eighteenth century, spring wheat had become the major staple crop of the Tucson basin and way beyond. Although it does better with irrigation, in a normal, nondrought year, it could also

Flaky Sonoran Pie Crust

This recipe comes from Joy Hought, executive director of Native Seeds/SEARCH and an expert in grains including wheat.

Makes two 10-inch crusts

1 stick cold unsalted butter
½ cup cold (solid) coconut oil or shortening
1½ cups all-purpose flour or White Sonora pastry flour
1½ cups White Sonora whole-wheat flour
1 teaspoon salt
1 tablespoon sugar
2 teaspoons baking powder
8 to 10 tablespoons ice water (Sonora flour absorbs more
    water than regular flour)

Preheat oven to 425 degrees Fahrenheit. Dice the butter and coconut oil and return it to the refrigerator while you prepare the flour mixture. Sift the flours, salt, sugar, and baking powder together in a large bowl. Add the butter and shortening. Use a pastry cutter or fingertips to quickly blend until the fat is the size of peas. Add the ice water until the dough begins to form a ball. Do not overmix.

Dump out onto a floured board and roll into a ball, then flatten into two disks. Wrap in plastic wrap and refrigerate for at least 30 minutes, or overnight. On a well-floured board, roll each piece of dough into a circle, rolling from the center to the edge, turning and flouring the dough to make sure it doesn't stick to the board.

Use to make two pie shells or one pie with both a top and bottom crust. For single-crust pies, prick the bottoms with a fork. Bake at 425 degrees for 15 minutes, then lower the heat to 350 degrees for another approximately 10 minutes. Keep an eye on the crusts so they don't overbrown. For double crust pies, follow the directions for your pie.

produce an excellent crop in marginal soils of low fertility and with no water other than winter rainfall. With the abundance of wheat, women began making tortillas from flour instead of corn. Originally these tortillas were small, about the size of corn tortillas.

The various varieties of White Sonora spread, and it was grown throughout the California coast and into Oregon. At the turn of the twentieth century until about 1920, millions of acres of White Sonora were grown throughout the West. It was the staple wheat for the western United States for almost 200 years.

The 1920s and 1930s were the beginning of the Green Revolution which advocated increasing grain yields through application of copious amounts of water and high nitrogen fertilizer. White Sonora did not thrive under those conditions. Mill technology also changed, making it more difficult to grind the soft, powdery wheat berries, which tended to absorb water.

The market also changed. Soft wheat varieties like White Sonora are used for crackers, cookies, biscuits, and pie crust. Bakeries were producing more bread and what they wanted was the hard red wheat. The soft heritage wheats fell out of favor.

Then came the closing of many flour mills in Sonora due to a multitude of economic factors. It was a downward spiral because without a means to get their grain ground, more farmers quit growing it.

Some Tohono O'odham families, however, continued to dry-farm White Sonora wheat up through the 1970s even though they had to take it all the way to Phoenix to be ground at the Hayden Flour Mills.

White Sonora wheat berries cooked until tender and combined with vegetables make a hearty salad.

White Sonora Wheat-Berry Salad

This is modified from a dish made by chef Janos Wilder and served at his Downtown Kitchen + Cocktails. Chop all the fruit into pieces about the size of raisins. If you have any fruit-flavored vinegars or olive oil, this is a good place to use them. Date vinegar from Iskashitaa Refugee Network also works well.

1 cup dry wheat berries
⅓ cup chopped dates (about 6)
⅓ cup chopped apricots or golden raisins
½ cup chopped apple
1 shredded carrot
⅓ cup hulled sunflower seeds, roasted
1 cup shredded baby spinach
⅓ cup crumbled goat cheese

Dressing:
4½ tablespoons olive oil
1 teaspoon honey or agave syrup
1 teaspoon mustard
2 tablespoons fruit vinegar

Cover wheat berries with 2 cups water, bring to a boil, cover, and turn heat down to a simmer. Cook 45–60 minutes until tender but chewy. Transfer to a medium bowl and add fruit, carrot, and seeds.

To make the dressing, put the oil in a cup and stir in the honey and mustard. Dribble the vinegar in while whisking vigorously with a fork. Add to other ingredients and stir to combine. Refrigerate. Just before serving, stir in shredded spinach and top with crumbled goat cheese.

WARNER'S MILL

During the time that wheat was being grown locally, there was need for a mill to turn it into flour. In early 1871, Solomon Warner, a Tucson storekeeper, purchased a partially constructed mill located on the east slope of Sentinel Peak. It was another three years before he began work on the mill and another year before it opened in 1875.

The mill was in a two-story building with the first floor of stone and the upper level of adobe. It was powered by water from springs to the south brought by a canal Warner had hired someone to dig. The water was enough to power machinery that turned a pair of giant millstones. According to archaeologist J. Homer Thiel, the mill was immediately successful, grinding more than 180,000 pounds of locally grown wheat into flour during the first four months of operation.

And there continued to be a need for Warner's services: According to U.S. Territorial Papers of the Interior Department, in 1881 the county produced one million pounds of both wheat and barley.

With water always an issue in a desert, in 1883 Warner constructed a dam to store water for the mill, leading to disputes with farmers who also relied on that water.

In July 1884, he even received a legal notice that stated:

> You are hereby notified that you are interfering with the water in the Santa Cruz and obstructing the free and continuous passage of the same at your mill and lake and water being taken from and prevented from flowing in the public acequia without the consent of the water overseer and to the damage of landowners thereto. You are also notified that unless you desist from interfering with and using said water in the manner you are now doing that you will be proceeded against in accordance with the law.

Eventually the issue was resolved, and Warner's Lake became a center for recreation for the dusty town. The water attracted ducks and became an attractive place for hunting. It was also stocked with carp.

Warner sold the mill in 1886 and a dozen years later, with less wheat being grown in Tucson, the mill shut down. The mill was dynamited in the 1930s and only its foundation remains along Grande Avenue. However, the adobe home Warner built for himself still stands.

Other small-scale farmers continued to grow minimal amounts, but commercial sources of White Sonora wheat had disappeared by around 1975.

In late 1970s and early 1980s, the then doctoral student Gary Paul Nabhan was interested in heritage crops and went on a hunt to see if anyone was still growing the White Sonora wheat. He found two farmers along the Mexican border, one in Big Fields on the Tohono O'odham Reservation and one in Sonora about a mile into Mexico. He helped the farmers sow a crop with draft horses and later went back with friends to harvest it with sickles and thresh the grain with mules.

When crops disappear, the knowledge of the best way to grow them disappears as well. As interest in heritage crops grew during the early years of the twenty-first century, millers, brewers, and bakers were looking for something new. Around 2010, several Southern Arizona forces coalesced to start the latest chapter of the White Sonora story. At the University of Arizona, folklorist Maribel Alvarez was looking at Norteño cultural identity in regard to local wheat. In Phoenix, miller Jeff Zimmerman, who was reviving the Hayden Flour Mills brand, and the James Beard Award–winning chef Chris Bianco were looking for heritage wheat. Bianco was interested in using it in his acclaimed pizza.

In 2012, Native Seeds/SEARCH, a Tucson nonprofit seed bank specializing in arid-land heritage seeds, was awarded a two-year grant from Western Sustainable Agriculture Research and Education, a program of the U.S. Department of Agriculture (USDA), to reintroduce into sustained production two heritage grains with historical presence and good potential for adaptation in the arid Southwest: White Sonora wheat and Chapalote flint corn.

Joy Hought of Native Seeds/SEARCH writes: "Unlike vegetable crops, bringing back local production of grains involves rebuilding the complex supply and processing chains that went extinct in many American communities at the turn of the twentieth century. This project required an ambitious collaborative strategy that engaged researchers, community nonprofits, producers and end-users from farm to table."

Today the heritage wheats, both White Sonora and Pima Club, are making a strong comeback due to their sweet flavor, disease resistance, and drought tolerance. The green leaves are resistant to rust, and the grain resists the *Fusarium* fungus. Their low gluten content makes them a good choice for people with gluten sensitivity. Specialty bakers advertise breads made with local heritage wheats, and local beer brewers use them as an ingredient. Users even collaborate with some local breweries offering their spent grain to bakers for inclusion in bread.

One of the most enthusiastic producers of heritage grains is BKW Farms north of Tucson in Marana. Ron Wong, one of the partners in the family farm, said that in 2013 he was looking for something new to grow organically that didn't have a shelf life. The White Sonora wheat the Wongs planted found a ready market, and they have increased the acreage every year. In 2018, BKW planted 60 acres of White Sonora and harvested 2,000 pounds an acre. They sold two-thirds as berries to more than a dozen craft brewers and one-third as flour that was ground at their facility. BKW Farms also grows small amounts of Khorasan and Red Fife heritage wheats for baking. The drawback for commercial farmers is that durum wheat produces 7,000 to 8,000 pounds of berries per acre, four times as much as heritage wheat. A single White Sonora plant and a single durum plant each produce about the same amount of grain, but the durum variety can be planted more densely.

White Sonora is also grown by San Xavier Co-op Farm, 9 miles south of Tucson, and Ramona Farms, about 80 miles to the north, both of which sell it commercially.

The benefit of White Sonora wheat remains its superior flavor, its drought heartiness, the way it malts (sprouts) for use in brewing, and the flakiness it imparts to pastries. Many people with gluten sensitivity are thrilled to report that they can eat bread and pastries made with White Sonora with no adverse health issues.

CHINESE GARDENERS, RESTAURANT OWNERS, AND GROCERS

The arrival of the railroad in Tucson in the spring of 1880 changed what Tucsonans ate in a number of ways. It brought a greater population of European-Americans from the East. They were used to a wider selection of food than the tortillas, beans, squash, beef, and wild foods that had been Tucson staples for generations. Some folks were growing a few of the European vegetables and herbs introduced by the Spanish, but these were mainly subsistence gardens and there wasn't enough extra to supply the market. Merchants could order vegetables and fresh seafood from California via the railroad. The building of the tracks also brought Chinese workers who decided to settle in Tucson once the tracks made it to the little desert city. Many of them had come from farming areas of China and knew how to garden. If the market needed vegetables, they knew how to grow them.

When the Chinese entered Tucson, they joined what was already a multiethnic community with Anglos and Mexicans living side by side and Native Americans nearby. Because of this, their reception wasn't as hostile as it was in some other communities. There were no inflammatory newspaper articles or ridiculing cartoons. In Tucson, they found work in laundries, mines, and ranches. They also elevated the food choices in this remote community when they went into business setting up restaurants, grocery stores, and vegetable gardens.

The information we have on the early Chinese in Tucson comes from newspaper accounts, census data, archaeological digs, memories of a few non-Chinese living at the time, and a few family memories of Chinese living in Tucson today. Although some of the Chinese learned to speak enough English and Spanish to conduct business, they weren't fluent. There are no letters or interviews conducted at the time.

The earliest documented Chinese resident was a man named Wong Tai, who had opened a restaurant in Tucson by July 1876, even before the railroad arrived. A newspaper advertisement for his Celestial Restaurant read:

The Wong family poses inside their market at 546 North Stone Avenue. From left are Wong Yan Sing, Bing Kun Wong, Bing Gan Wong, Jimmy K. Wong, and Moy Youk Lang. Photo was taken around 1926. (Courtesy of the Wong family)

This first-class restaurant is on Congress street near the Church Plaza. The Chief Cook and Baker is "Louy," one of the very best and who is well known to be such. Patronage is solicited. Fare Excellent and Charges Reasonable. (*Arizona Weekly Citizen*, July 15, 1876)

In 1879, a newspaper article estimated the total number of Chinese residents in Tucson at about 30. After more Chinese settled in the city when the Southern Pacific Railroad reached the Tucson railhead in March 1880, the federal census taken in June 1880 counted 160 Chinese residents, about half of them working in food service.

Those Chinese who wished to farm moved to areas at the base of Sentinel Peak where they rented farmland from some of the town's leading citizens, among them Leopoldo Carrillo. Carrillo had a home on his land, but after he rented it out, he moved into town, living in what is now the Sosa-Carrillo-Frémont House, currently part of the Arizona Historical Society.

Small groups of single male Chinese would join to rent and work some fields, always with the thought of making as much money as possible so they could return home with capital to start a good life in China. Typically, several relatives worked one farm. Eventually more than 150 acres were under cultivation in the area, watered by ditches off the river. In lush and green gardens, these farmers specialized in fruits and vegetables usually not grown by their Hispanic neighbors.

A typical Chinese diet at the time included more vegetables than Americans generally ate. Dena Cowan, the supervisor at Mission Garden during the planning of the Chinese Garden, did extensive research by speaking to the Chinese community and looking at historic documents. She put together a long list of crops grown by the Chinese gardeners for their own use. They included long beans, winter melon, bitter melon, Chinese cabbage, water spinach, Chinese broccoli, goji berry (leaves eaten), fuzzy melon, kohlrabi, soybeans, garlic, cilantro, snap peas, chives, leek, snow peas, Chinese radish, mustard green, spring onion, small cabbage, watercress, Ceylon spinach, peanuts, eggplant, winter squash, and summer squash (what the Mexicans called *calabasa*).

Chinese-Style Turkey Stuffing

Mary Wong grew up in Barrio Anita where the Chinese adopted Mexican and American food traditions mixing them with their own Chinese customs. Here is a turkey stuffing using rice, a favorite Chinese food. Mary, who was 94 years old when she shared this recipe, was a dear friend of my mother-in-law.

¼ cup dried shrimp
6–7 dried Chinese black mushrooms
2 cups glutinous sweet rice
1 cup long grain rice
Sprinkle of salt
1 cup diced hard Chinese sausage
1 cup diced ham
1 small onion, chopped
1 teaspoon oil
1 teaspoon soy sauce

Three hours before beginning to cook, soak the dried shrimp in a small bowl. In a separate bowl, soak the Chinese black mushrooms.

Put the rice to soak in water to cover for one hour.

When you are ready to cook, drain and rinse the rice. Put in a pot with 2½ cups water and sprinkle of salt. Cook over low heat until water is absorbed, and rice is tender.

While the rice is cooking, dice the hard Chinese sausage and the ham, and chop the onion. Heat the oil in a large, heavy frying pan and sauté the meat and onion. Add the soy sauce and set aside. When rice is finished, add it to the frying pan and mix with the meat. Cover the frying pan and cook over very low heat for 20 minutes. Use to stuff a turkey or chicken.

Additionally, they grew produce particularly for their Tucson customers including strawberries, artichokes, cabbage, corn, potatoes, sweet potatoes, chiles, carrots, various melons, grapes, apples, lettuce, spinach, and turnips.

Fruits included jujube, peaches, kumquats, mulberries, plums, apricots, figs, tangerines, Valencia oranges, grapefruits, pomelos, lemons, limes, grapes, and pecans. Since many of these fruits grow on trees, the farmers were making a commitment to spend enough time for the trees to mature.

This intense method of gardening required lots of irrigation. The Chinese farmers wanted to water every day, and if it wasn't their turn to get water in their canal, they took 5-gallon pots down to the river, filled them up, and took them up to irrigate their fields and seedlings. (A more complete discussion of the problems this caused is on page 50.)

In 1887, fifteen-year-old Clara Ferin, who grew up to be a schoolteacher and valued community volunteer, wrote an essay about Chinese farmers in Tucson. From the level of detail and her keen observations, we can assume that she had visited one of the farms. The work is rendered in her lovely handwriting, and at the end she writes: "My first essay to be read in public." Here are sections of her essay:

Jimmy K. Wong and Moy Youk Lang sit on the running board of a car in front of the family grocery store. (Courtesy of the Wong family)

About fifteen years ago the vegetable Chinamen first came to Tucson to live and cultivate farms and raise vegetables. . . .

They are of a very industrious and preserving nature, independent and quick-tempered. They all speak enough English to make themselves understood. . . . Most of the vegetable gardens are situated in the outskirts of the city, some as far out as Fort Lowell while others are on the road to the Tucson mountains. Adjoining their gardens are small huts built of adobes and ornamented by tin cans, barley sacks and bushes in which two or three partners, or "cousins" as they call each other, live together.

When working on their farms, they present a very comical appearance with their trousers rolled up above their knees, barefoot, and sometimes shirtless. They wear large straw hats like inverted wash basins and with a shovel in hand go about in the mud getting the vegetables ready for the morning. The Chinamen take very good care of their gardens. The get up early in the morning and while one goes to town the other one or two plow the grounds carefully all day. They do most of the work by hand, pushing steadily along behind the plow until the ground has been laid in smooth furrows. After the soil has been well tilled, the vegetables are planted in long rows from one side of the field to the other. As soon as the plants begin to grow, they are covered with coal oil cans to protect them from the sun.

Chinese farmers delivered their produce house to house in wagons like this one. (Arizona Historical Society)

After discussing how beautiful the gardens were, Clara discussed the marketing.

The one who sells the produce comes into town as early as five o'clock in the morning so that the vegetables will not be withered by the sun and will be fresh when they arrive in the market.

When in town, [the farmer] wears dark blue overalls and a loose china jacket; his pig-tail is wound around his head in a cue under his large straw hat. All the morning he goes from house to house selling vegetables from a strong but shabby wagon. His horse is fat and sleepy and goes down the street at a jogging pace.

Their methods of business are very exact. They sell their vegetables in small quantities and will not be induced to come down in their prices however high. They have their special customers and keep the accounting by marking down on the casement of the door the amount bought each day and at the end of the month they have not the trouble of making out bills.

Years later, Maria Urquides, whose father owned a few of the rented lots, recalled the Chinese gardeners:

There were little stables there, and there would be about four Chinese vendors who would keep their wagons there to have an early start. And they would take their vegetables—and you know how artistic they are—they'd pick the carrots and the onions and the calabacitas (little squashes) and they'd arrange them on their wagons, cover them with gunny sacks, and wet them. And this was in the evening, and I can often remember going to sleep with the sing-song of their patter. They'd sprinkle the gunny sacks with water, and it was just like an evaporative cooler to keep the vegetables fresh overnight. And then they'd start early in the morning and come back at night with empty wagons. They were a terrific people. I had a very soft spot in my heart for the Chinese. Of course, we used to steal a little carrot every now and then from them.

The 1900 federal census listed 34 Chinese farmers in the Tucson area. They were apparently astute marketers, for one newspaper story read: "Mou Op, a Chinese vegetable gardener who lives in the valley just west of town, says he will have a box of ripe strawberries next week. He will very likely sell them at auction and with the proceeds go back to China on a special steamer and be a wealthy member of the emperor's court for the rest of his days."

Another Chinese farmer had fields where El Encanto Estates is now, near Broadway Boulevard and Country Club Road. He supplied Albert Steinfeld's gourmet store with fancy vegetables, all of them needing to be uniform in size and color.

Because the Chinese community kept much to themselves, not a great deal was known about how they lived. However, in the early 1990s, work needed to be done on a drainage along Mission Road near the modern Spruce Street. Because of the requirement for cultural mitigation, the Center for Desert Archaeology was hired to investigate the area, which turned out to be the site of an early Chinese garden and household.

By sifting through the household's trash, the archaeologists were able to find evidence that the family had eaten pork, chicken, and beef with the bones cut into small pieces to facilitate eating with chopsticks. Also present were butchered cat remains and land turtle carapaces.

Seafood was a typical part of the diet of Chinese people and one report said that early Chinese railway workers near Yuma were so starved for fish that they left their work one day and went to fish in the Colorado River. At the Mission Road site, researchers found bones from several species of fish, including some large saltwater varieties probably brought to Tucson from California packed in ice on the Southern Pacific Railroad. Fish could be found closer to home when merchant Chan Tin Wo leased nearby Warner Lake to raise carp for his Chinese customers.

In a talk to the Tucson Metro Chamber of Commerce in 1985, civic leader Esther Tang recalled:

> My father Don Wah owned the first bakery in connection with a grocery store on Simpson and Convent St. He delivered bread by horse and buggy with a bucket of burning coal to keep warm. Eventually he parlayed this same neighborhood market into a chain of successful grocery stores. . . . The Chinese grocery stores were the convenience markets of today—the difference was they acted as bankers for their customers and charged groceries in a manner no banker or businessman would dare practice. I remember my parents gave customers a "cartera," a notebook recording purchases but returning the notebook to the purchaser without a record for themselves . . . that's trust. In transactions, a handshake was sufficient.

Another Chinese grocer who came with the railroad was Wong Yan who was assisted in his business by his wife, Moy Youk, and his children. When their eldest son, Bing Kun Wong, was a young adult, he realized that the people living 15 miles north in Marana and out at the Tohono O'odham Reservation had little access to groceries and began delivering in both places. With frequent trips to Marana, Bing saw the potential in farming there, bought some land, and planted cotton. Since he had made friends on the reservation, he invited some Tohono O'odham farmers to come to work for him. Today his sons and a grandson run BKW Farms in Marana. They are still principally cotton growers, but they have branched into durum wheat, which they sell for pasta, and heritage grains such as White Sonora, Khorasan, and Red Fife wheat varieties.

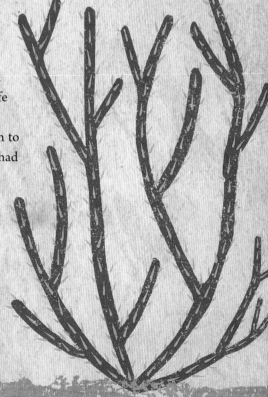

By 1952, the list of Tucson Chinese grocery stores had grown to 114 along with several dozen other stores. Every neighborhood had several Chinese markets; busy mothers could send a child to pick up an item since the store was only a block or two away. Everybody in the family was expected to pitch in, even small children. One woman recalls waiting on customers when she was as young as eight, even selling beer and cigarettes. In the 1970s there were still more than a hundred groceries owned by Chinese families; in 1988, 41 grocery stores remained along with 77 Chinese restaurants.

GARDENING IN THE DESERT

GROWING YOUR OWN VEGETABLES, TUCSON STYLE

FOR MOST OF HUMAN EXPERIENCE, growing your own food, or most of it, was a given. The Santa Cruz Valley has a 4,000-year history of people doing just that. However, with increasing urbanization, people began drifting away from gardening. Then in the 1940s, World War II and the need to send a great deal of food production overseas brought U.S. home gardeners back to the vegetable patch. President Franklin D. Roosevelt championed "Victory Gardens" and by 1943, 20 million Victory Gardens supplied more than 40 percent of American produce grown that year. However, once the war was over, interest in vegetable gardens and orchards waned, and Americans fell in love with all things modern, including frozen vegetables.

Now local interest in growing our own food is on the upswing again. Americans are becoming more health conscious and are learning about and embracing the benefits of fresh local food and its superior vitamin content. By 2013, one-third of American households reported growing some of their food.

Growing food in our desert climate can be daunting. Gardeners can improve their chances of success with seeds from the Pima County Public Library's free seed library and from Native Seeds/SEARCH, which specializes in heritage seeds from the arid Southwest.

COMMUNITY GARDENS OF TUCSON

Not everyone who wants to garden or is considering raising a portion of their own food has suitable yard space or the knowledge of how to get started. Some people like the idea of a community experience, working with others. The Community Gardens of Tucson can fulfill the needs of all these folks at twenty gardens located all over the Tucson basin.

Gardeners who sign up with Community Gardens are assigned a plot equipped with drip irrigation and pay a user fee of $18 per month that covers water and use of tools. Tucson Water has instituted special water rates for community gardens to encourage local, community agriculture. Scholarships are available to cover costs for those who can't afford the monthly fee. Everyone who is assigned a 3-by-20-foot plot must agree to a list of rules, including using only organic gardening amendments and keeping their plot fully planted in herbs, vegetables, and flowers throughout the year in order to use water efficiently. Most of the rules are common-sense requirements for any shared-use venture.

Community Gardens of Tucson offers classes to help families learn to garden together. This garden is located at Congregation Chaverim. (Erin Brown)

I visited retired University of Arizona scientists Jennifer Hall and David Mount as they were uncovering their garden plants after an uncharacteristic freeze. Because they had planted vegetables that could take cold weather, they were happy to see little damage. Their garden, in three 3-by-20-foot plots behind Saint Demetrios Greek Orthodox Church, is at a site run by Community Gardens of Tucson. They are experienced gardeners with flourishing beds of turnips, chard, fava beans, two kinds of spinach, and three kinds of peas. Each exuberantly growing cauliflower, broccoli, and artichoke plant takes up a circle about a yard across, which is a benefit of the larger garden plots: lots of space.

Despite the fact that their plots appear to be healthy, Hall and Mount have faced challenges. Bermuda grass is persistent, aphids love the broccoli leaves, and Mount had to plant the peas four times to get them to come up. But after years of experience, they know how to figure a way around the issues. As the volunteer managers of this garden, Hall and Mount can contribute their expertise to new gardeners who might be daunted by early failures.

According to Elizabeth Smith, executive director of Community Gardens, at some of the long-established gardens, participants see growing food as only one of the advantages. "These people have been gardening together for a very long time. Getting to know their fellow gardeners is an important bonus. Community is built when the gardeners work together helping each other with harvests and weeding. This leads to potlucks and friendships."

Community Gardens of Tucson is overseen by a community board of directors and run by a staff of three who collect dues, pay bills, and see to the overall organization. In addition, each garden has a site coordinator to make sure everything runs smoothly and to help with education for beginners.

The Community Gardens of Tucson doesn't own any of the garden properties. They are located on vacant lots on loan or on land that is part of churchyards or schoolyards. This makes access of water and electricity more convenient. If the gardens are on school property, teachers can work them into their curriculum as illustrations for topics such as local food systems, nutrition, math, and botany. When vacant lots are lent by property owners, Community Gardens asks the owners to commit for a minimum of five years.

Establishing a new community garden in previously undeveloped land is a more complicated process than one might expect. In mid-2018, people on the far east side of town located a plot of land near Houghton and Valencia Roads that would work as a community garden. They knew they would face considerable costs, so they wrote grants and had bake sales and garden tours. Before putting a spade into the ground or accessing one packet of seed, they had months of legal work. The zoning allowed a garden, but since it was previously undeveloped land, first they needed to prove there were no protected species on the property, then came adherence to the City of Tucson Native Plant Preservation Ordinance. Detailed drawings needed to address topographical watershed runoff, buffer zones, property boundaries, and easements. Then it was on to irrigation and rainwater harvesting.

In some parts of town, neighbors have set up community gardens on their own. They have found an unused plot, obtained permission to use it, and forged ahead. If the property is not undeveloped land like that out on Houghton, the process is much simpler. This is the case with university neighborhoods Rincon Heights and Iron Horse, whose members determined that the monthly fee for the Community Gardens of Tucson would preclude too many of their low-income neighbors from participating. Rincon Heights rents land from the University of Arizona for a nominal fee, and Iron Horse uses land in the city-owned Iron Horse Park.

REFUGEES BRING GARDENING SKILLS TO MIDTOWN GARDEN

Among the gardeners working in the community gardens are refugees settled in Tucson by the International Rescue Committee (IRC). Many of these people come from a gardening background in their home countries and are anxious to grow the foods that are part of their culinary tradition.

The IRC sponsors them for plots in community gardens nearest to their homes. Once again, it's not just about the vegetables. It's also about forging friendships in a strange land. Gardeners hail from many different countries including the Democratic Republic of the Congo, Burundi, Syria, Rwanda, Congo, and Afghanistan.

For those who enjoy gardening and wish to expand to grow more than just food for themselves, the IRC conducts a farming program for participants who have spent at least one successful year in a community garden plot. It offers an eight-week program in a "microproducer academy," where garden-ers learn the intricacies of small-scale farming in the United States. They learn not only how to scale up their farming but also how to market their surplus.

"They are so excited to use their skills," explains Katrina Martinez, Nutrition and Food Security program supervisor of the local IRC office. "They know quite a bit about plants, but to be successful, they need to learn about gardening in the desert, things like irrigation, and to adapt to what Americans like to eat."

Some of the refugees who are graduates of that program are farming land at Las Milpitas, the Community Food Bank of Southern Arizona garden, where they are growing broccoli; cabbage; root crops like beets, carrots, and onions; and greens. Even in the summer, they have had good luck with peppers.

In early 2018, Literacy Connects, a program that promotes literacy for all ages, wanted to put to use an empty plot of land next to their offices and offered it to the IRC for a garden. In a true community endeavor, volunteers from Habitat for Humanity dug the garden plots, installed irrigation, and built a shed. Literacy Connects agreed to pay for the water. The IRC pays for seed, materials, and equipment. By fall, twenty-five refugee families were working the new Literacy Garden.

Having access to the vegetables and foods you grew up with makes the transition to a new home easier. So the refugees living in the Desert Courtyard Apartments on North Alvernon Way decided to grow their own. With help and encouragement from the apartment owners and help from Iskashitaa Refugee Network, they took over an empty plot south of the apartments. Many of the residents were experienced farmers in their homelands, and now the garden is lush year-round with leafy greens and twining vines. In 2019 they took over an unused plot to the north and began more gardens.

GARDENING WITH THE COMMUNITY FOOD BANK

The Community Food Bank of Southern Arizona is committed to helping its clients get access to fresh vegetables. Because the freshest produce is what you grow yourself, the Food Bank offers gardening classes at Nuestra Tierra, a small garden beside the main Food Bank headquarters on South Country Club Road. Once they have gained sufficient skill, clients can take over a plot at the Food Bank–operated community garden Las Milpitas or at one of the many community gardens around Tucson. If clients have room in the yard at their home, Food Bank staff will help them plan a garden and work out a system of irrigation to make the best use of scarce water.

It's clear that Tucsonans do want to learn to garden. More than a thousand participants come to the Community Food Bank gardening workshops each year. They say they want to improve their health and the health of their children and they have gotten the message that eating more fresh vegetables is the way to do it. Participants learn not only gardening basics but also worm composting, beekeeping, how solar devices can help in growing fish and plants, and wildlife conservation. If they need seeds,

LAS MILPITAS GARDEN

It's a muggy morning in mid-August when Angela Soliz gets to work in her plot at Las Milpitas de Cottonwood Community Farm. She is taking over the plot, one of sixty available for gardeners, from someone who moved out of Tucson and gave up the space. She clips overgrown basil, eyes a small green chile, and checks the golden cherry tomatoes and a few small plants that will eventually produce eggplants. Tonight, the basil will go into a bruschetta for Angela's dinner.

Las Milpitas is on Cottonwood Lane, along the west bank of the Santa Cruz River. Shaded in the summer by ancient mesquite and acacia trees, it was farmed for thousands of years by native people who lived in the area. Before erosion, the Santa Cruz ran level with the land and annual flooding fertilized the soil.

In 2011, the Community Food Bank began working to turn the 6 acres of county-owned land (which they rent for $1 a year) into today's garden. City High School, a charter school, had begun work on the property but didn't have the resources to fully develop the concept. When the Food Bank organizers stepped in, they began by envisioning the space as a community project. Neighbors were brought into the process over a series of meetings.

Elena Ortiz, the garden manager, says, "We didn't want it to be a place where someone comes on their own and gardens and leaves." In fact, gardeners meet each other by participating in classes and by volunteering time on garden functions other than their own plots. Since research has shown that people are healthier physically, mentally, and emotionally when they are connected to others, the garden promotes social health as well as all the healthy vitamins in the vegetables that clients grow.

Priority for plots goes to families who identify as low income or who live close to the farm. About half the gardeners have a family income of $2,000 a month or less; one-third of gardeners receive benefits from the federal Supplemental Nutrition Assistance Program (SNAP) or from Arizona's Women, Infants, and Children nutritional program called WIC. Nearly 90 percent of the gardeners report being able to decrease the size of their grocery bills because of the produce they grow.

The 4-by-20-foot plots are free to use and come equipped with drip irrigation. Gardeners can receive free seeds, fertilizer, mulch, fencing, and shade cloth. They are asked to attend classes on subjects like irrigation and composting, and to volunteer to participate in the larger projects. There are even cooking classes to let gardeners learn how to prepare unfamiliar vegetables, such as kale.

In addition to the individual plots, other garden areas produce vegetables that are sold at the Community Food Bank's farmers' market or used at its community kitchen, Caridad, where meals for the homeless and others are prepared.

Four plots are used by immigrant farmers sponsored by the International Rescue Committee. They have graduated from a gardening-for-market program and are now selling their produce at farmers' markets.

Volunteer help is central to running such a complex endeavor and Las Milpitas attracts many willing hands—around three thousand volunteers a year from such community groups as the

Angela Soliz works in her plot at Las Milpitas de Cottonwood Community Farm, a function of the Community Food Bank of Southern Arizona.

University of Arizona's Eller College of Management, local schools, and businesses doing service projects.

Having a farm and teaching people to grow food was a departure from the typical food bank program of handing out supplementary food boxes. But in Tucson's mild climate where you can garden nearly year-round, it seemed like a logical move to help people get access to more produce. One-third of the gardeners have a family member managing a diet-related disease and are learning about the health benefits of the fresh produce they grow.

Meanwhile, Angela is finishing up her chores and the freshness of early morning is giving way as the sun rises higher in the sky. Some children who have accompanied their parents are feeding the two dozen chickens the remains of their white pomegranates. It's a happy place this morning. People are collaborating on projects, sharing information on gardening, and taking home healthy food. It's just what the organizers hoped for.

they only need to ask. The Food Bank maintains an annual goal of distributing 10,000 seed packets and 300 fruit-bearing trees.

That number of new gardening enthusiasts is more than the Food Bank staff can keep up with. In turn, they have decentralized by training community members as garden leaders to help install gardens and irrigation systems and troubleshoot issues for new gardeners.

STARTING EARLY: GETTING KIDS INTO THE GARDEN

What child doesn't love to dig in the dirt? And when the result is food, that can be an awakening to the miracle that is gardening. But advocates for teaching children to garden emphasize that lessons extend beyond the production of food. Gardening helps with math skills, communication, perseverance, science, and cooperation. Tucson's best vegetable growing season coincides with the school year, so teachers can conveniently work gardening into their lesson plans.

University of Arizona Community and School Garden Program

About 30 first-graders march into the cafeteria at Manzo Elementary School and are soon clad in kid-sized aprons and plastic gloves too big for their tiny hands. They are excited to see in front of them piles of fragrant basil harvested from the school garden. They are going to make pesto.

Leading the lesson is a calm Rani Olson, coordinator of the Farm to School and Food Literacy programs at the Tucson Unified School District (TUSD), assisted by University of Arizona interns, some of whom are completing requirements for becoming registered dietitians. Others are enrolled in the UA Community and School Garden Workshop.

With the goal of introducing students to healthy eating, the Community Food Bank installed gardens in dozens of schools, many in low-income areas. They did not have the staff, however, to maintain the gardens, and the already-overburdened teachers didn't have the time—and in many cases the knowledge—to make them flourish.

Help has come from interns enrolled in the UA Community and School Garden Workshop. The popular class is always fully subscribed at 60 students a semester.

"The interns, the teachers, and the schoolchildren all love the school gardens," says Sally Marston, director of the program. "There are so many things the kids can learn—what makes good soil, how to harvest rainwater, even entrepreneurship when they sell their organic eggs and fish in a school-run farmers' market."

Also part of the Community and School Garden Workshop team is Moses Thompson, who acts as a coordinator between the UA and TUSD. Thompson, originally a school counselor, had nationally

While the children at Manzo Elementary School love taking care of the chickens, they also learn entrepreneurship when they sell their organic eggs at the market. (Chris Richards)

recognized success in developing the garden at Manzo Elementary School. Manzo's many awards for its ecology programs have led to it calling itself "the greenest elementary school on the planet."

Students in the UA Community and School Garden Workshop come from such diverse majors as art, nutrition, plant science, Latin American studies, speech and hearing, public health, and education. A neuroscience student studied the social and emotional effect on the children of spending more time outside.

Before the university students begin their internships in the gardens, they learn to implement a healthy garden and maintain garden infrastructure—like the compost systems, water-harvesting cisterns, and cultivating a healthy space for chickens.

But it's not all about the plants. Marston adds, "Especially important is a session on managing children in the garden—how to keep the kids organized and focused on learning. While the gardens are fun for both younger students and the interns, learning is the ultimate goal: turning outdoor spaces into classrooms for social studies, math, science, culture, and art through direct experience rather than passive learning."

A hiccup in the program occurred when usually vegetable-shy students wanted to taste what they had grown. The Arizona Department of Health Services, which oversees school lunches, was wary of

Teachers at schools with gardens try to incorporate lessons in math, science, and nutrition into the daily ritual of caring for the gardens. Kids are introduced to unfamiliar vegetables. (Chris Richards)

serving kids anything that didn't originate from standard commercial equipment, but working in collaboration with the Community Food Bank, they eventually put together a comprehensive garden-to-cafeteria list of requirements for school gardens that includes an analysis of soil composition, fertilization, and water sources. Now, depending on how much is harvested from each garden, the occasional school lunch can include school-grown produce.

The garden program serves twenty low-income schools in TUSD, two in the Sunnyside Unified School District, and three community gardens, all places the UA students can travel to in a reasonable amount of time.

Classroom teachers who wish to learn more about the science of food production and about using the gardens for teaching and research are invited to the Green Academy, a set of courses for which they receive professional development credit.

While the garden program has an undeniable feel-good component, it also provides impressive measurable results. A program evaluation by the University of Arizona's Southwest Institute for Research on Women showed 90 percent of students reported that working in the garden made them want to learn more about plants, water, and animals, and a similar percentage said that the program taught them about biodiversity and healthy foods. Sixty-nine percent of elementary students and 72 percent of high school students said that school gardens helped them to learn subjects like math, reading, and science.

Most students said that the school garden had a positive impact on their emotional well-being, an important factor since research shows that a child's sense of emotional stability is central to their academic success.

The Community and School Garden Program appears to be a win-win on all counts. Tucson children learn about gardening and healthy food through direct experience while UA students learn about community and how their efforts can contribute to a better world. And the interns' participation is crucial. As Moses Thompson said, "The school gardens would fall apart without them."

Tucson Village Farm

Tucson Village Farm is a quarter acre of lushly planted vegetables on the University of Arizona's farm on North Campbell Avenue, called the Campus Agricultural Center. Here, 13,000 schoolkids every year learn that bees make honey (and get to taste it), that popcorn actually comes from an ear of corn, and that carrots grow underground (and are encouraged to pick and eat one).

"That's why we say we're saving the world one carrot at a time," says farm manager Alex Atkin.

The grant-funded, child-oriented environmental center was started in 2010 by Leza Carter, who found partners for her dream garden in the Pima County Cooperative Extensive Service, the University of Arizona, and the 4-H organization.

During the school year, nine AmeriCorps volunteers help a small farm staff host trips for groups from kindergarten through twelfth grade. The students learn increasingly complex lessons in how food grows, which pollinators are important, how to raise chickens, and why eating vegetables is important for nutrition. They readily plunge their hands into the vermiculture box, looking for the worms that make the farm soil so healthy. There are even specially designed raised beds to accommodate students with disabilities.

In the summers, children as young as four attend a day camp where they can feed the dozen clucking gold, brown, and black-and-white hens, gather the eggs, and harvest vegetables for lunch. The adult staff is assisted by teenage 4-H Healthy Living Ambassadors who have been through earlier camps themselves.

A FARMacy program is particularly aimed at nutrition for families. Affiliated with El Río Clinic, parents and their children who are at risk for nutrition-related illnesses can learn about gardening and healthy meal prepara-

David Berk has been working with Tucson Village Farm for several years and has now become a Healthy Living Ambassador, helping with the smaller children.

Solamon and Emile get acquainted with some chicks at Tucson Village Farm. (David Gilmore)

tion. Teenage 4-H students do peer teaching of other children directed to the program.

In 2018, the Tucson Village Farm was the recipient of a $445,000 grant from the Angel Charity for Children to fund a culinary education center that includes a certified kitchen and expands the ability of the staff to teach not only growing healthy vegetables but also cooking them into delicious, kid-approved meals.

There is always more to do than the regular staff and volunteers can manage and Tucson Village Farm welcomes community volunteers who are willing to get a little dirty for a morning or a day of prepping soil, pulling weeds, or planting the acre of popcorn it takes to make snacks for all those young farmers. Tuesday afternoons are U-Pick days when Tucsonans can go to the farm and pick their own vegetables for the week.

LIBRARY CARD CATALOG DRAWERS NOW HOLD SEED PACKETS

All gardening starts with seeds. This is the story of how one librarian's dream of building community through seeds has led to one of the largest seed banks in the United States.

Take Susie Morris, who prides herself on growing a variety of flowers and feeding herself and her husband vegetables from her midtown backyard garden. An inventive cook, she also grows a big plot of culinary herbs. For the last three years she has gardened exclusively with free seeds from the Pima County Library.

"I love our library," Morris says. "I use the Internet there, I check out lots of books, so using library seeds seems natural. It's another way to connect with my library community."

Anyone with a library card can check out seeds, up to ten packets a month. The small, precisely labeled seed packets that Morris finds at Woods Memorial Library reside in repurposed Dewey Decimal System card catalogs there and at eight additional branches of the library. People looking for seed types not available at their home library and patrons of the branches without seed libraries can reserve seeds from the online listing and have them sent where they want to pick them up, just as one would reserve a book.

More than 50,000 seed packets leave the library for Tucson gardens every year. A cruise through the online catalog is enticement for anyone to get out the gloves and shovel. What gardener could resist taking home seed for bull's blood dark red beets, King Richard leeks, or golden honeymoon cantaloupes?

Tucson's seed library is the inspiration of librarian Justine Hernandez. "It was a confluence of ideas," she recalls. "I had listened to a radio interview on how supermarket tomatoes are devoid of flavor and nutritional value. And I was impressed with what the Community Food Bank's Santa Cruz River Farmers' Market was doing to make good food accessible to people in low-income neighborhoods."

Hernandez started an online search for seed libraries and got more intrigued. "I thought that this was revolutionary. The library could be involved with the physical health of the community," she says. "In libraries across the city, we were seeing more people who had to leave their own countries

Librarian Justine Hernandez organized the seed library at the Pima County Public Library in 2012.

Tucson gardeners access more than 50,000 packets of seeds from the Pima County Public Library each year.

SQUASH UNDER THE BED
By Ofelia Zepeda

There was always crooked-neck squash
   under our beds.
The space under the bed met the criteria of a
   cool, dark, dry place.
These large, hard-skinned squash with
   speckled, serrated,
green and yellow designs shared space under
   our beds
with new cowboy boots, lost socks, forgotten
   toys,
dust, and little spiders.
The squash rested under there with our
   memory of summer.
Awaiting winter darkness.
With the cold weather, we split the hard skin
   and expose the
rich yellow meat inside, the bounty of large
   seeds entangled
in the wetness of their origin.
We saved the seeds for next summer.
We eat the soft, sweet meat of the winter
   squash.
We swallow the warmth of summer.

From *Where Clouds Are Formed: Poems by Ofelia Zepeda*
Used with permission

who had strong agricultural traditions. This is a way they could participate, and we could reach out to them."

She got in touch with the few seed libraries operating in other parts of the country and received guidance from some staff members at Native Seeds/SEARCH. Then she pitched the idea to her bosses at the library. They not only liked the idea, they urged her to go even bigger than she had planned.

Hernandez wrote to seed companies and cruised farmers' markets to ask for donations of open-pollinated seeds to begin the collection. The seed library opened in January 2012.

While the idea is for Tucson gardeners to save seeds from their harvest and return a portion to keep the seed library fresh and active, no one is fined for not returning seeds. The organizers are more focused on encouraging people to start gardening, even if it is one pot of lettuce. As they become more proficient, they can begin returning seeds for others to use.

When gardeners return seeds, they are encouraged to give the details on the variety and as much about the gardening experience as possible to guide future users of the seeds. Currently, 30 to 40 percent of the seeds are local seeds. Those are obviously varieties that thrive here. Others are donations from seed companies of types of vegetables known to do well in the Tucson climate.

The efficient running of the seed library requires considerable community support. When donated seeds arrive at a library, they are looked over by librarians who determine if they are appropriate for the collection. Everything is then refrigerated at near-freezing temperatures to kill any insects along for the trip. Volunteers separate, package, and label the seeds. Each packet gets a bar code just like a book and each accession has its own inventory number. Volunteers can be anything from teen advisory groups to retired folks who want to help out at their library. Two sisters like to work together as they watch television.

The seed library has been a hit since the first season it opened. Hernandez is thrilled with how her idea has taken off and gives the credit to the library users. "Tucson is a dynamic, engaged community," she says. "They go for gardening and these seeds in a really big way."

FOR FURTHER READING

Burgess, Martha. "In Padre Kino's Veggie Garden." *Edible Baja Arizona*, November–December 2013: 115–118.

———. "Replanting History: A Walk Through Tucson's Mission Garden." *Seedhead News*, Native Seeds/SEARCH, Summer 2014.

———. "Interpreting Ethnobotany at Mission Garden, Tucson, Arizona. Part 1. What AZNPS's Wild Desert Garden Teaches Us for the Future." *The Plant Press*, the Arizona Native Plant Society, Volume 38, Number 2, Winter 2015.

Doelle, William H. "Tucson Underground: The Archaeology of a Desert Community." *Archaeology Southwest*, Volume 24, Numbers 1–2, Winter–Spring 2010, Center for Desert Archaeology.

Thiel, J. Homer, and Jonathan B. Mabry, editors. *Río Nuevo Archaeology Program, 2000–2003: Investigations at the San Agustín Mission and Mission Gardens, Tucson Presidio, Tucson Pressed Brick Company, and Clearwater Site*. Technical Report No. 2004–11, Center for Desert Archaeology, Tucson, Arizona, 2006.

NATIVE SEEDS/SEARCH PRESERVES LEGACY OF DIVERSITY

Thousands of years of agricultural heritage of the Southwest rests in jars on shelves in a 45-degree, 600-square-foot walk-in refrigerator at the headquarters of Native Seeds/SEARCH, a Tucson-based nonprofit. Corn kernels come in rusty red, gold, and smoky blue. The most striking squash seeds are long ovals aptly named Silver Edge. Beans are as small as a grain of rice and as large as your thumbnail and come in brown, red, gray, and speckled.

This priceless collection of heritage seeds is the result of Mother Nature's adaptation of the seeds to growing conditions in the Southwest and of selection by untold generations of Native American and pioneer farmers who chose their best seeds to save for planting.

The seeds in the jars will eventually make their way into paper seed envelopes to be distributed through the Native Seeds catalog, website, or retail store to home gardeners or farmers committed to growing these heirloom varieties of vegetables, dyes, and fibers. Planted and tended in gardens, the seeds will produce huge hard-shell squashes, purple spotted beans, watermelons with sweet golden flesh, deep blue ears of corn, and tiny, fiery chiltepin chiles—varieties of fruits and vegetables that have never seen the inside of a grocery store.

Unlike other seed companies, the Native Seeds/SEARCH employees are working to have fewer repeat customers. Rather than striving to sell ever more seed packets, they encourage gardeners to save their own seeds. To facilitate this, they provide frequent classes in both Spanish and English in the art of seed saving. And they have put together lesson plans to help educators teach children about seeds and plant growth.

In addition to selling seeds, Native Seeds/SEARCH also gives them away through twice-yearly seed grants. Native Americans living in the greater Southwest region or belonging to tribes in the Southwest may request up to ten free seed packets in a calendar year and may purchase others at reduced price. There is a resurgence of interest in farming among young Native Americans throughout the Southwest. They have received

Native Seeds/SEARCH volunteer Linda Peck winnows seeds at a garden workday.

heritage seeds originally donated by their relatives—seeds that would have been lost without Native Seeds/SEARCH acting as conservator.

Other donations of seeds go to organizations working on educational, food security, or community development projects, particularly those benefiting underprivileged groups. The organization normally gives around 170 seed grants per year with more than half going to school gardens. Not only do the grants benefit the recipients by providing food and enhancing their health, they also keep locally adapted crop varieties alive and in active use in farms and gardens.

Native Seeds/SEARCH volunteers bag heritage sunflowers to protect the seeds from hungry birds.

History of Native Seeds/SEARCH

Native Seeds/SEARCH (the acronym stands for Southwestern Endangered Aridland Resources Clearing House) had its formal beginning in 1983. Several years previously some of the founding members had been working to help Tohono O'odham farmers get access to seeds for traditional crops, many of which had almost disappeared. Farming as an occupation had been falling out of favor and with each farmer who retired with no successor, heritage varieties hundreds, sometimes thousands, of years in development were being lost.

The four founders—Gary Paul Nabhan, Karen Reichhardt, Barney Burns, and Mahina Drees—were all in their thirties and shared a vision dedicated to "the conservation and promotion of native, agriculturally viable plants of the U.S. Southwest and northwest Mexico."

Nabhan wrote a grant request to the National Center for Appropriate Technology. As part of the grant, the group was tasked with "growing out traditional crops in order to supply seeds to native farmers."

But first they had to find seeds for these ancient varieties. They sought out farmers who were growing small amounts of heritage vegetables along with their cash crops and begged and purchased small amounts of seed to grow out. They met Hopi farmers who were retiring and were happy to pass on seeds handed down in their families for generations so the precious germ plasm would not disappear. They rode mules deep into the mountains to Mexican farming regions not accessible by roads to find varieties of corn not grown elsewhere. When they encountered military checkpoints on back roads in Mexico, passage was eased by long conversations about the various corn varieties they were carrying and comparisons with varieties familiar to the soldiers.

Native Seeds/SEARCH collects, stores, and distributes about 2,000 arid-adapted types of seeds for traditional crops used as food, fiber, and dye.

In the earliest days, there was no walk-in refrigerator, not even an office. Reichhardt's parents lent them a refrigerator she kept in the garage and the seeds were stored there in baby food and Mason jars. A fellow graduate student studying birds asked to keep a dead vulture in the freezer compartment for a few weeks, and they obliged. When it was time to get the refrigerator ready for storing the fall harvest, Drees discovered that at some time the electricity had gone off and she was facing a soupy heap of putrid turkey vulture. It is a testimony to her dedication to the cause that she cleaned up the mess and aired out the refrigerator in time to safely store the next collection of seeds. She maintains that some of the early collections still have a whiff of "eau de vulture."

In talking to others about their project, the founders sensed interest from several quarters. They bought a couple of mailing lists and put out a one-page, front-and-back listing offering fifty seed varieties, mainly corn, beans, and squash. The response was encouraging, even surprising. Gardeners wanted to grow these heritage seeds, and they were willing to pay for them.

By this time, the organizers had moved the collection to the basement of Drees's stone cottage near Sabino Canyon and the seed amounts had graduated from baby food jars to gallon pickle jars sourced from Whataburger.

Further growth and generous benefactors allowed the purchase in 1997 of 60 acres of rich floodplain fields in Patagonia for seed growouts followed by the construction in 2010 of the modern Conservation Center offices and a laboratory off River Road where Native Seeds/SEARCH has resided since. It is ringed by small demonstration gardens where visitors can see lush plots of tepary beans, squash, melons, and towering sunflowers. Today the full-color catalog is 50 pages long with 200 varieties of seeds for sale. Hundreds more varieties are offered through the organization's website, ranging from peppers to lentils, chickpeas, cilantro, and more. The seeds include those heritage varieties gathered from early farmers and from Native American tribes, including the Apache, Gila River Pima, Havasupai, Hopi, Maricopa, Mayo, Mojave, Mountain Pima, Navajo, Tarahumara, and Tohono O'odham.

Besides collecting, storing, and distributing seeds and growing information, Native Seeds has a legacy of research and advocating for the important role of the food grown from the seeds they conserve. In 1990, Native Seeds worked with the northwestern Mexico Tarahumara, from whom they had collected 450 seed varieties, to set up nurseries and farms, develop erosion control, and plant gardens and orchards. The importance of the conservation work became clear twenty-two years later in 2012 when the Tarahumara had widespread crop failures due to extreme weather conditions. Native Seeds/SEARCH was able to repatriate 400 pounds of traditional seed to the Tarahumara farmers so they could continue growing the vegetables that had been part of their lives for generations. Without access to the Native Seeds seed bank, these heritage varieties would have been lost forever.

In the late 1990s, Native Seeds was instrumental in getting protection for the native chiles found growing in the mountains south of Tucson; a 2,500-acre parcel in the Coronado National Forest is now called the Wild Chile Botanical Area. It marked the first time that the federal government had set aside habitat to preserve the wild relatives of domestic crops.

In 2012, Native Seeds led the way in the reintroduction of Sonora White wheat to Arizona. With the help of a two-year grant from the USDA's Western SARE (Sustainable Agriculture Research and Education), the staff organized a program to revive the production, milling, distribution, and marketing of both Sonora White wheat and brown-hued Chapalote corn. The grant supported research to help answer specific questions for growers such as optimum planting and harvest times, the most efficient cleaning and storage methods, and the effect of farm management on nutritional content and flavor.

Since 1983, the staff and a corps of many hundreds of volunteers have collected and cared for the seeds that reflect the vast and important biodiversity of heritage food of the Santa Cruz basin and beyond. They strive to fulfill their mission statement: "We envision the Greater Southwest as a place where farms and gardens, kitchens and tables, stores and restaurants are brimming with the full diversity of arid lands–adapted heirloom crops; people are keeping the unique seeds and agricultural heritage alive; and the crops, in turn, are nourishing humankind."

> Native Seeds/SEARCH seeks to find, protect, and preserve the seeds of the people of the greater Southwest region so that these arid-adapted crops may benefit all peoples and nourish a changing world.

MISSION GARDEN:
A WALK THROUGH TIME

Enter through the rustic wooden gates and wander behind the adobe walls of the Mission Garden and you can easily imagine walking through a magic door back to a Spanish colonial garden in an earlier Tucson. To the right, a thick grove of fig, pomegranate, orange, and quince trees forms a towering green wall. In the summer, grapes hang in bunches and ripening figs are thick. Tucked behind the trees are vegetable and flower gardens. Should you visit there in late spring, to your left you'll see a field of golden ripe White Sonora wheat. Beyond that a half dozen chickens scratch in the dirt.

As you stroll through the garden, you will be walking on ground farmed for thousands of years by people who fashioned a simple desert existence next to a life-giving river. Beneath your feet will be four pit houses, carefully covered over to preserve them.

The History

The 4-acre Mission Garden is on the site of the original garden of the San Agustín Mission. In 1694, two years after founding San Xavier Mission, Father Eusebio Kino, accompanied by two Spanish soldiers, traveled a day's ride north along the Santa Cruz River and visited a Piman Native American community located at the base of what is now known as Sentinel Peak, or "A" Mountain. Captain Juan Mateo Manje, one of the Spanish soldiers, described the area: "Here the river runs with much water . . . there is good pastorage, and agricultural land with many canals to irrigate it. From this land they harvest much maize, beans, cotton from which they make their clothing, and other fruits of squash, cantaloupe and watermelon."

Dena Cowan harvests White Sonora wheat at Mission Garden.

The people who lived there called their village S-cuk Son, meaning "Black Spring," after the water they found at the base of the adjacent black hill. The village Father Kino saw in 1694 was only the latest habitation of the fertile site that had provided a living to people for thousands of years.

When the City of Tucson made plans to widen and straighten Mission Road through the area in the mid-1980s, the Institute for American Research (later Desert Archaeology, Inc.) conducted test trenching from Congress Street south to Mission Lane. They found evidence of centuries of habitation there on this rich floodplain. The deepest layers from around 800 BC to AD 50 contained at least 14 pit houses and 10 possible pit houses giving the investigators an exciting look back to this ancient time. Scattered across the floor of one house were sherds from five large jars that once held seeds that were to be used either as food or for the next year's planting. The jars could have held hundreds of pounds of maize and beans. (You can see a re-creation of a pit house in the southwest corner of the garden.)

Above the pit houses, there were several levels of Hohokam settlements showing successive eras of occupation between AD 850 and 1300. By this time, the inhabitants had perfected irrigation and in later investigations researchers found more than a dozen irrigation canals bringing Santa Cruz River water to the fields around the houses. One canal, close to the base of Sentinel Peak, was the largest found to date in the Tucson basin. This canal was about 26 feet wide and 7 feet deep, large enough to divert the entire flow of the Santa Cruz River at that time. When we recall that the canal was dug with nothing other than digging sticks, baskets to move the dirt, and backbreaking labor, we can marvel at what an engineering feat it was.

But Father Kino knew none of this. Those earlier civilizations were gone and what Kino saw was a few hundred souls whom he wanted to bring to God. He made several trips to the

Membrillo

Membrillo is a sweet, thick jelly, sometimes called quince paste. It is eaten with cheese, stuffed in pastries, or eaten alone as a sweet confection.

6 quinces
Juice of ½ lemon
2 cups sugar (approximately)
Pinch of salt

Peel and core the quinces and cut into large wedges. Keep the wedges in water as you work to avoid discoloration.

Place the fruit in a pot and cover with water. Add the lemon juice. Bring the water to a boil and cook the fruit until it's very soft. That will be 30–35 minutes after the boiling starts.

Drain and let cool for 5 minutes. Transfer to a food processor or blender and process until it is smooth, about the consistency of applesauce.

Measure the fruit—you should have about 2 cups—and place it in a heavy-bottomed pot. Add sugar equal to three-fourths of the amount of fruit and stir the sugar into the fruit. Add a pinch of salt.

Bring the sugar and fruit to a low boil in the heavy-bottomed saucepan and simmer, stirring frequently, on low heat. Cook slowly, keeping the mixture barely at a boil and stirring often to prevent burning, until the mixture thickens. Here the recipe needs your full attention. Continue to cook over low heat, stirring constantly, until mixture is a thick paste that stays together in a ball. The mixture should seem stretchy and almost dry. The fruit will change color and become a bright orange-red, or maybe just pink.

Pour into a lightly oiled dish, flatten, and let cool. Score into small pieces.

area and set up San Agustín to be a visita of San Xavier, arranging for it to be attended regularly by priests stationed at Bac. There was never a permanent priest at San Agustín, although Father Bernardo Middendorff spent a few months there in 1757. The local Native Americans asked that a church be built at San Agustín, and a simple one was completed in 1771. That sufficed for about twenty-six years. It appears that after construction of the Franciscan structures at San Xavier were finished in 1797, the workers moved to San Agustín and built a two-story convento (a priest's residence and possibly a trade school), a chapel, a granary, cemetery areas, and a surrounding compound wall.

The garden to the west of the San Agustín Mission appears to have been built in the early 1800s and was surrounded by thick walls to keep out desert critters such as javelina, deer, and rabbits as well as domestic livestock such as cattle and sheep. An acequia (canal) brought water from the river to the garden. The people grew a subsistence garden of traditional vegetables along with varieties introduced from the Mediterranean and fruit trees cloned from those Kino introduced to missions to the south.

The original mission garden didn't function long. The local Native American population was declining and by the 1820s, the San Agustín Mission was largely abandoned. The chapel fell into ruins between 1862 and 1880. When Leopoldo Carrillo built his house on the south side of Mission Lane, he helped himself to the roofing timbers from the convento, hastening the destruction of that building. The 1887 earthquake may have contributed to its collapse. The proposed widening of Mission Road would have gone over the ruins of Carrillo's house.

Fortunately, an outcry and lawsuit by historic preservationists and Menlo Park residents convinced the City of Tucson to abandon the Mission Road project. Then in 1999, a popular proposition passed directing a percentage of the Tucson city sales tax to Tucson Origin Heritage Park, of which the Mission Garden was a part.

With funding in hand, in the fall of 2001 the Center for Desert Archaeology took a closer look at the Mission Garden site, building on extensive investigations that had been conducted between Congress Street and Mission Lane in 2000. A series of backhoe trenches revealed pit houses occupied over a thousand years by two distinct cultures. There were also two caches of stone hoes and eight Hohokam burials and cremations. All the identified burials were excavated and repatriated to the Tohono O'odham Nation.

In 2008 the city built a wall around the garden. The project languished for several years until some of the people who had been with the project earlier decided to start a nonprofit to begin the development.

The Mission Garden Vision

Mission Garden is run by Friends of Tucson's Birthplace, a nonprofit operated by a tiny staff and forty regular docents, although throughout the year, more than two hundred volunteers give time regularly or for special events. Volunteer time totals more than four thousand hours a year. According to Diana Hadley, one of the early advocates, the original idea had been to re-create the garden as it had been in the time of San Agustín Mission, but when the archaeology showed that the history of the site was much deeper, the organizers decided the gardens should reflect all the residential periods.

Posole de Trigo

This is a traditional soup always served at Mission Garden's Feast of San Ysidro.

4 pounds of mixed beef bones (for example, neck and tail)

4–5 quarts water

2 teaspoons salt

⅔ cup dried beans

⅔ cup dried garbanzos

1 bulb garlic, sliced in half crossways

1 white onion, chopped coarsely

1 cup fresh wheat berries (trigo)

3 small potatoes cut into pieces the size of a walnut

1 unpeeled sweet potato, cut into pieces the size of a walnut

3 carrots cut into inch-long pieces

1 pound of green beans cut into 2- or 3-inch pieces

3 summer squash cut into inch-long pieces

2 ears fresh white corn, cut into 2-inch sections

Options for accompaniments:

Flour tortillas

Queso fresco

Chiltepins

Limes

Cilantro

1 roasted green chile, chopped, optional

Cooked or raw nopalitos, optional

Purslane (verdolagas), optional

Wild greens (such as amaranth), optional

Combine the bones, water, and salt in a pot that has a capacity of at least 6 quarts. Bring to a boil, and when foam appears at the top of the pot, lower the flame and skim off the foam. Add the beans, garbanzos, garlic, and onion. Cook the wheat berries separately in 2 quarts of water until they are tender.

Posole de Trigo is a traditional soup served on the Feast of San Ysidro, incorporating the newly harvested wheat berries.

When the meat is cooked and the beans and garbanzos are tender, remove the bones and meat. Add the vegetables to the pot, potatoes, carrots, and green beans first, then a few minutes later, add the squash and corn. When the meat is cool enough to handle, pick off the meat.

Add the cooked wheat berries, add additional water if needed, and cook until all the vegetables are tender, approximately 30 minutes. Remove the two halves of the garlic bulb. Add the meat. Taste and adjust salt. Warm through.

Serve with flour tortillas, queso fresco, chiltepins, a squeeze of lime, a sprinkle of chopped cilantro, and your choice of additional garnishes.

The author (in pink), Ford Burkhart, and two volunteers plant the first trees in the Mission Garden orchard in 2012. The West University Neighborhood Association sponsored this Seville orange.

Then came the question of what to plant. The first crops to be planted in the garden in 2012 were the fruit trees. Botanists working with the Arizona-Sonora Desert Museum's Kino Heritage Fruit Trees Project had located trees growing in Tucson's historic neighborhoods and propagated them for planting in the garden at Tumacácori Mission to re-create the Spanish colonial orchard. It was obvious they belonged in the Mission Garden as well.

Jesús García, a Mexican-born ethnobotanist, had scoured the older neighborhoods in Tucson and communities in Southern Arizona for varieties of trees introduced by Father Kino. Once the site was prepared, Tucson citizens and organizations were offered the opportunity to choose a fruit variety, help plant it, and dedicate it (with a nice plaque) for $1,000.

In the first round of planting in February 2012, 138 heritage fruit trees went in the ground. They included 30 pomegranate, 30 quince, 15 fig, 13 Mexican sweet lime, 6 Seville orange, 6 apricot, and 2 pear trees.

Next the organizers considered the vegetable gardens. Native Seeds/SEARCH, a Tucson-based seed conservation organization, had been seeking out and conserving traditional food-crop seeds for thirty years and generously provided precious heirloom seed. The varieties included Old World

Mission Garden supervisor Emily Rockey grooms the Seville orange planted in 2012. Good soil and proper care allowed this sapling to reach about 15 feet tall in just seven years. It is the same tree shown in the accompanying photo planted by the author, Burkhart, and two volunteers!

pulses that Father Kino would have brought—lentils, garbanzo beans, and fava beans. Root vegetables included a purple garlic from Hermosillo, Sonora, and I'itoi's onion, a bunching shallot introduced by the Spanish. They chose two types of heritage wheat—Sonora White and Pima Club—for the winter garden.

The grapes in the Mission Garden are a cultivar of Mission grape from Mission San Borja that ethnobotanist Gary Paul Nabhan sourced through the University of California–Davis germ-plasm repository.

Jesús García contributed seeds from plants grown on his family's land along the Río Magdalena— heirloom fava beans, Magdalena cilantro, and a green called *acelgas* or chard.

In "Replanting History," Martha A. Burgess, a knowledgeable and longtime volunteer at Mission Garden, recalls, "When we began the project, the land had not been farmed or gardened since the 1800s. When we took on the job of soil prep, it felt like mud cement. The waffle squares gave our crew of dedicated volunteers a good workout, digging by hand and shovel to loosen the soil and then amend with compost. I still remember how, as I lifted my pickaxe to cleave the compacted floodplain hardpan of the Santa Cruz to break ground for vegetables, I was struck with deep respect for these ancient desert gardeners and farmers. It still moves me, now, that it is our turn to turn the soil here."

The deep fertile soil of the Santa Cruz floodplain that nourished Tucson residents for thousands of years has turned the small saplings of 2012 into towering trees that in season hang heavy with fruit—oranges, pomegranates, quinces, and figs—and provide deep shade in the summer heat. The labor of hundreds has brought the dream to reality.

A Stroll Through Agricultural History

As time, funds, and volunteer hours made possible, new gardens have been developed and have begun to fill the property. To the west of the orchard lie a series of timeline gardens, where you can learn about the food plants cultivated by Santa Cruz River Valley residents over the last 4,000 years. Turn your face to the sun, pick up a handful of this ancient soil, inhale the dust as it sifts through your fingers. If you squint a little to block out the power poles and ignore the Mission Road traffic, you can transport yourself back a thousand years to the time when a Hohokam farmer worked this very spot.

EARLY AGRICULTURE GARDEN. We date the beginning of agriculture in the Tucson area to about when the first tiny ears of corn arrived from the south and the native people began to replace their nomadic life with a more settled way of living. This simple life persisted for 2,000 years.

HOHOKAM GARDEN. Beginning around AD 500, the Hohokam, with their highly organized culture, were inhabiting the Tucson basin. Extensive series of canals radiating from the Santa Cruz and other rivers allowed them to expand their reliance on agriculture.

O'ODHAM GARDEN. The Tohono O'odham are the indigenous people of the Sonoran Desert descended from the earlier Hohokam. During the summer, they grew 60-day corn in fields that captured runoff from slopes. They also grew domesticated tepary beans, which were tolerant of heat, drought, and alkaline soil.

MEXICAN ERA GARDEN. Beginning with the establishment of the Presidio in 1776, Tucson was a Mexican town. Farmers grew barley, wheat, onions, chiles, beans, and melons. Around their homes, they grew fruit trees, flowers and herbs, grapes and vegetables.

ANGLO-TERRITORIAL ERA GARDEN. Tucson became part of the United States with the Gadsden Purchase in 1854. New residents brought foods they were used to, such as potatoes.

CHINESE GARDEN. Chinese farmers had fields near the river and supplied most of the vegetables for the Tucson population in the late nineteenth century. They also grew vegetables for their own use such as bitter melon, long green beans, and Chinese broccoli.

YOEME (YAQUI) GARDEN. The Yoeme people of northern Mexico fled to the Tucson area in 1890 to avoid persecution. They brought their edible and medicinal plants.

AFRICAN-AMERICAN GARDEN. After the end of the American Civil War, freed slaves set out for a new life and some ended up in Tucson and Marana where they planted their traditional crops.

Z GARDEN. The Z Garden exhibits in microcosm three distinct native plant communities that meet in the Arizona Upland desert. The shade ramada demonstrates how the Tohono O'odham traditionally used mesquite as upright posts and crossbeams, and ocotillo branches for lattice roofing. The Z Garden honors the life work of longtime native plant enthusiast Nancy Zierenberg.

MICHAEL MOORE MEDICINAL GARDEN. Named after the late ethnobotanist Michael Moore, this garden features the plants early residents relied on when homegrown remedies were all that were available.

Organizers are currently working on a design for the Garden of the Future.

There's real food growing in all those gardens—heritage varieties that taste great and have been bred over generations to stand up to the challenging Tucson climate. Volunteers from the nearby neighborhoods have cooked traditional specialties for fundraisers, and the gardens are so productive that local chefs are using the products in their menus. Pivot Produce has worked as an intermediary to distribute the heritage produce to the kitchens at Time Market, EXO Roast, La Estrella Bakery, Mama Louisa's, and Maynards Market & Kitchen. Mei Mei's has made use of vegetables from the Chinese Garden in various dinner menus. Barrio Bread has included Mission Garden tomatoes in a focaccia, and Janos Wilder has used squash and squash blossoms at his Downtown Kitchen + Cocktails. Recently organizers have added an occasional farmers' market to sell seasonal produce.

Festivals

Throughout the year, the Mission Garden opens its gates for festivals that celebrate harvests and traditional holidays. Late April brings the Agave Festival with a demonstration of pit roasting of agave hearts. The San Ysidro Festival in May honors the patron saint of farmers and attendees are always treated to a bowl of *posole de trigo*, a traditional stew with wheat berries prepared by Mission Garden volunteers. In the fall of 2018, a traditional grinding stone was donated and used to grind some of the heritage wheat harvested by volunteers and threshed by horses during the spring festival.

The Membrillo Fest in late October honors the flourishing quince trees in the orchard. Quinces do very well in Tucson and have been grown successfully in barrio gardens for hundreds of years. During the festival, one of the elders of the neighborhood demonstrates how to turn quince into membrillo paste.

SMALL-SCALE COMMERCIAL AGRICULTURE

CONTRACTING TUCSON'S FOODSHED

T UCSON'S OUTER FRINGES ARE RINGED by small farms providing fresh fruit and vegetables to consumers willing to seek them out and able to pay a little more for produce grown locally and organically. There are even some small farms tucked discreetly into midtown neighborhoods.

A 2019 report by Megan Carney and Keegan Krause on Tucson food entrepreneurship found that there are 855 farms in Pima County and 80 percent of them operate on 50 acres or less. Approximately 70 percent of these small farms sell less than $10,000 worth of product a year.

Despite the fact that people have been farming in the Tucson basin for millennia, scarce water and rocky soil make coaxing vegetables from the earth difficult. What's promising, however, is how many young farmers are taking on the challenge. Their youth is encouraging as farmers over the age of sixty-five now outnumber farmers under thirty-five countrywide by a margin of six to one. Nearly two-thirds of farmland nationally is currently managed by someone over age fifty-five. If we aren't going to cede the produce business to big ag, we're going to have to make things easier for these young farmers so they can take over as the current contingent retires.

Tucson's young farmers face the same issues as young farmers across the country. In the summer of 2018, after a couple of false starts, a group of young agriculturalists growing plants and animals for food and fiber organized the Southern Arizona Young Farmers and Ranchers Coalition (SAYFRC). The mission of the organization is to provide support for beginning and established food producers, and to build connections between urban and rural areas. They work together to lobby for policies that increase the resiliency and diversity of the local food system. Another goal is to facilitate mentorships, apprenticeships, continuing education, skill building, and labor sharing among its members. The website proclaims: "We will also demonstrate to the public and younger generations that farming, ranching and food processing are honorable and invaluable professions."

Because the success of a new generation of farmers is important to our national security, SAYFRC joined with other farmers nationally to lobby Congress for attention to their needs. The 2018 Farm Bill increased permanent funding to train the next generation of farmers as well as veteran farmers, farmers of color, and indigenous farmers. It also established permanent funding for programs that support local food and expand regional markets, dealt with issues of making farmland affordable, set up a beginning farmer and rancher coordinator in each state, and worked to make organic certification more affordable.

Finding land to farm is not as difficult in the Southwest as it is in some more highly developed areas. In some cases, Tucson's young farmers are taking over lands previously used for agriculture, such as Rattlebox Farm going into an old pecan orchard. In other cases, such as Wild Child Gardens, they are copying the pioneers and using their youth and energy to turn raw desert into productive farms.

While the idea and benefits of eating locally have seen a resurgence over the last decade, the burden and risk of making it happen fall on the small farmer while the customers can choose to shop or not on a given weekend, leaving the farmer with a batch of wilting spinach.

A popular way for farmers to sell their produce is at farmers' markets, and a thriving group of markets serves to connect Tucson farmers with the people seeking their just-picked produce.

Farmers also find customers through CSAs and small-scale middlemen. CSA stands for Community Supported Agriculture and customers pay up front for a share of a farmer's produce, giving the farmer both working capital and an idea of how many people will be eating his or her vegetables. The vegetables vary through the season and the farmers are usually tuned in to what their customers like to eat. And the offerings are abundant, often more than 20 pounds of produce a week.

Farmers with the capacity to grow more than they can sell at a farmers' market or through a CSA can take part in the Farm to Institution program run by the Community Food Bank of Southern Arizona. The Food Bank acts as a go-between, facilitating contracts, and accepting and dispersing the produce. It is discussed in more detail beginning on page 185.

Let's visit a few of the small farms located in the Tucson basin. Please notice that many of these farmers are women, a trend seen nationally.

RATTLEBOX FARM

It was already quite warm on an April morning while husband-and-wife team Dana Helfer and Paul Buseck cleaned mud and outer leaves from 60 pounds of deep red beets the size of tennis balls. We talked in the shade of their washing and potting shed at the end of their spring growing season. They would let the fields on their 1-acre farm lie mostly empty until the rains began in midsummer, signaling time to put in crops for sale in the fall.

In June, they'll start tomatoes, squash, and peppers in a shady greenhouse; the little plants will go into the ground as soon as the monsoons start, along with seeds of zucchini, melons, green beans, long beans, and okra. There will be zinnias as well, large colorful blooms hardy enough to withstand the summer sun. In August and September, they will begin winter veggies in the greenhouse: broccoli, cabbage, chard, kale, bok choy. The starts will be transplanted into the garden in October.

At Rattlebox Farm, everything is grown from seeds, started in the greenhouse or in the ground. The field is watered with drip tape, long black ribbons embedded with emitters. Each plant gets the water it needs with no waste.

Helfer and Buseck began farming on a quarter-acre plot in the west-side Menlo Park neighborhood before moving to the far east side of the Tucson basin. "If there is one thing that has helped us, it is the process of starting small and growing incrementally," Helfer says.

When they found the former pecan orchard with a producing well, they were ready to take the next step. They sell their produce through the Santa Cruz River Farmers' Market, to restaurants through Pivot Produce, and to members of their own CSA. They limit their CSA to fifty shares of a 24-week season from September to April. The shares are a balance of greens, roots, and familiar vegetables.

Dana explains that it is advantageous to mix the CSA, farmers' market, and wholesale. The most profitable is the farmers' market, but they can't sell all they can grow there. The CSA is a guaranteed market. Restaurants buy wholesale, and it's easier because they don't need so much packaging. "For a small farm, it is insurance to have a diversity of items and markets," she says.

Despite the fact that farmers' markets bring better prices, Helfer and Buseck confine themselves to just one because with small elementary-school-age children they did not want to be gone from home so frequently.

Rattlebox Farm is not yet at capacity for what they could grow in terms of land, but the farm couple says that when looking at expansion, they need to consider water needs and labor. In the next extension, they are thinking of planting perennial crops like figs, pomegranates, and grapes which aren't so labor intensive.

Neither Helfer nor Buseck came from farming families, but they studied agriculture at the University of California–Davis. At the student-run organic farm at Davis, they gained in-depth knowledge of soils and nutrient cycling. With their academic background, they tend to think deeply about how the community infrastructure can support family farms.

"It's easy to gush about family farms, but how do you support people like the Rattlebox Farm that want to grow at a larger scale?" Helfer asks. "Farmers need to work and talk with each other—share resources, planting times, technical information. We want others to be successful. There is so much more demand than any of us can supply."

She feels that there are many ways communities can support small farms. Among these are tiered water rates for farms and places in addition to farmers' markets where farmers can sell their products. Extension agents at the university could focus more on the issues facing the small farmer. The community needs to build an infrastructure that can support new and learning farmers with land and water resources. In other places, she says, cities and counties have identified arable land that would be appropriate for farms. Land trusts could be formed and offer long-term leases.

"The community working together can reduce the considerable risk for the small farmer," Helfer says.

DREAMFLOWER GARDEN

The modest and tidy house fronting the street in a midtown neighborhood gives no indication of the delights in the almost-an-acre backyard where Lorien Tersey grows forty to fifty different culinary herbs along with fruits and vegetables.

Tersey has been cultivating this garden since 2003, expanding little by little, adding land when her neighbors sold out. The plots are surrounded and shaded by trees and bushes which not only cushion the plants from the worst of the sun, but also give the place the look of a home gardener's project gone way overboard rather than the locus of a commercial enterprise. A row of yellow and pink rose bushes divides a path from tables of herbs in small pots.

Two rows of lacinato kale grew throughout the summer and in late October are 3 feet tall and still producing long, crinkly leaves in the distinctive deep green with a bluish tinge. Next to them are rows of Egyptian onions, some ready for harvest, others just set out. Shiny purple eggplants and purple pod beans planted in mid-August got a boost from the rain and are now bearing. Strawberry plants grow in 50-gallon barrels cut lengthwise and mounted on cement blocks.

Forty hens and three roosters are spread over three spacious cages and their clucking and occasional squawking provide the background music to the garden.

Tersey sells her vegetables and eggs to neighbors and through Pivot Produce and Abundant Harvest, the co-op arm of the Community Food Bank that sets up shop at the Santa Cruz River Farmers' Market on Thursdays. In her stall at the market, she sells potted herbs, ornamental succulents, and a small selection of vegetable bedding plants. The most popular sellers are the well-known herbs: oregano, marjoram, peppermint, thyme, parsley, and chives. But customers looking for the unusual can also find salad burnet, French chervil, anise, germander, clary sage, chocolate mint, orange bergamot, and even catnip.

MERCHANT'S GARDEN

With the arrival of the heat of late May, Tucson home gardeners are down to only the heartiest plants, and area farmers are putting in summer crops or fallowing their plots altogether, waiting for the rainy

Tabbouleh

This recipe from Lorien Tersey of Dreamflower Garden makes good use of the herbs she grows in her garden.

¼ cup fine bulgur
3 cups finely chopped flat-leaf parsley (Italian parsley)
2 medium Roma tomatoes, chopped
½ cup chopped I'itoi onion tops, green onions, or chives
¼ cup chopped mint leaves

Dressing:
Zest of one lemon
2 tablespoons lemon juice
¼ cup extra virgin olive oil

Soak the ¼ cup of fine bulgur for 30 minutes and then drain. Combine bulgur with other ingredients in a medium bowl. Combine the lemon juice, lemon zest, and olive oil in a cup, and use a fork to whisk together. Pour the dressing over the bulgur and vegetable mixture and stir to distribute.

Lorien Tersey grows herbs and vegetables and raises chickens on her urban farm of about an acre tucked into a midtown neighborhood.

season to begin in July. But inside the greenhouses at the hydroponic Merchant's Garden, robust heads of crisp romaine march in a row and voluptuous rosettes of Boston lettuce grow beside fluffy magenta leaf lettuce.

The lettuce is grown in water recirculated from nine fish tanks in which tilapia lazily swim. The fish are fed bugs, leftover lettuce, and protein-rich fish food and excrete nutrients in a form of nitrogen that the plants use to grow.

While a typical American vegetable travels 1,500 miles from farm to table, Merchant's Garden founder and co-owner Chaz Shelton cuts that down to an average of 4 miles. Not only does decreasing food miles help reduce greenhouse gas emissions, it also ensures that the food is fresher and more nutritious because it was harvested the day it was delivered. A salad might be served by a waiter the same day the lettuce was picked.

The AquaBox, the system Merchant's Garden uses, produces ten times the volume of food per square acre than that of traditional farming while using only a tenth of the water. After seeds are germinated under grow lights, the seedlings are transferred to a frame set over water circulating from the fish tanks. As the plants grow, their roots dangle in the nutrient-dense water.

While in-ground farms are located on Tucson's outskirts where acreage is available, Merchant's Garden AgroTech is designed to be an urban farm, close to the chefs, food markets, and schools it serves, only a mile and a half from the downtown hub of trendy restaurants. Shelton leases property that used to be the campus for the former TUSD Howenstine High School.

Shelton sends half a million pounds of lettuce out to Tucson tables each year, 600 pounds of which goes to TUSD for their

Lettuce and herbs at Merchant's Garden are hydroponically grown in nutrient-rich water recirculated from nine fish tanks. (Emily Derks)

schools every week. The delivery schedule rotates so that all schools have the opportunity to include local lettuce on their lunch menu.

Despite being responsible for growing all this produce, Shelton's background is in economics, entrepreneurship, and finance. Working in the health-care field, he recognized the importance of making fresh food available. He hired University of Arizona scientists to put together the system that allows him to supply greens to fifty restaurants, some grocery stores, and the eighty-eight TUSD schools.

While this high-tech operation lacks some of the cozy glamour of the family farm, this might be the future of desert farming. Shelton explains that Merchant's Garden houses the entire supply chain: "We build, grow, harvest, and deliver locally produced food. This is a local production for local consumption."

Shelton adds, "We got into this business as a farm, but we want to change the world."

WILD CHILD GARDENS

In 2017 Miguel and Maria Quijada, both in their mid-thirties, bought 5 acres of creosote-covered desert in Marana and began to prepare their farm. The land came with a well with an unusually high water table for the area. The first month, they dug trenches and brought in fertilized compost and added more manure from the goats and horses their neighbors raised. Taking the long view of their venture, they also planted forty fruit trees. While waiting for them to bear, they harvest fruit from trees their elderly neighbors can no longer care for.

The two weren't total neophytes to growing vegetables. Maria had a large garden in Tempe and had gardened for years, using seeds passed down in her family, mainly heirloom varieties.

The Wild Child Gardens produce flowers as well as vegetables, seeds, and eggs.

Today they grow cut flowers and vegetables with those seeds and also sell extra seeds in tiny manila packets so home gardeners can take advantage of the climate-adapted varieties that Maria has been growing for years. Fifteen chickens provide eggs for sale and manure for the garden.

Miguel mans a table at the Santa Cruz, Steam Pump Ranch, and Rillito Park Farmers' Markets with tempting packets of greens and vegetables. He also gathers flowers into charming, small bouquets that seem to be a hit with shoppers.

One early December afternoon a customer was thrilled to find a basket of green tomatoes. "I was raised with these," she said while calling over a friend to decide how many they should buy. (They decided on four large ones.)

Why would a young couple head out to a patch of raw desert and try the admittedly difficult life of farming?

"We wanted to do something that didn't harm the earth," Miguel explains. "I wanted to live and work from home and to work with my wife. I want to be around plants all the time. To pass one's life tending to a garden makes the most sense."

BRECKENFELD FAMILY GROWERS

Early November is garlic planting time at the Breckenfeld Family Growers farm. That's twelve different varieties of garlic.

Why twelve? "Some are sharp and hot, some come on slow and stay with you, others come on sharp and go quickly," Donald Breckenfeld, the farmer, explains. There's a mild French garlic with a floral flavor, two Italian varieties with a buttery taste, and one out of Sonora with a peppery undertaste. The garlic will grow all winter and be harvested in May.

Breckenfeld also grows a dozen different kinds of peppers, four different varieties of kale, and three kinds of beets including yellow beets. "I want people to see that there are other kinds of vegetables with better taste," he says. Especially popular are their no-heat jalapeños.

Donald Breckenfeld's partner is his wife, Cristina, who keeps all the planting records, makes sure the crops are rotated in the fields, and starts all the tomato and chile plants from seed.

Customers at their stand at the Santa Cruz River Farmers' Market and at the Rillito Park Farmers' Market get an education along with their vegetables as both are willing to explain in detail the advantages of each vegetable. "It's the teacher in both of us," Breckenfeld says.

The Breckenfelds' one-and-a-quarter-acre farm south of Irvington Road is in the ancestral floodplain of the Santa Cruz River, a back slough where water came in with sediment, adding lots of organic carbon. The soil is rich enough that a casually discarded nectarine seed grew into a 12-foot tree with little attention. A chiltepin seed dropped by a bird has grown 6 feet high and taken over the grape arbor.

As a retired soil scientist, garlic farmer Donald Breckenfeld makes sure his fields are healthy by encouraging bioactivity. The tiny white speck that looks like a grain of rice is full of mycorrhizae, a fungus that breaks down the organic matter in the soil.

Best Garlic Dip

With fields of fragrant garlic right outside her back door, Cristina Breckenfeld devised this simple recipe to showcase the different varieties she and her husband grow.

5 to 7 garlic cloves (or to taste)
16 ounces unflavored Greek yogurt
Salt and pepper to taste

Using a garlic press, press (do not chop) the cloves into the yogurt and mix well. Add salt and pepper. Place mixture in a covered container and refrigerate for about an hour and a half. Mixture can be used as a dip for vegetables or chips, or as a topping on baked potatoes. It will last if refrigerated for about a week. You may substitute sour cream, cream cheese, or lebna (yogurt cheese) for the Greek yogurt.

As a retired University of Arizona soil scientist, Donald Breckenfeld pays a great deal of attention to what's going on underneath his plants. He rotates his small fields keeping one-third to one-half acre in production at a time. He rototills the fallow plots, turning under the remains of whatever he was growing, letting it compost naturally in the ground.

Breckenfeld picks up a handful of the rich deep brown soil in a fallowed field and points out a tiny white speck about the size of a grain of rice. "That's the mycorrhizae," he says. Later he explains that the fungus helps by breaking down the organic matter in the soil, setting up a symbiotic relationship between the bioactivity and the plants' roots.

"You know that sweet smell some soil has?" Breckenfeld asks. "That's the bioactivity."

Along with most other Tucson farmers now and in the past, Donald wishes he had more water. He supplements his 1,800-gallon rain-collection tanks with city water and plans to add more tanks.

"I use a lot of techniques in order to conserve water," he explains. "I plant the vegetables close together so they shade the ground. I'm also careful not to over-irrigate. I try to have a twenty-four- to thirty-inch wetting profile in the soil so when the roots get down, they have something to tap into."

DESERT TREASURES

Pete Larsen has watched over the Desert Treasures citrus grove since 1972. He knows each tree by variety and history. As he drives his golf cart slowly through the trees, his dog trotting along, he points out special trees and their characteristics. There are Duncan, Marsh, Star, and Triumph grapefruit. Another section is home to Persian and Palestinian limes, Eureka and Meyer lemons, small citrus like kumquats and calamondins, and deep red blood oranges. Around 300 trees are spread over the property and to Larsen they are not a grove, they are individuals.

Larsen became the caretaker of the orchard when he moved to Tucson to become an agricultural agent and was looking for a place for his family to live. When he saw the house on the north side, he knew it was perfect for his family, although it also came with hundreds of trees that were not in good shape. Over the years he has brought the trees back to health, experimenting with different types of fertilizer and watering schedules.

The property also came with 10 Medjool date palms, and Larsen harvests those as well.

Larsen sells his citrus directly to the Food Conspiracy Co-op. Eleven cartons of harvested fruit were on a table ready for delivery during my visit. His son-in-law maintains a table at Rillito Park Farmers' Market on Sundays. Shoppers wanting access to noncommercial citrus varieties available nowhere else in Tucson know to seek them out.

The neighborhood has a long history as a citrus-growing region. In 1923, Maurice Reid, who had come to the desert to recover from tuberculosis, noticed that there was a swath of land on the north side where cold air currents were diverted by the mountains, leaving the land warmer and often frost free in the winter. Reid bought 450 acres and called it a "thermal belt."

David Leighton continued the story in the *Arizona Daily Star* on June 3, 2014:

> By 1935, Reid had transformed 26 acres of sunbaked land, formerly covered with mesquite trees, prickly pear, and cholla cactus, into a virtual Garden of Eden producing oranges, lemons, figs, tangerines, grapefruit, mangoes, papayas, pineapples, olives and dates, along with tropical flowers.

That year, Reid shipped Christmas boxes of Arizona fruit to every state in the United States and the Territory of Alaska. That was also the year he sold an adjoining piece of the property to Reverend George W. Ferguson of Saint Philip's in the Hills Episcopal Church, who planted the property with five varieties of citrus trees. Ferguson also commissioned local architect Josias Joesler to design the home that still stands in the center of the property.

In 1936, Reid petitioned the county to change the name of the road that ran by his property to Orange Grove Road. His son Gene, who majored in horticulture at the University of Arizona, rose through the ranks at the City of Tucson to become the first director of the Parks and Recreation Department. Reid Park is named after him.

Eventually H. W. "Bill" Taylor acquired Reverend Ferguson's property, planted more trees, and called the business Desert Treasures as the name remains to this day.

In 1947, Reid sold his retail, mail order, processing, and manufacturing business to his neighbor Taylor who combined it with his own business. Many longtime Tucson residents recall going to the shop on the property to buy citrus for their own use or to send as gifts to family.

Seventy percent of the original trees are still alive and bearing. The other 30 percent Larsen has replaced over the years.

In 2018 the Desert Treasures orchard and the Ferguson home were awarded Pima County Historic Landmark status, protecting this Tucson architectural treasure from future development.

HIGH ENERGY AGRICULTURE

Anne Loftfield and her son, Greg McGoffin, farm on an 80-acre parcel in western Marana. Part of their land is a designated riparian area with a pond that attracts egrets and owls. Since it also attracts critters that like succulent vegetables, the beds are all fenced, and some are reinforced with corrugated panels.

Loftfield was a corporate accountant and her son was a landscape contractor when the 2008 recession hit. Looking for something to replace his dwindling business, McGoffin settled on farming, and Loftfield agreed to help. McGoffin handles the heavy labor while Loftfield starts the seeds, waters, and weeds. She also harvests the produce every Wednesday for the Thursday Santa Cruz River Farmers' Market and harvests again on Saturday for the Sunday farmers' market at Rillito Park.

And despite being in her early eighties, that is a schedule she keeps year-round. During the late fall, her display table is piled with leafy greens like bok choy, White Russian kale, rainbow chard, deer tongue lettuce, and mesclun—each head crisp and deep green, practically pulsing with vitamin A. Later in the winter, she'll bring broccoli and carrots. In the warmer months she displays both small and large tomatoes, summer squash, and peppers in a blend of shapes and colors. She is always eager to chat with her customers about the advantages of one variety of green over another and how to prepare them.

Loftfield stresses that the health benefits of her vegetables come from the healthy soil in which they are grown. When a field isn't being used for market produce, it is planted with a cover crop of grasses or legumes. That crop is then cut and fed to their goats whose aged manure is spread on the soil in an age-old cycle. "In ten years, we've gone from hard desert soil to rich brown," Loftfield says.

As a way to use some of the produce that doesn't sell at the market, Loftfield puts up 500 to 600 quarts of fermented vegetables every year that she sells alongside the fresh vegetables.

On a typical market day, you'll find quarts of raw sauerkraut made from cabbage, salt, and caraway seeds; bok choy kraut with carrots, onions, thyme, horseradish, and sea salt; and spicy pickled jalapeños bright with slices of slender carrots. Occasionally Loftfield will have something new to offer like the intense green mesclun pesto that appeared on a cloudy mid-December market day and went home to be dinner for a lucky shopper.

SAN XAVIER CO-OP FARM

The food production at the San Xavier Co-op Farm straddles thousands of years of the history of the Tohono O'odham, from mesquite pods to broccoli. The farm is located on land that was worked by the ancestors of today's farmers who lived in the village of Wa:k. These early farmers dug some of the first irrigation ditches in the country, bringing water from the Santa Cruz River to their fields.

The farm is located in the San Xavier District of the Tohono O'odham Nation, not far from the now-dry Santa Cruz. In 1887, the U.S. Congress passed the Allotment Act in which residents of some Indian reservations were given permission to select a portion of land, an allotment, to farm as family. In 1971 about a thousand of the Tohono O'odham allotees decided to piece some of the lands back together and form a cooperative, and in turn to farm it as a whole.

The soil was rich floodplain, but overpumping by others had drawn down the water table. The problem was solved when the U.S. Congress passed the Southern Arizona Water Rights Settlement Act in 1982, which gave 24,000 acre-feet of Central Arizona Project water to San Xavier each year.

This poshol soup was served at the San Xavier Co-op Farm recently. With the ingredients of tepary beans, 60-day corn, and cholla buds, it could well have been dinner for a local native family a thousand years ago. The tepary beans and corn were grown on the farm and the cholla buds were wild-harvested nearby (see recipe on page 37). (Roger C. Wolf)

On a crisp early winter morning, a 3-acre field shows a haze of green as broccoli, cauliflowers, onions, garlic, cabbage, and kale are getting their start. Much of the produce is bound for Tucson Unified School District schools through the Community Food Bank's Farm to School program. Under the shade of an ancient mesquite tree, sprouting frames hold thousands of inch-high plants that will be ready to go in the ground when the first round of vegetables is harvested a few months in the future.

In the summer, the farm grows corn, tepary beans, yellow-fleshed watermelons, chiles, and the large hard-shell squash called ha:l, all heritage varieties grown by the ancestors of today's farmers. Some of the watermelons go to the University of Arizona cafeteria to cool off students sweating through summer school.

A double line of fruit trees separates the field from the more active part of the farm. Varieties include Anna apples, apricots, plums, peaches, and pomegranates, reminiscent of the fruit trees Father Kino brought to plant on this same spot at the beginning of the eighteenth century.

Elsewhere on the farm, fields of Pima Club wheat, another heritage wheat brought by the Spanish, will grow through the winter and be ready for harvest in late spring.

The age range of the food production staff, some as young as nineteen years old, offers hope for future food production in the Tucson basin because these farmers are much younger than the national average.

With diabetes high in the reservation population, the staff at the farm organizes seasonal workshops to teach people how to use the healthful wild plants that sustained their ancestors. The workshops stress gathering in a culturally sensitive and environmentally healthy way.

In spring, expeditions go into the desert to harvest cholla buds. Phyllis Valenzuela, who brings many years as a commercial cook to her job at San Xavier Co-op Farm, then teaches the workshop participants how to clean the spines off in the old way (by rolling them over a screen) and in the contemporary way (by tumbling them in a chile roaster without the heat). Ambitious gatherers can sell their harvest to the farm for drying and packaging and eventual sale in the farm store.

Early summer is mesquite harvest. Workshop participants learn to taste the pods before picking as the flavor varies from tree to tree. After drying, the pods are ground in a hammermill. The ground meal is in high demand so ambitious harvesters can sell whatever they don't want to use themselves to the farm. In September, it's time for prickly pear gathering as it has been for the Tohono O'odham for millennia.

In another workshop, Phyllis Valenzuela leads the group in the traditional manner of preserving the ha:l squash. The squash is peeled, cut into very thin strips, and hung on a clothesline. When it is dry but still pliable, it is bundled into hanks for storage. Rehydrated, it can be used in soups, stews, breads, or muffins.

San Xavier Co-op Farm is the embodiment of why Tucson was named a UNESCO City of Gastronomy: Ancient, indigenous foods of the Sonoran Desert are grown and consumed in both traditional and modern ways, reflecting a culinary heritage stretching over 4,000 years.

LARRY'S VEGGIES

You'll drive by cotton and cornfields—and in the late fall, gigantic rolls of cotton in the middle of the dirt road—to get to the fenced 6 acres of Larry Park's farm in Marana. Veggies of all kinds poke up under white row covers, there to protect the plants from scavenging rabbits. Beets and spinach grow low, but celery, broccoli, and cabbage push the row covers up. Small snow-white cauliflower heads are hidden in the middle of enormous crowns of leaves. All are watered with long black ribbons of drip tape.

A greenhouse provides warmth and humidity for one hundred thirty-five 45-gallon tubs that hold small lettuces, beets, turnips grown for the greens, bok choy, several types of kale, and other winter greens. They'll spend the colder months in here as protection from frost, which in this area of Marana near the river can be 20 degrees colder than in the city. Park lost a week's worth of green beans and zucchini in the field one fall when a frost came much earlier than expected. Come February, with the threat of frost passing, these vegetables will be planted in the field along with squash, bell pepper, eggplant, and green beans.

Park and his wife, Eunice, previously farmed in Cochise County but gave it up when they came to Tucson. Gave it up, but not for long. Park has been farming since he bought an 80-acre plot of land in Douglas when he was just a sophomore in high school. What he calls his "disease" lured him back to farming.

Larry Park grows some of his winter crops in his greenhouse. His fields in Marana are sometimes 20 degrees Fahrenheit colder than Tucson.

The piece of land he now farms was formerly planted in cotton but had lain fallow for 14 years. That was important because it means it was never contaminated by being fertilized with sludge from the waste-treatment plant, which would make the vegetables ineligible for the "naturally grown" designation. Park fertilizes with bone meal, cottonseed meal, and vermicast produced by worms in Oracle.

Park is always in his field by 5 am—with the sun just coming up in summer, still cold and dark in the winter. Sometimes he's there by 2 am if there is more work to be done before leaving for one of the four farmers' markets he attends (SaddleBrooke, Trail Dust Town, Oro Valley, and Rillito Park). He vows to his customers that the vegetables have been picked twenty-four to forty-eight hours before sale. But it could be as little as twelve. Having sold at the local farmers' markets since the early 2000s, the Parks have developed a following of faithful customers.

FELICIA'S FARM

While many of Tucson's small farmers face stress and a few sleepless nights after confronting their balance sheet, Sofia Forier-Montes, the manager at Felicia's Farm, has only to worry about whether her seeds are germinating and how to get rid of aphids. That's because all the high-quality organic produce from Felicia's Farm is given away.

Felicia Ann Cutler had a vision to "feed the people and teach them to feed themselves." When she passed away in 2009, her husband, David Cutler, decided to set up a farm in her memory behind his home along River Road. There was plenty of land back there—4 acres—that had formerly served as a plant nursery for a former owner of the property. Now four fields and a shade house produce fresh vegetables. A noisy and colorful mix of red, white, brown, and black chickens inhabit a bright and sunny enclosure. When they have fertilized the straw spread on the floor of their coop, it goes into the compost pile, part of a sustainable loop. Chickens past their productive life are donated to the Iskashitaa Refugee Network. People from other cultures are accustomed to doing their own chicken processing and have the skill to turn a freshly harvested chicken into a meal.

In Felicia's memory, the donations of vegetables and eggs benefit those most in need of fresh produce and protein: the homeless and poorest in our community. Felicia's Farm sends most of its donations to Casa Maria (see page 195), where the vegetables go into grocery bags sent home with people living in the neighborhood. The eggs are hardboiled and added to the sack lunches prepared by various community organizations. Among other recipients is Our Place Clubhouse, a program for adults recovering from mental illness, which also receives some of the vegetables and eggs. Flowers to draw pollinators get donated to Peppi's House, an inpatient hospice at Tucson Medical Center, and to Casa de la Luz Hospice.

Forier-Montes plants her fields with basic crops. "I just grow everyday vegetables," she says. "I don't need to grow exotic things to sell at a premium, so I stick to leafy greens, carrots, onions, garlic, radishes, and beets."

Many of the low rows of crops flourish under filmy white row covers. They are protection not only from frost but also from pests. "With the mild winter, pests are living through the year," Forier-Montes says. "Pest control becomes more complicated. The row covers are the first defense."

Although Cutler paid all the farm expenses initially, the group is also seeking grants to expand the work of the farm through its Izi Azi Foundation. Cutler remains dedicated to the cause and hopes that through the foundation Felicia's Farm will survive beyond him.

Felicia's Farm also sponsors free field trips for schools. The youngsters often reciprocate by volunteering. A high school student built an ingenious solar dehydrator for the herbs.

Just because Forier-Montes isn't worrying about production goals doesn't mean she isn't extremely successful in coaxing great vegetables from the Tucson soil. With the help of an army of volunteers, Felicia's Farm donated 600 pounds of fresh produce and 170 dozen eggs each week in 2019.

Every week Felicia's Farm delivers fresh organic vegetables like these just-pulled carrots to Casa Maria and other Tucson nonprofits working to provide produce to people who need it.

These hardworking hens at Felicia's Farm produce more than 8,000 dozen eggs a year.

OUR FOODSHED

Ever since the first farmer in the Santa Cruz Valley tentatively put a corn kernel into the ground, farmers in this area have dealt with the fact that we have irregular rainfall and no perennially running rivers. Now that the population of the greater city has exceeded a million residents, all of whom are using water domestically, the situation is even more challenging for farmers. To access organically and locally grown food, we must then widen our definition of "local" and expand our foodshed.

Here are a few of the small farms outside the Tucson basin who serve Tucson customers through farmers' markets and CSAs. All are within a hundred miles of Tucson.

Sleeping Frog Farms

Sleeping Frog Farms is an intensive 75-acre farm located in the Cascabel corridor of the San Pedro River Valley. It was started in 2008 by three farmers in their thirties and one in his late twenties. The group runs its own CSA program as well as contributing to the Tucson CSA. They offer both a traditional program, which runs for a specified number of weeks, and a one-year program. The farm, which focuses on heirloom fruits and vegetables, also sells directly to restaurants and through TUSD's Farm to School program and the Food Conspiracy Co-op.

SouthWinds Farm

Located near Benson, SouthWinds Farm offers a seasonal CSA program that focuses on either the summer or fall/winter growing seasons. CSA members can pick up their weekly share at the La Posada Farmers' Market in Green Valley or the Rillito Park Farmers' Market in Tucson. Joe Marlow, the farmer, also sells directly to restaurants. He looks at his farm through the eye of an economist and keeps data on everything. He started the farm in 2012, converting it from raw desert. The produce is organic, and all the vegetables are either heirloom or hybrid varieties adapted to our climate.

Forever Yong Farm

John and Yongson Rueb began their farm in the rich bottomlands of Amado in the late 1990s. Their main cash crop is garlic, most of which they sell wholesale. However, they grow a variety of vegetables they sell through the Food Conspiracy Co-op and the Santa Cruz River Farmers' Market. Some of their vegetables grow in two large greenhouses where they are protected from pests. In the summer customers seek them out for their wide selection of melons.

Aravaipa Creekside Growers

Andrew Carhuff and Nicole DeVito transitioned from producing oyster mushrooms in a shed behind their rented Tucson house to a 5-acre farm in Aravaipa Valley. Now in addition to both oyster and shiitake mushrooms, the young couple also grow greens, vegetables, and cut flowers as well as manages an orchard nearby for another property owner. Their goal is to create a sustainable diversified farm using mushroom compost, rainwater harvesting, and permaculture methods. They have a table at the Rillito Park Farmers' Market and sell directly to Time Market.

Ramona Farms

Ramona and Terry Button began their farming venture with a 26-acre plot of tepary beans on the Gila River Indian Reservation near Sacaton.

Today Ramona Farms has expanded to 4,500 acres of commercial and heritage crops. They honor Ramona's Pima and Maricopa heritage by growing white, brown, and black tepary beans. They grow durum, Pima Club, and White Sonora wheat and sell each variety as berries and as flour. They also sell several preparations of the heritage Pima corn they grow, such as polenta and grits.

BEES: BUSY DESERT POLLINATORS AND HONEY MAKERS

Bees are integral to the farming scene in Southern Arizona. You can't take a spring hike in the desert surrounding Tucson without encountering bees. If the winter rains have been decently spaced, the bees will be visiting the wildflowers, dipping from blossom to blossom. A bit later mesquite trees will fairly hum with bee activity when their long, pale yellow blossoms appear. And in town, citrus season brings out every bee in the neighborhood. Several farmers host hives for beekeepers in their fields, taking advantage of resident pollinators.

Tucson is bee heaven. Experts estimate that there are possibly as many as 1,300 species of wild native bees distributed within the Sonoran Desert bioregion. This is not unusual as bees tend to be more abundant in deserts and savannas. The region around Tucson is thought to host more kinds of bees than anywhere else in the world, with the possible exception of some deserts in Israel. Wild desert bees are solitary. A native bee makes a nest by digging a burrow in the ground or finding an abandoned beetle tunnel in a snag of wood and gathers pollen and nectar for her own use and to feed her larvae.

Native bees are crucial for pollination of food plants as they wrap their hind legs around a flower, vibrate their wings to gather the pollen, then fly off to another plant. This is called buzz pollination and is done only by wild native bees.

Honeybees are European imports and were brought to the Santa Cruz Valley by the Jesuit and Franciscan missionaries. The priests needed wax for the candles they burned in their churches and for reading at night. They were accustomed to using honey as a sweetener because sugarcane doesn't grow in Europe. Resupply from Europe or even Mexico City was too far away so they had to be prepared to produce their own honey. Later, when the Mexicans migrated north from Sonora, they brought crop seeds and fruit tree cuttings and no doubt bees as well to pollinate their crops and make honey.

Chris Brinton of Life'Sweet Honey Farms works with his bee boxes to check on his bees' health. (Michelle Kilander Heirloom Photos)

According to a paper published by the Arizona-Sonora Desert Museum, at least 30 percent of our agricultural crops require both native bees and honeybees to move pollen between flowers, meaning that without the pollen that bees transport, many plants can't produce fruits, vegetables, and seeds. Tucson field crops that need bee pollination include cucumbers, cantaloupes, watermelon, and fruit trees.

When the domesticated bees take the pollen back to their hives, they make honey to feed themselves and to raise their young. Fortunately for us, bees make more honey than they need to survive, and since 10,000 BC humans have been raiding hives to satisfy their own sweet tooth. The smartest honey gatherers leave enough behind so the bees can survive and repopulate the hive. (Since the typical worker honeybee in the spring and summer is worn out from work after as little as 20 days, the queen must continually produce replacement bees.)

Tucson shoppers eagerly seek out raw local honey for its health benefits. Raw local honey is easy to find in roadside stands, at farmers' markets, and on the shelves of health-oriented grocery stores. It differs from typical grocery-store honey, which is pasteurized and filtered, with the pollen removed. Commercial honey is sold clear and stays that way.

Local beekeepers tell us that all raw honey will eventually crystallize, turning more solid, taking on a lighter, creamy color, and intensifying the flavor slightly. It melts easily and can be temporarily reliquefied by setting it in a pan of hot water.

Tucson homeowners are becoming more aware of the importance of bees in our ecosystem but are reluctant to have them living in their attic or under their shed. While some bee removal services kill the bees, others rehome them in their own hives and put them to work.

In an attempt to increase honey production in 1956, Brazilian beekeepers introduced bees from Africa as an experiment. Twenty-six swarms escaped, interbred with the Brazilian European bees, and began spreading north arriving in the southern United States around 1990. There is general agreement that all honeybees in the Southwest are now Africanized and because they are more defensive, they are more likely to attack if disturbed. Beekeepers have different ways to deal with their aggression. Some introduce a European queen thus changing the genetics of the colony and making the bees less aggressive. Others actually embrace the sturdier Africanized bees and learn to work with them.

All Tucson beekeepers also must deal with tiny red-brown varroa mites. "Mites are blood feeders," says Chris Brinton of Life'Sweet Honey. "Mites get into the hive, make their way to the interior, and attack the bee larvae." Varroa mites can also infect the bees with harmful viruses.

Many local beekeepers, both professionals and hobbyists, credit Jaime Zubeldia with teaching them the ropes. In 2016 Zubeldia decided to have the honey from his hives and that of two other beekeepers tested for pollen source.

Analysis showed that from 75 to 80 percent of honey produced during the spring and early summer was from mesquite pollen. Since most of the pollen found in these honey samples was from a single plant species, they could be labeled and classified as a "unifloral" mesquite varietal honey.

However, one honey sample produced between fall and early spring was dominated by a plentiful mix of 20 distinct wildflower-pollen types. Since the primary pollen in this honey sample was less than the accepted 45 percent threshold, it would be labeled and classified as a "multifloral" wildflower honey. We can assume that this analysis would be more or less true for most honey produced across the Tucson basin.

There is a great interest locally in keeping bees by folks who might have a hive or two or aspire to have a free source of honey. They are actively looking for information and more than 1,700 people are followers of two Facebook pages devoted to local beekeeping. Many of the posts come from those knowledgeable in the field. Experienced beekeepers always advise newcomers to the business to buy full protective gear, and even at that they should expect to get stung.

Meet Some Local Honey Producers

Monica White of Southwest Bee Supply sells honey from 90 hives located on the eastern side of the basin in Vail. She says there are benefits to the Africanized bees. "African bees are a studier, heartier breed, more resistant to disease and parasites," she explains. "They don't get sick as easily. Anyway," she adds with a shrug, "most of them aren't that bad. Bees get to know the beekeeper and they tolerate us."

According to White, knowing exactly when to collect the honey is crucial to the taste. "As the honey sits in the hive, it develops flavor and color. Even after you take it out, it continues to develop."

Many people seek out honey derived from specific desert plants for health reasons. White explains: "If you buy honey made from the pollen of the plants that you're allergic to, you build up your immune system every time you eat a little bit."

On the western side of the valley, Life'Sweet Honey has its 650 hives spread in desert areas from Picture Rocks to Three Points. Chris Brinton, the beekeeper, is particular about what pollen his bees bring back to their hives. "I keep all my bees away from agriculture," he says. "I want them to have only desert pollen. My customers want wildflower honey to help with their allergies. Customers are also very interested in mesquite honey."

Because Brinton keeps his bees in rural areas, usually on state land, he needs to check often to make sure they have water. And because the Tucson rains are so spotty—drenching some areas, leaving others dry—he'll keep a close eye on what's blooming and move his hives to areas with more flowers if necessary. When the drought of the 2017–2018 winter left wide swaths of the desert dry and without blooms, Brinton's honey production dropped by a quarter.

Tucson ice cream lovers may have eaten Brinton's honey without realizing it. A local business, Screamery Ice Cream, buys Life'Sweet raw honey by the five-gallon bucket to use in several of their flavors including Sweet Cream Honey Comb and Bees Knees.

Dave Benton of Tucson Honey Company locates many of his hives on the farms of small local growers. The farmers are happy to have the pollinators and are less likely to be troubled by bees buzzing around their home. They are also happy to get a small percentage of the honey from the hives on their land. While the bees visit the crops, they don't just stick to the farm. According to Benton, research shows that desert bees will travel up to 8 miles during their foraging expeditions as they seek out mesquite and wildflowers.

Like other beekeepers, Benton says that his bees are semi-Africanized. He sees that as an advantage as he finds them hardier and more resistant to varroa mites and finds that his bees aren't especially aggressive. "They have mellowed incredibly since Africanized bees arrived in 1990," he says. "Tucson has feral honeybees and the new bees have interbred with them."

True Love Honey was the result of Anthony Tubbiolo losing his job in the 2009 recession. Someone offered him two years' worth of stored honey. He laid out all the cash he had for part of it and began selling it on the side of the road. He made his money back and then some. His wife-to-be, Hilda, was a customer. She was having trouble getting her food truck business going and he needed help with the honey stand. They decided to combine forces and, with Hilda's small daughter in tow, moved the honey stand from corner to corner throughout Tucson.

Eventually they bought some hive boxes and captured some bee colonies. They now have their hives in Marana, mainly in the Ironwood Forest National Monument.

The Tubbiolos now sell their honey both wholesale and in their own tasting and sales room on 4th Avenue. Hilda guides customers through the flavors of the desert-blend honey compared with the wildflower honey, passing out tastes on tiny straws. She also infuses their honey with flavors such as cayenne, lavender, and cinnamon.

Education about raw honey and the importance of bees in the ecosystem is an important part of the honey business, but Noel Patterson has made it a full-time job. In 2009 he was working as a wine salesman when he received a hive as a birthday present. Intrigued with his gift, he talked about the honey he was producing as he visited the restaurants that were his wine clients.

The chefs were interested in buying his honey, but with just one hive, he didn't have enough to provide for their needs. He asked them if they'd be willing to go into partnership and front the money for the hive (in the range of $300–$400), and in return share in the honey. Peter Wilke of Time Market restaurant/grocery store and the B Line restaurant was his first client; Wilke even put a hive in his own backyard. Patterson's business, Dos Manos Apiaries, was born.

While Patterson continues with his cooperative hives, he now has an additional job. When he talked to Miraval Arizona Resort & Spa about sponsoring a hive, they were so enthusiastic they asked him to talk to their new committee on sustainability. In turn, they hired him to set up some hives on their property—there are now sixty—and educate their guests about honey and the role of both European and native bees in the food system. Miraval uses the honey the bees produce in the spa kitchen and in several spa treatments.

"Everything I know about wine applies to honey," Patterson says. "Honey tastes totally different from place to place and from year to year."

People looking to get rid of bees or to acquire some bees can look to Monica King, a third-generation beekeeper. King removes unwanted swarms and takes them to her own property

Honeybee Ice Cream

This recipe was developed by local beekeeper Linda McKittrick. In addition to the basic ingredients below, she suggests adding organic edible flower petals, which will be pesticide free. Elderberry trees have lovely white blossoms in the spring. Yellow palo verde flowers would give a golden hue. Or you can use scented geraniums. To freeze your ice cream, you can use the older-style ice cream maker with ice and rock salt or the type where you freeze the container and stir the milk mixture with the attached paddle.

2 cups organic milk
⅔ cup local honey
½ teaspoon sea salt
2 large eggs
2 cups heavy cream
1 tablespoon vanilla

Over medium to low heat, and being careful not to scald it, heat the milk in a stainless-steel pan, about 5 minutes, whisking in the honey and salt as the milk warms.

Beat the eggs in a small bowl, then add half of the milky mixture in the pan by whisking it—slowly—into the eggs. Stir this milk/egg mixture back into the milk in the pan and heat again over the medium-low heat for another 5 minutes, stirring constantly so that you don't scorch it.

Remove from heat and pour mixture into a glass or ceramic bowl and let it cool completely. Once cooled, whisk in the heavy cream and vanilla. Pour into your ice cream device and freeze.

between Three Points and Sasabe where she keeps from 50 to 75 hives. If they are Africanized, she re-queens them with a European queen. "The Africanized bees are too temperamental," she says. "I don't like their unpredictability." She always uses a strain of European queen bees bred for disease resistance.

Mainly, King breeds queens. For people wanting to get into the honey business, King offers "nuncs," a starter hive consisting of five frames of bees, with a queen, a brood, and some worker bees. Her bees feed on wildflowers and mesquite, whatever's in season. Because she's trying to increase her number of bees to pass along new colonies, she feeds the bees when there is no natural pollen. King is encouraging to new beekeepers, teaches classes, and has passed along her knowledge as the 2019 president of the Southern Arizona Beekeepers Association.

MEAT EATING THROUGH THE MILLENNIA

Until Father Kino arrived in the Santa Cruz River Valley with cattle, pigs, sheep, and goats, the local meat diet was largely confined to rabbits and other small mammals with the rare deer brought in by a hunter who had good luck. At least that is what all local archaeological excavations have shown. How-ever, in the San Pedro River Valley, the next valley to the east and a little south near Hereford, scientists have uncovered a large prehistoric butchering site with remains of twelve immature mammoths, one horse, one tapir, several bison, one camel, one bear, several rabbits, and a garter snake. They have dated the site to between 11,000 and 13,000 years ago.

This was an accidental discovery in 1952 when rancher Edward Lehner found bones in the sidecut of an arroyo after a particularly heavy rain and notified the University of Arizona.

In the years after the disappearance of the megafauna, it appears from the bones left behind that even getting a deer was only a very occasional event. To me, Paul Mirocha's poem supposes the thoughts of a hunter contemplating such a kill. Mirocha thinks it could apply to a mountain lion as well as a human hunter.

MULE DEER
Odocoileus hemionus
By Paul Mirocha

I go to bed hungry and thirst for the rain
You chew on the flower, the thorns, and the leaf.
I dream of the blood that flows in your veins.
You are standing alone
at the edge of the world.
I wake with the taste of dust in my teeth.

From *The Sonoran Desert: A Literary Field Guide*

Used with permission

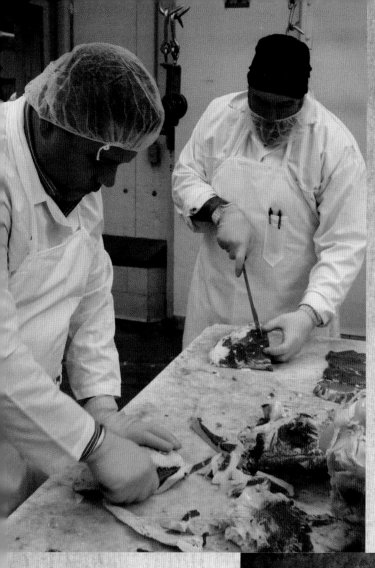

Samuel Garcia, professor and head of the Food Products and Safety Laboratory (sometimes called the meat lab) of the UA's College of Agriculture and Life Sciences, and Kirk Klosowsky are two of the dozen or so teachers, butchers, and agriculture students who provide custom butchering services for small commercial animal raisers and for those who just raise one or two animals for their own use. (Roger C. Wolf)

Father Eusebio Kino introduced hardy criollo cattle to the To-hono O'odham in the 1690s. To-day, Southern Arizona ranchers are adding them to their herds. (Bill Steen)

In the years subsequent to Father Kino arriving in the Tucson area with cattle in the 1690s, the Tohono O'odham began a transition to a cattle-raising culture. Father Kino had introduced cattle to the Tohono O'odham to keep the animals near the mission, but the Native Americans had other ideas. They drove their herds out to their ancestral lands, keeping them in areas where they could provide for their copious water requirements.

When the Spanish soldiers arrived at the Presidio, they brought along cattle and grazed them on lush grass next to the Santa Cruz River. In the centuries since, ranchers have pushed farther to the margins of the valley and into the foothills as the open spaces were fenced off. Now they are in the outer fringes of Pima County and in the surrounding counties that have more open space.

Navajo-Churro sheep, introduced by the Spanish, do well in Arizona's arid conditions. (Bill Steen)

It was never easy for ranchers. According to historian Thomas Sheridan, early ranchers raised a mixed breed of longhorn called criollo, but drought and constant Apache raids carrying off their stock led to most ranchers giving up by the 1840s.

The cattle business began to grow again after the Civil War. As windmill technology improved, ranchers could pump water into ponds, allowing cattle to graze away from streams. The federal government stimulated the growth by buying large numbers of cattle for U.S. Army posts and Native American reservations. But cycles of drought continued to be a problem. In the late 1890s, the combination of drought and overgrazing led to an almost total collapse of ranching in Southern Arizona. After a few years of rebuilding, the drought of 1921–1925 led to the loss of 18,000 cattle in western Pima County, most on Tohono O'odham lands. Ranchers learned they needed to consider the carrying capacity of their land and develop stable watering places to sustain their enterprises.

Despite the challenges, ranching still takes up a fair amount of land in Pima County. A report prepared by Sheridan for the Sonoran Desert Conservation Plan states that in eastern Pima Country ranching stretches over approximately 1.4 million acres, comprising a mosaic of private and public landownership, dedicated to ranching. Most ranches are family-owned enterprises, often run by the descendants of original homesteaders who set up the ranch in the late 1800s. There generally will be a small core of deeded land surrounded by federal and state land on which the rancher holds grazing permits. Today the Tohono O'odham control about 2.5 million acres, most of it in the far western part of Pima County, on which they graze cattle and horses.

Economically, ranching is a good use of land in the Santa Cruz Valley. Valuable meat is produced on land that cannot be used to grow crops. Mild winters allow cows to calve in the field whereas in colder climates they must be kept in a barn.

Yet, ranching in Pima County is a shrinking business. The 1997 federal agricultural census counted 39,000 cattle in the county. In 2012 it was down to 18,312. The 2012 agricultural census also lists about 10,000 hogs and pigs being raised in Pima County, 570 sheep and lambs, and 3,100 laying chickens.

Just as consumers are becoming savvier about where and how their vegetables are grown, they are increasingly concerned about where and how their meat is raised. They want local and organic.

Tucson custom butcher Ben Forbes is a link between the Southern Arizona rancher and the consumer who wants locally raised meat. Forbes learned to butcher whole animals when working at Whole Foods and says that until the resurgence of custom butchery, it was a dying trade.

As Forbes builds his business, it is his goal to make it possible for ranchers to concentrate on raising animals properly and let him do the marketing rather than having to go to farmers' markets themselves. They'll still make more money than if they were selling on the whims of the commodity market.

Every year Forbes buys 50 to 60 steers and a couple of hundred pigs from local ranchers. The animals will be slaughtered at the Food Products and Safety Laboratory (usually called the meat lab) of the UA's College of Agriculture and Life Sciences. There, they will be skinned and quartered and delivered to Forbes's 36-degree-Fahrenheit workshop.

Forbes knows each muscle of the cow and how to get the most out of it. "The cuts from the front and back of the animal are the hardest to sell," Forbes says. "But to be sustainable, you need to use the whole animal. If you braise these cuts properly, they are twice as flavorful as the tenderloin.

"My customers come to me with an open mind. Rather than asking for a specific cut, they ask what's good. I have cuts you don't find at a grocery store. For example, I offer a sierra steak. There are muscles within the chuck shoulder that are more tender. I separate them out and give the customer a tender steak that is more economical and more flavorful."

All the meat Forbes butchers is 100 percent grass fed, which savvy consumers know is more healthful with a better ratio of omega-3 to omega-6 fatty acids. "There is a delusion that grass-fed meat has no marbling," he says. "But at the Lazy J2 near Patagonia, Sidney Spencer raises her Angus-Hereford animals for four years and there is plenty of intramuscular fat."

At least half of the pigs that Forbes butchers each year are for families who have raised just one for their own table. "It takes only six to eight months to raise a pig," he said, "versus at least two or two and a half years for a cow."

Forbes admits that the increased cost of local meat is an issue for some people. "But," he says, "our cooking and buying practices have to change if we want to support local ranchers. Local meat might cost a little more, but you don't need an eight-ounce steak. Since grass-fed beef is tastier, it is more satiating. You can do with less."

Tucsonans also have access to naturally raised grass-fed meat from several other Southern Arizona ranches. Paul Schwennesen took over some operations of Double Check Ranch in Pinal County from his folks in 2007. He is a familiar sight at Tucson farmers' markets where he arrives with a freezer full of beef that he has raised and that was butchered in a packing-house right on the ranch. Customers have watched his children grow from infants to young "cowhands."

Many Tucson Mexican butcher shops keep a grill going on the weekends. Customers can choose a cut and have it cooked right there.

Schwennesen says he tries to manage his lands holistically and is "reinventing local small-scale agriculture in a way that respects land, animals, and people." He contends that not trucking the animals to an off-site slaughterhouse is more humane and leads to less stress and better-tasting meat.

Deborah and Dennis Moroney have chosen to concentrate on heritage breeds through their Sky Island Brand at their 47 Ranch near McNeal in Santa Cruz County. They raise crossbreed cattle and criollo cattle, a breed that evolved in the semiarid Canary Islands and was brought to Mexico by the Spanish. Not fussy about what they eat, criollo cattle will browse on prickly pear, oak leaves, or tumbleweeds. The meat, which is available in Tucson at the Food Conspiracy Co-op, is tender and the flavor robust. The Moroneys also raise Navajo-Churro sheep, another breed brought by the Spanish that adapts well to arid conditions. Consumers like the flavor, which reflects the fresh range of plants that the sheep have been eating, the terroir.

Tucsonans wanting locally raised pork turn to E & R Pork where Erika Pacheco and Rod Miller raise several heritage breeds of antibiotic- and hormone-free pigs—up to 1,500 at a time—on several local properties. The pigs enter the cycle of the local food system by dining and fattening up on spent grain from Hamilton Distillers, Sentinel Peak Brewing, and Borderlands Brewing. They also eat wheat germ from Hayden Flour Mills in Tempe and feed from Bonita Bean Company in Willcox.

PRESERVATION OF
PIMA COUNTY RANCHLAND

In order to preserve open space, Pima County has purchased six ranches using voter-approved open-space bonds. The ranches are the King 98 Ranch and Rancho Seco, both in the Altar Valley to the west of Tucson; the Six-Bar Ranch in the San Pedro River Valley; the Bar V Ranch, southeast of Vail; the Carpenter Ranch in Marana; and the A-7 Ranch on Redington Road. The total of 18,094 acres with 75,000 acres of associated grazing leases maintains not only open space but also land for cattle raising. The historic Empire Ranch just north of Sonoita is now managed by the Bureau of Land Management and is open to anyone who wants to camp for up to two weeks to get the flavor of what it's like to wake up on a ranch.

The E & R Pork pigs are slaughtered and packaged by the UA meat lab and sold to restaurants and to the general public at farmers' markets.

For city residents who wish to raise some of their own animal food, regulations permit property owners to raise chickens, ducks, geese, and miniature goats. Hen houses must be at least 20 feet from the neighbor's house and the number of animals permitted is based on the size of the lot.

SELLING TO SCHOOLS AND HOSPITALS:
BIG CUSTOMERS, BIG CHALLENGES

For small farmers, large, guaranteed sales can be a step toward solvency. Small commercial farms would be happy to gear up to grow and sell more if they could rely on a stable market. And big customers such as schools and hospitals are as interested in the flavor and freshness of local food as the homemaker or chef. Although regulatory and planning hurdles stand between small farmers and large markets, the Community Food Bank of Southern Arizona is working to bridge the issues.

Major local purchasers such as Tucson Unified School District (TUSD) and Tucson Medical Center (TMC) need large amounts of the same thing and need to rely on delivery to fulfill menus planned months in advance. The small farmer sometimes cannot produce the quantity needed, and even if they could, they would face complex regulations in selling to these larger accounts. For example, TUSD was set up to award just one bid for all their produce. Wanting to include some local vegetables in the children's menus, the school district added one more bid option for local food. But just one. No small local farm could produce the variety of vegetables in the quantity required. To make it work, the Community Food Bank of Southern Arizona stepped in through their Farm to Institution Value Chain Initiative and became that one central distributor. Now the Food Bank uses its infrastructure of warehouses and refrigerated trucks to gather, deliver, and invoice produce from participating local farms to TMC and the University of Arizona as well as TUSD.

Everybody displaying maximum flexibility is also part of the equation. For the program to work, the institutions need to plan menus seasonally and the farms need to gear up to grow what the institutions need in the quantity they require. TUSD dietitians have been modifying the school menu rotation to connect with harvest times of each vegetable. Specifically, they are looking for fruits and vegetables that grow well here and can be harvested in Tucson between September and December and January and April. The dietitians also must coordinate with regulations from the National School Lunch Program, which dictates that each meal must contain certain nutrients and a mix of colors. Additional regulations specify the portions of foods that must be served to each age group.

The Community Food Bank representatives pull everyone together to decide who is going to supply what, during what time frame, the frequency of delivery, and the quantity. They also work out a fair price and everyone signs a contract. The program works with 15 to 18 local farms to sell more than 12,500 pounds of produce (that's 295,000 servings) to the large institutional markets.

A big success has been the locally grown cherry tomatoes that TMC has put on their salad bar. While standardization is sometimes an issue, the varying colors, shapes, and flavors of the tomatoes are an asset. Another popular item is greens. Since the summer of 2015, local farmers have been supplying TMC with kale and Swiss chard year-round. While the local schools couldn't use the heritage yellow-fleshed watermelons grown by San Xavier Co-op Farm because of a perceived choking hazard from the seeds for the young children, students at the University of Arizona loved them.

Merchant's Garden employees pack up 600 pounds of lettuce every week to be served to TUSD students as part of a project to include locally grown produce in school lunches. (Emily Derks)

Rani Olson, TUSD coordinator of the Farm to School program, says, "We look at those items kids already enjoy so we don't need to sell it. Fruits are great. We have cantaloupes, honeydew, and watermelon in the early fall. Kids love steamed broccoli. Asian pears from a farm near Aravaipa Canyon were a big hit."

Kids readily eat carrots, but buying them from local farms is hindered by the processing needed. "Carrots need to be scrubbed and chopped," Olson says. "We don't have the labor to do that, but we are looking at processing equipment that might help."

To see how the system is working, let's take a look at TUSD food headquarters. The school year has just gotten underway in mid-August when a stack of boxes holding a thousand pounds of sleek, green cucumbers sits in a small corner of the basketball-court-sized walk-in cooler. The cucumbers came from a small farm in Patagonia and will be sliced into rounds and served at lunch with ranch dip to students at a few Tucson schools. The cucumbers will provide vitamins and welcome hydration on a warm afternoon.

Next week, another locally grown farm vegetable will go to another group of schools. When the fresh vegetables arrive, they are not slipped in hoping the students don't notice. Rather, they are treated like the rock stars of the meal. Teachers discuss them, and posters in the lunchroom tell specifics about the vitamins. There is even information about the farmer who grew the vegetables. Sometimes the farmers come to the schools to answer questions about the produce. They also talk about the various skills they need, such as a knowledge of mathematics, to become a successful farmer.

Lindsay Aguilar, a registered dietitian and director of food services for TUSD, is responsible for overseeing 40,000 student meals a day including breakfasts, lunches, after-school snacks, and now even some suppers. With 74 percent of TUSD students coming from low-income families and eligible for free or reduced lunches, TUSD has accepted the challenge of making sure each student has enough food, and the right food, to be able to fully participate in classroom learning.

Each of the 86 school lunch locations gets a mix of local and commercial produce over the course of a week. For example, if Merchant's Garden, which grows salad greens for TUSD, harvests 500 pounds of lettuce, that is enough for just 10 schools. Another 10 schools will get the local salad after the next harvest.

The programs that Aguilar and her staff are overseeing are forward looking and beneficial. But they are also expensive. "Our grant team is constantly applying for grants," she says. For example, a Sprouts Neighborhood Grant has funded field trips to Merchant's Garden so students can see where their salad is grown.

The hope is that children exposed to a wide variety of fruits and vegetables and to meals from other culinary traditions will not be afraid to try a new vegetable. The extensive time and extra money TUSD funnels into its food program aim not only to feed the students while they are at school but also to set up a lifetime of healthy food choices.

FARMERS' MARKETS HELP FARMERS AND CUSTOMERS CONNECT

"Know your farmer," we are advised. The easiest place to meet them is at the markets where you can chat with the person who picked your squash just before loading up the truck.

After attempts to start farmers' markets in Tucson fizzled in the late 1980s and early 1990s, the local farmers' market movement really got going in 1999 when Richard and Erzebet Bruner organized an open-air market at Saint Philip's Plaza, hoping to replicate the abundant market found in Erzebet's native Budapest, Hungary. Today farmers' markets have grown in popularity in Tucson with about a half dozen scattered over the valley, mostly open from Thursday through Sunday. Local producers are joined by farmers from outside the Santa Cruz Valley, places an hour away with cooler summer weather and more water, who are drawn by greater Tucson's million residents.

Farmers spend lots of time alone in their fields during the week and say they like getting to meet their customers and having the opportunity to share their enthusiasm and the health benefits of their vegetables. These markets are also one of the few places people looking for organic animal products like eggs, cheese, and meat can connect with growers. Small producers of food items like jams, pastries, and tortillas also take booths.

Farmers' markets serve the consumer and the farmers in different ways. The markets give small farmers access to customers in several different neighborhoods without having to invest in a regular storefront. They are able to get higher prices for their produce when they sell a single head of lettuce to a shopper than when they sell a crate of lettuce to a store or restaurant. Most farmers are facing a tight margin of cost of production to income. Some even lose money. The extra money that they can bring in from shoppers willing to pay a bit more for vegetables where they can meet the farmer and be sure of the growing conditions is sometimes the difference between making it or not.

There are numerous benefits to both customers and communities when people shop at farmers' markets. Usually the time from when a vegetable is picked to when it is offered at the farmer's display table is hours, rarely more than a day. Since fruits and vegetables lose nutrients as soon as they are picked, customers get a more nutritious product. And the fresher the vegetable, the better the flavor. Additionally, small farmers are able to choose varieties that provide the best flavor, not just varieties that will hold up for a weeklong trip across hundreds if not thousands of miles. Farmers growing for local customers know what their customers want and are able to cater to small groups of consumers who are not only willing but eager to try vegetables they are not familiar with. Shoppers are frequently offered small samples to taste.

Shoppers see value in buying produce, honey, and meat from somebody whose face they recognize and name they know. They learn who has the sweetest peaches ("Come back next week, honey—we've got another variety just ready to pick") and the crispest lettuce ("Brought it in an hour before I headed over here"). They get advice on how to cook a particular cut of meat.

Sleeping Frog Farms in the San Pedro River Valley brought these beautiful radishes to the Rillito Park Farmers' Market.

Even more important is health. A shorter distance between your farmer and your kitchen table leads to less chance of contamination. During several recent lettuce scares when greens disappeared from grocery shelves because of contamination, I didn't flinch. I knew exactly where my lettuce had come from, I knew who grew it, and I knew it was healthy.

Who Shops at Farmers' Markets?

The simple answer to why shoppers frequent farmers' markets is to get food. But the reasons are deeper and more complex than that. Melanie Wallendorf and Matthew Godfrey, of the University of Arizona Eller College of Management, looked into who exactly shoppers were at Tucson farmers' markets and why they were there.

The shoppers seemed to fall into four broad categories: those looking for the most healthful produce, those seeking the best produce for the money, people who consider strolling through the market as recreation, and others who are there as a community-building event.

The first group, the researchers say, are "consumers for whom ethical or environmentally sustainable food acquisition is a critical moral choice tied closely to their lifestyles and identities." They are interested in environmental sustainability and organic, locally grown produce and avoid genetically modified organisms and pesticide-sprayed crops. They accept the expense as a worthwhile investment in their health. These consumers enjoy visiting the same vendors weekly and hope the relationship will allow them to go home with the best food.

The second group is looking for the best value in food at the lowest cost and farmers' markets are only one of several venues where they shop. Generally, these shoppers make a trip through the entire market before making a purchase, checking prices and availability.

The third group, according to the study, attends a farmers' market "as a leisure activity that provides entertainment and an escape from routine daily life." They are drawn by the free samples, snacks, tasty beverages, and live music that offer a bright spot in their lives. They don't necessarily work the visit into their normal food shopping, although they may buy a few items. The experience is more like going to a movie or window shopping at the mall.

The fourth group "employs the market to reinforce relationships with others who consumers regard as like-minded individuals." These shoppers are looking primarily for a social experience rather than a shopping trip. They see their attendance at the local farmers' market as community networking where they build and maintain social connections.

One of the criticisms of farmers' markets nationally has been that they tend to be located in areas of high- or middle-income households, although it is people of lower income who tend to live in food deserts—that is, places where easy access to fresh wholesome foods is lacking. It is also true that the produce at farmers' markets is a little more expensive than that at the lowest-price supermarkets, pricing out lower-income shoppers.

To counteract this problem, the two farmers' markets run by the Community Food Bank (the Santa Cruz River Farmers' Market at the Mercado San Agustín and the smaller market at their headquarters

The farmers' market at Steam Pump Ranch has a friendly rural atmosphere and is convenient for people who live in Oracle, Marana, and the northern parts of Tucson.

At the Abundant Harvest stand at the Santa Cruz River Farmers' Market, the white tags on the baskets identify which farmers will get paid for the sale of their produce.

on South Country Club Road) and those run by Heirloom Farmers' Markets accept SNAP benefit cards (SNAP stands for Supplemental Nutrition Assistance Program, the successor to food stamps). Customers can trade SNAP benefits for vouchers that can be used at individual farm stands. In fact, participating markets have begun a Double-Up SNAP incentive in which the Community Food Bank matches SNAP customers' spending up to an extra $20. This program was implemented to attract SNAP customers to the market and improve their nutrition by nudging them to buy local fresh fruits and vegetables.

The Double-Up Food Bucks are also a benefit to farmers as they can be spent only on Arizona-grown fruits and vegetables. At the end of 2018, Heirloom Farmers' Markets reported that 150 shoppers every month used the Double-Up SNAP program, putting an extra $3,000 into farmers' pockets each month.

Tucson's Farmers' Markets Spread over the Basin

Tucson-area farmers' markets stretch from Picture Rocks in Avra Valley in the west to the base of the Rincon Mountains in Vail in the southeast and from River Road on the northwest side to 36th Street on the south side of town. Each market has its own personality and client base. Hours of the markets vary by season so do check before heading out.

University of Arizona Mall, Wednesdays Midday

The university academic schedule dictates when this market is open selling to students and university staff.

Santa Cruz River Farmers' Market, Thursday Afternoons

This market is held at the Mercado San Agustín on West Congress Street and Avenida del Convento at the western terminus of the streetcar line. The Mercado is fashioned after a Mexican plaza with shops facing an interior courtyard. Farmers and other merchants set up stands on the outside perimeter of the building and in the courtyard as well, claiming the same spot every week so customers can easily find them.

The Community Food Bank of Southern Arizona sells vegetables through the Abundant Harvest Cooperative. Successful gardeners who grow more zucchini or lemons or kale than their families can possibly eat have a place to sell their excess without having to set up a farm stand in their neigh-

Dana Helfer of Rattlebox Farm assists a customer at the Santa Cruz River Farmers' Market.

borhood. Gardeners can bring in anything from a few bags of greens to a bushel or two of oranges. Gardeners with produce for sale arrive in the hour before the market opens to have their fruits and vegetables tallied by volunteers.

On a cool fall day threatening rain, Dan Harrigan, a grower, was volunteering as a market ambassador. He has a 900-square-foot garden which he rotates by planting two-thirds of the space and leaving one-third fallow. He brought in kale, elephant garlic, lettuces, spinach, escarole, and endive. He generally goes home with $40 to $50; on his best week he made $100.

Next in line was Josepha Ntakirutimana, who learned to garden in her native Rwanda and brought two varieties of kale and basil. She gardens in her own backyard and in a nearby community garden and averages about $20 a week in sales.

Antonio Torrez showed up with plump figs that will be sold for $5 a pound. Torrez's 20 fig trees at his place on West Valencia produce from June through December. He also brought almost 15 pounds of tangerines, their skins so tender they almost peeled themselves. In the summer he brings peaches and apples.

The Food Bank also maintains a smaller farmers' market on Tuesday mornings at their main campus on South Country Club Road.

Rattlebox Farm, Breckenfeld Family Growers, High Energy Agriculture, Wild Child Gardens, and Dreamflower Garden are among the other local regulars. Farmers also come from Benson, Patagonia, Saint David, and Willcox.

Morris K. Udall Park Farmers' Market, Friday Mornings

Tables and tents set up on the grass give the Udall Park a country feeling although it is just off busy Tanque Verde Road. Aromas of roasting chiles and a guitarist crooning country western songs add to the atmosphere. Shoppers find a good selection of fresh and roasted vegetables, tempting baked goods, salsa, jam, honey, pasta, and organic grass-fed beef. One winter morning there were even Turkish sweets, tiny brown and cream quail eggs, and CBD-infused dog treats.

Banner–University Medical Center, Fridays Midday

This is a smaller market catering to the lunch crowd, drawing customers from the medical, nursing, and pharmacy colleges as well as the hospital. It includes a few vegetable vendors and local cooked food.

Oro Valley Farmers' Market at Steam Pump Ranch, Saturday Mornings

Set on the site of the old Steam Pump Ranch, this market is a good choice for residents of the communities north of Tucson. The name comes from the fact that in 1874 two German immigrants bought a portion of the Cañada del Oro Ranch and used a steam engine to pump water from the shallow aquifer and develop an oasis. One of the men was George Pusch, for whom Pusch Ridge in the Santa Catalina Mountains just to the east is named.

The market has a rural feel with the shade structures built of wood. Just by being 15 miles out of downtown, there's a more leisurely vibe. Some merchants, such as Tortilleria Arevalo, bring food to sell, and people can pick up a burrito for breakfast on a chilly morning.

Every month, the second Saturday brings music or demonstrations or something for family fun. Steam Pump Ranch hosts special tours, historic and cultural presentations, concert series, and activities for children.

East of the market area is a small garden that replicates a Hohokam garden from around AD 500–1100. There is also a replica of a Hohokam pit house of the type that was found near Pusch Ridge by archaeologists working through Pima Community College in the 1990s.

Rincon Valley Farmers' Market, Saturday Mornings

This market serves those who live in Vail and the far east side of the basin. At about 20 miles from midtown, it's also a good destination for those heading for a hike in Saguaro National Park East or anybody needing to escape the city bustle for a spell. The one vegetable seller when I visited was from outside Tucson, but Queen Creek could be considered our foodshed. You'll also find honey made by bees feeding off Vail mesquite trees, homemade tortillas of several varieties, raw milk, and organic meat from E & R Pork, a local farmer.

Anne Loftfield of High Energy Agriculture ferments some of the vegetables she grows and sells that product alongside her fresh produce.

An old barn houses small-craft makers in the former horse stalls—everything from aprons to jewelry to lamps made from teapots. Every third Saturday of the month there's the addition of a sale where folks are invited to bring everything from furniture to still-good tools.

Rillito Park Farmers' Market, Sunday Mornings

Set between the Rillito Park horse racing track and the Loop Trail along the Rillito River, the Rillito Park Farmers' Market is the largest in Tucson. In 2015, Pima County and the Rillito Park Foundation built this permanent farmers' market space with three shade pavilions, a center entertainment circle, and public restrooms. It is leased to Heirloom Farmers' Markets, which brings in the vendors.

If a farmer in the Tucson basin or Tucson's foodshed grows it and it's in season, you'll find it here. Because it attracts so many shoppers, farmers come from the far edges of our foodshed to bring their tomatoes, melons, peaches, and greens to the market. In addition to raw foods, many vendors bring cooked offerings such as breads and baked goods, including gluten-free items; coffee; salsas; and specialty teas. You can even find home-baked biscuits for your canine pal.

It is possible to buy a family's entire weekly produce needs here from fruit for breakfast to salad for lunch to vegetables for dinner. There are also numerous animal products including organic beef, chicken, goat, and lamb as well as honey, eggs, and jerky. And to make it easier to turn that chicken and vegetables into a tasty stew, you can have your good knife sharpened while you shop.

A booth in the entertainment circle, called Taste of the Market, features food demonstrators cooking up vegetables from the local vendors. You can get a generous sample of whatever the featured vegetable is, information about the nutrients it contains, and some recipes. It's worth stopping by.

Picture Rocks Farmers' Market, Sunday Mornings

Picture Rocks is a small, rural community in Avra Valley, and this market serves the local population. For shoppers coming from elsewhere, the beautiful drive through the lush desert surrounding the community makes the trip there a special treat. You'll find a small selection of fresh vegetables sourced from several farmers, eggs, and honey. Several booths have baked goods, fudge in a dozen flavors, and some crafts. You can pick up lunch or a snack from a food truck. Local, live music sets a nice tone to the morning.

PIVOT PRODUCE

Erik Stanford of Pivot Produce arrives at the Santa Cruz River Farmers' Market just before it opens on a late-May Thursday afternoon and heads directly to see Anne Loftfield at the High Energy Agriculture booth. There he picks up 25 pounds of yellow and green mixed summer squash—flat pattypans the size of a small bagel and shiny-skinned zucchini and Mexican gray squash. He also hefts a 10-pound bag of leeks and onions.

Two booths down, he stops at Dreamflower Garden, where he gathers up bags of epazote, wild arugula, fragrant marjoram, oregano, spearmint, and chives that farmer Lorien Tersey has packaged for him. Purchases completed, he makes the rounds, chatting with other farmers, maintaining contacts and friendships. Looks like it's going to be a good tomato year, they all agree.

Stanford isn't feeding a large family with all that produce, nor does he have a restaurant. He is buying the vegetables that he has a hunch that local chefs will want. Farmers don't have time to peddle their wares from restaurant to restaurant, and chefs don't have time to drive to the fields or even cruise the farmers' markets. That's where Stanford comes in. His website says he has been "bridging the gap between local farmers and chefs since 2016."

At the beginning of the year, Stanford sends the chefs a month-by-month estimate of what probably will be available and some chefs plan their menus around that availability. Today, after leaving the Santa Cruz Market, he'll return to his office and email forty-five Tucson chefs a list of the items he just picked up along with the beets, collard greens, wheat berries, and freshly ground Sonora White wheat flour that other farmers delivered to him earlier in the day. The chefs will email or text back their orders, and Friday morning, he'll make his deliveries, giving the busy chefs access to just-picked produce without having to leave their kitchens to go out to the farms or markets. An average of sixteen restaurants a week take him up on his offerings.

At the Santa Cruz River Farmers' Market, Erik Stanford of Pivot Produce checks the herbs he ordered from Dreamflower Garden. All the herbs are destined for Tucson's chefs.

Among his customers this week are Scott Girod, chef at Anello, a small pizza restaurant. Girod said, "Having fresh organic produce makes our menu complete." For his popular seasonal vegetable plate, he purchased the summer squash, cooking the zucchini whole in the coals of their wood-fired oven and pickling thin-sliced pattypans, then topping them with pistachios, basil, and mint.

Executive chef Brian Smith at Maynards Market & Kitchen purchased mustard greens, beets, and arugula that he used in a salad, and collard greens that he sautéed with onions, garlic, and pepper flakes, a recipe he picked up when he worked in the South. He always plans to use the fresh vegetables in his nightly fish special.

"If I could buy everything I need from Erik, I would," Smith says. "The flavor of his vegetables is a hundred percent better than commercial. The celery he gets is off the charts. Also, he has things not available elsewhere, such as I'itoi onions. The same for some of the melons that will come in later in the summer."

Early the next week, Stanford let his customers know that San Xavier Co-op Farm had the season's first peaches. Two days later, Reilly Craft Pizza & Drink was offering a special of dry-aged pork porterhouse with peaches and collard greens. The menu also mentioned that Pivot Produce had provided heirloom tomatoes, spring onions, and basil for the pizzas.

In choosing what to buy from the farmers, Stanford thinks like a chef because for years he was one. His idea for Pivot Produce was born from his love of interacting with farmers, and he soon discovered that other chefs were willing to pay him to do the same sort of shopping he had done for himself. It wasn't without a few hiccups, though. Restaurant chefs are accustomed to ordering large and standard quantities of vegetables from commercial conveyors. They can dictate a certain size and delivery date. Stanford, on the other hand, offers them what the small-scale local farmers have available that week in the random

Erik Stanford keeps track of chefs' orders for local produce on a large whiteboard.

sizes that come out of the field. The chefs had to be flexible.

But with the ever-increasing farm-to-table enthusiasm sweeping the culinary world, customers were interested in local produce and chefs found that the flavors of the fresh vegetables not only spurred their creativity but also outweighed the inconvenience.

Stanford sells vegetables not picked up by the chefs at a small Sunday farmers' market in a lot near the 5 Points Market & Restaurant. Anything left over goes to the Casa Maria Soup Kitchen, expanding the reach of these delicious organic vegetables.

FOR FURTHER READING

Carney, Megan A., and Keegan C. Krause. *The State of the Tucson Food System, 2018–2019*. Center for Regional Food Studies, University of Arizona College of Social and Behavioral Sciences, 2019.

Haury, Emil W., E. B. Sayles, and William W. Wasley. "The Lehner Mammoth Site, South-Eastern Arizona." *American Antiquity*, Volume 25, Number 1, July 1959.

Sheridan, Thomas. *Arizona: A History*. University of Arizona Press, Tucson, 1995.

———. "Ranching within Pima County: An Overview of Ranch Conservation." Education session for the Sonoran Desert Conservation Plan Steering Committee, August 14, 1999.

U.S. Department of Agriculture. 2012 Census of Agriculture. National Agricultural Statistics Service, 2014.

Wallendorf, Melanie, and Matthew Godfrey. *Food Accessibility in Southern Arizona: Mapping the Growth, Trajectory and Market Base of Tucson Farmers' Markets*. Making Action Possible in Southern Arizona (MAP Dashboard), White Paper #3, University of Arizona Eller College of Management, September 2016.

TUCSON'S ARTISAN FOOD PRODUCERS

I F TUCSON INDEED DOES TASTE like nowhere else, much of that has to do with local food producers who combine Tucson's flavorful raw ingredients into delicious new combinations of foods and beverages.

MADE IN TUCSON: SMALL KITCHENS ABUZZ WITH ACTIVITY

The term "desert terroir" is a fancy term for the fact that foods made from our local indigenous and heritage ingredients taste of our sunny, arid home. Foods produced by small entrepreneurs in home and commercial kitchens in the Santa Cruz Valley have flavors found only here, and many have loyal followers.

The number of unique local food products totals well over 150. Here are a few of them.

Barrio Bread

Only the rim of the sun is visible over the Rincon Mountains when Don Guerra begins loading the first batch of bread into his Italian deck oven. He has been at his Barrio Bread bakery in historic Broadway Village since 5 am. Each of these loaves has spent the 12 overnight hours nestled in a terrycloth towel in a wicker basket as they slowly rise in the fermentation chamber, a large refrigerator kept at 43 degrees Fahrenheit. They are the first of the 600 loaves he will bake that day in an oven that customers can see in the front of the store.

Guerra is a champion and promoter of local heritage grains and credits them with giving his bread such rich flavor.

"As an artisan baker, these grains have opened up my world tremendously," Guerra says as he slides the third tray of 15 loaves into the oven. "It's not the shape or the flavoring. It's about the grain itself. Like an artist that blends paints, I blend grains to produce the color and the flavor profile of the bread. It's just flour, water, and salt, but it's how you combine them that is key."

To source the specialty grains essential to his bread, Guerra works with the Wong family at BKW Farms just up the highway in Marana. In addition to planting their usual crops, they support Guerra's mission by growing small plots of spelt, White Sonora wheat, Einkorn (the most primitive form of wheat), and Khorasan (marketed as Kamut), an ancient form of durum wheat from Iran. They also supply Guerra with organically grown durum and hard red spring wheat, the more modern varieties.

"BKW and I have an awesome collaboration," Guerra says. "We are working on developing a local grain economy. Some of these varieties were in danger of disappearing. But through our partnership we have an opportunity to change the course of history."

Guerra's method of producing bread is costly. His flour costs 50 percent more than commodity flour and each loaf takes 24 hours from flour to fragrant brown goodness. This is reflected in his prices, but there are plenty of people who see the value in his exceptional product and are willing to pay.

Guerra calls himself a community baker. When he isn't baking, he is sharing his passion, spreading the word about heritage grains. This educating, this sharing that he does constantly, is as important to Guerra as the flavorful golden loaves with the deep brown crust that he turns out five days a week.

"I've taught six hundred people how to bake the way I do," he says, and he doesn't worry about competition. "There are no shortcuts in this business," he says. "If they are able to pull it off and go out and do it for themselves, great. I'm trying to create a sustainable future for the community. If I don't teach these folks to make bread, who will be our bakers in the future?"

Cheri's Desert Harvest

The kitchen area of the modest factory that produces Cheri's Desert Harvest products always smells heavenly. There's the musky unmistakable scent of prickly pear if it's a day to make prickly pear jelly or syrup. Habanero-chile jelly day might make your nose tingle. And the day Cheri makes margarita marmalade, it's citrus all the way.

Cheri is Cheri Romanoski, a former schoolteacher who liked to make jelly from produce growing in her yard. When she made more than her family could consume, she gave it away to neighbors. By 1985 it seemed like a good idea to start making the products commercially. She started with pomegranate jelly, Arizona red lime marmalade, and green chile pepper jelly.

The business grew slowly, and today she offers sixteen different preserves, four syrups, five candies, and six quick mixes that include a preserve in every box. All of these are made with fresh fruits and vegetables harvested in the Sonoran Desert or frozen citrus concentrates from fruit grown in the southwestern United States.

Don Guerra of Barrio Bread lets his dough, made with wild yeast and heritage grains, rise all night so the loaves are ready for the oven when the sun comes up. (Mike Christy)

How to Make Bread with Wild Yeast

Don Guerra's bread is made with flour, water, and salt. But those ingredients would be a hard lump if it were not for the next ingredient: wild yeast. Experienced bakers might like to try Don Guerra's method for making bread with wild yeast. He explains that wild yeast spores are abundant on the grain and in the air. Millions of them, in fact. You just have to give them the proper environment in which to grow.

Here are his instructions:

Mix 2 cups of flour and 2 cups of water in a bowl and let it stand on the kitchen counter loosely covered with a clean kitchen towel. After 24 hours, you should notice some bubbles. The wild yeast are digesting the starches in the flour, burping carbon dioxide and pushing out gas.

After 48 hours, multiply the yeast colony by taking a portion of the mixture out and adding more flour and water. (Discard the extra flour-and-water mixture or share with a friend.) Again, put it aside. After another 8 to 10 hours, it will be strong enough to leaven your bread. Make a mixture that is 30 percent by weight of the leavening mixture added to other flours, knead, shape, and proceed as you would with other bread recipes.

For the last rising, let the dough rest for 12 hours at around 43 degrees Fahrenheit before baking.

Cheri Romanoski of Cheri's Desert Harvest processes 35 tons of prickly pears every year to make her jellies, syrups, and candies.

Although each of her products has its fans, it is the prickly pear jelly and syrup that are the biggest hits. Romanoski is a big champion of the local fruit, saying, "It defines us as Arizonans."

As soon as the prickly pears begin to ripen in late summer, Cheri's picking crew is out in force at 5 am to harvest on certified organic ranchlands away from pollution and car exhaust. She uses exclusively Engelmann prickly pears, believing they have the best flavor and color. In a typical harvest season, her employees will hand-pick the 35 tons of fresh cactus fruit that she will use throughout the year in her various products.

During harvest season, Romanoski and her team rush to steam and press the fruit into juice while it is still at peak freshness. She manages to get an 80 percent juice yield, which comes out to about 7,000 gallons of juice. She freezes the juice until she's ready to make jelly, syrup, or candy and she also sells juice to other local food artisans.

Although Romanoski cooks in amounts larger than you would make in your own kitchen, her batches are considered small for commercial production. "With smaller batches you get better nutrient value, color, and flavor," she says. "The fruit is so wonderful that we don't want to destroy any of its attributes."

Every year, Romanoski typically sells more than 60,000 bottles of prickly pear cactus syrup, 145,000 jars of prickly pear cactus jelly or marmalade, and about 650,000 pieces of prickly pear cactus candy.

Prickly pear fruits have an interior of hard seeds and with the quantity of fruit she uses, that is a great mass of unusable material. Unusable until recently that is, when a market began to grow for prickly pear seed oil for use in cosmetics. With anti-aging properties, the oil is now in high demand. Romanoski ordered a specially built seed oil expeller from Europe to deal with the stone-hard seeds, and she now has the seed oil for sale. The oil is high in vitamin E and omega-6 fatty acid, both of which are healthy for the skin.

Flor de Mayo Arts

Flor de Mayo Arts is the creation of Martha A. Burgess, ethnobotanist, environment educator, and purveyor of desert foods. Burgess studied for years with Tohono O'odham elder Juanita Ahil and gained a deep spiritual appreciation for the wild and cultivated foods that over many generations were strong enough to survive and even thrive in the harsh Sonoran Desert climate.

To Burgess, a bean is not just a bean. "What you see are edible jewels," she says. "These colorful gifts from the Southwest are genetic treasures—genetic diversity before your eyes. They are ancient treasures of sustainability saved from one generation to the next as appropriate agriculture—adapted and fit for the dry southwestern land long before deep groundwater pumping and commercial fertilizer came along."

A longtime board member and volunteer for Native Seeds/SEARCH, Burgess urges her customers to save a few of the beans from the package and try to grow them in their own summer garden, perpetuating the long line of desert dwellers who saved the healthiest seed from each harvest to plant the next season, adding to the natural selection process of continual adaption to the environment.

Burgess sells domestic tepary beans, mesquite meal, and chia seeds in her online store, but her signature product is Tom's Mix—a fourteen-bean Southwest heritage soup mix. Burgess sources the beans from various growers in the desert Southwest and triple-cleans them before packaging them, but notes dried beans still need sorting and washing before cooking. Tom's Mix honors ace gardener and woodcraftsman Tom Swain who grew out many Southwest heirloom varieties for the seed conservation organization Native Seeds/SEARCH, and who designed this delicious bean combo.

Tom's Mix Bean Soup

To adapt this soup to your own taste, Burgess suggests adding fresh or dried herbs such as oregano, basil, cumin, or epazote. A sprinkle of chopped fresh cilantro to the warm bowl of soup adds flavor and color. You could also make your own mix of beans.

2 cups (1 pound) Tom's Mix, sorted and washed
3 quarts drinking water or stock
1 to 2 onions, chopped
3 to 4 cloves garlic, minced
2 stalks celery, chopped
2 potatoes diced
2 carrots, chopped
1 to 2 fresh tomatoes, chopped, or 28-ounce can chopped tomatoes
Ham bone, bacon, or other meat (optional)
1 dried red chile or 1 tablespoon chile powder (optional)
Dried or fresh herbs to taste
Salt or soy sauce to taste

In a large pot, put cleaned, rinsed beans with water or stock and bring to a boil. Add all flavorings but salt or soy sauce. Cover and cook over low heat 2 to 3 hours until beans are soft and liquid has thickened. Cover can be removed in last hour of cooking to speed thickening. Add salt or soy sauce to taste.

The mix contains at least fourteen of the following bean varieties: Anasazi, Aztec black (black turtle), scarlet runner, Aztec white runner (bordal or mortgage lifter), Maicoba (azufrado), ojo de cabra, Rio Zape (Hopi purple string), moon bean (soldier), yellow-eye (butterscotch calypso), 4-Corners gold (Zuni gold), bolita, Colorado River (cut-short bean), Tohono O'odham pink, cranberry bean, yellow Indian woman, appaloosa, and flor de mayo.

We B' Jamin Farm

Show Barbara Carr a fruit and she'll turn it into jam. She originally learned the skill in Alaska, but she has managed to transfer it to the flavors of the desert. There are prickly pear jellies and syrups of course, but she also indulges Tucsonans' love for spiciness by adding chipotle to a prickly pear sauce. Working in her own commercial kitchen, she mixes jalapeño with raspberries and mangos. For those who like it even hotter, she offers habanero with pineapple or blackberries.

Carr grows her own peppers and vegetables in a greenhouse on her 4.5-acre property. When she sets up her display at the Oro Valley and Rillito Park Farmers' Markets, it's a riot of color, and when the morning sun shines through the jars, they appear to be glowing.

San Xavier Co-op Farm

Stopping into the store at the San Xavier Co-op Farm is a treasure hunt—you're never sure exactly what you'll discover. Sometimes you'll find fresh vegetables from the farm next door, honey from the hives on the farm, or baked goods put together from San Xavier–grown wheat. Maybe you'll score some lemon scones or mesquite cranberry bars. There's a mesquite cookie mix if you want to do your own baking.

At We B' Jamin Farm, Barbara Carr makes more than a dozen varieties of jams and jellies plus pickles and syrups using Southwest ingredients.

You can usually find Pima Club wheat flour and White Sonora wheat flour, both from soft heritage wheats grown on the farm and perfect for cookies and pie crust.

And, of course, there are beans, both red and white varieties of the teparies that sustained these people for generations, as well as Pima lima beans, all grown right on the farm. Several delicious soup mixes contain various mixtures of dried corn, wheat berries, beans, and cholla buds. A limited supply of traditional dried foods and fresh vegetables along with some quick mixes and baked goods are available in a store at the farm. Phyllis Valenzuela emphasizes, "Everything is grown or wild-harvested, cleaned, and packaged here." And if it's a mesquite cookie that catches your eye, it was baked right at the farm.

The farm holds seasonal workshops for residents of the San Xavier section of the Tohono O'odham Nation to remind folks of the methods their ancestors used to gather the wild Sonoran Desert foods. If they gather more than their household can use, they can sell the excess mesquite meal, saguaro syrup, and cholla buds in the store.

You can read more about the San Xavier Co-op Farm on page 104.

Desert Tortoise Botanicals and Desert Forager

John Slattery knows what's edible on the Sonoran Desert, from the tiniest flower that's good in tea to the prickly pear fruit that provide delicious juice.

After studying with indigenous healers using powerful botanicals growing on the desert, Slattery started Desert Tortoise Botanicals in 2005, concentrating on salves, tinctures, and teas all made from wild-foraged ingredients.

The six tea blends, three of which relate to the seasons, include wild-crafted ingredients such as flowers from ocotillo, elder, prickly pear, and desert lavender and herbs such as lemon balm, spearmint, chamomile, nettle, malva, dandelion leaf, and plantain.

Slattery's other business, Desert Forager, includes beverages based on prickly pear juice gathered locally. Slattery says, "The shrub syrups are all made with prickly pear juice and feature a second local fruit such as pomegranate, peach, pear, apricot, apple, orange, and grapefruit. Sometimes I sneak some additional foraged ingredients in there such as manzanita berries or elderberries. Our shrub syrups have been used to make drinks sold at cafes and restaurants downtown since 2014." The shrub syrup is sold locally for home consumption.

Slattery also makes tepache, a lightly fermented beverage in several fruit flavors, and natural sodas in rotating flavors such as elderberry; prickly pear; Sonoran Sunrise with prickly pear, saguaro, and peach; and vanilla crème with mulberries and African sumac berries.

Slattery teaches frequent workshops and is the author of the book *Southwest Foraging: 117 Wild and Flavorful Edibles from Barrel Cactus to Wild Oregano.*

Big Skye Bakers

Bodie Robins of Big Skye Bakers is one of the folks who have brought mesquite baking into the twenty-first century and he sells his mesquite baked goods at farmers' markets in Tucson and Sierra Vista.

Robins, an architectural designer, began baking with mesquite as therapy in 2008 when construction took a dive with the recession. His first experiment produced some dog biscuits that he shared with his neighbors. He decided there might be a future in mesquite baking when his neighbors admitted they were eating the dog biscuits themselves. With salsa!

Robins took his product to a farmers' market. But it turns out not enough people were willing to pay for high-end mesquite dog biscuits (many dogs are willing to just chew the pods, unbaked), so he began to experiment with other baked goods, trying various combinations of flours until he produced a version he liked.

Today he sells mesquite cookies and cupcakes and pies with mesquite crust. Many of his customers are attracted by the gluten-free nature of Bodie's mesquite pie crust. A perfect loaf of gluten-free bread eluded Bodie until recently when extensive experimenting finally led to a mixture of mesquite meal, brown rice flour, tapioca, and sweet potato flour that turns out a delicious loaf.

Robins gathers the mesquite pods he uses and has them ground at the Baja Arizona mill at the Sierra Vista Farmers' Market. He goes through up to 200 pounds of mesquite flour a year and if he runs out, he can grind a few pounds in his Vitamix. He produces his goods in his home kitchen under Arizona's Cottage Food Program.

You can find Robins and his Big Skye specialty baked goods at the Rillito Park Farmers' Market in Tucson and at the Sierra Vista Farmers' Market.

Mano y Metate

Amy Valdés Schwemm opens the double doors of her industrial refrigerator and displays a collection of herbs and spices that would make Marco Polo and any Arab spice trader swoon. Plastic tubs and glass jars hold nine kinds of chiles, three kinds of nuts, sesame and pumpkin seeds, raisins, prunes, tortilla meal, cinnamon sticks, herbs, cacao nibs, imported chocolate from Oaxaca, and a secret ingredient—dried bananas.

These are the ingredients she uses to make the six dried mole mixes she sells through her company Mano y Metate. She has a stringent non-GMO policy for every one of them.

Amy owns a three-room professional kitchen with five large refrigerators, a huge black stove, and an array of health department–endorsed sinks. But she works her spice magic out of a room about 15 feet square. Just herself, a small scale, and that well-stocked fridge. The rest of the facility she rents on an hourly basis to other small food businesses—a caterer, two women who make kimchi, a baker of cheesecakes, and a couple of food trucks.

Mano y Metate mole mixes including the classic mole negro on a retail shelf.

Mano y Metate Mole Dulce Brownies

Schwemm says, "I like the brownies thinner, so there's more spicy, chocolaty topping per bite. Feel free to take them out of the oven sooner or bake them in a smaller pan if you like them gooey, but the edges of the pan always seem to go first around here."

4 eggs (room temperature)
2 cups sugar
2 sticks softened butter (8 ounces)
1¼ cups cocoa powder
1 teaspoon vanilla
½ cup flour
¼ teaspoon salt
3 tablespoons Mole Dulce powder
Mole Dulce powder for topping, 5 tablespoons or so,
    to taste

Preheat the oven to 300 degrees Fahrenheit. Line a 9-inch × 13-inch baking pan (or two 8-inch square pans) with parchment paper.

With an electric mixer, beat the eggs just until fluffy. Beat in sugar. Add remaining ingredients except topping and beat. Pour batter into pan(s) and spread to level. Shake Mole Dulce powder though a wire strainer to evenly distribute over the batter as a topping. Bake for 35 minutes, or until a toothpick inserted comes out with crumbs instead of batter.

Schwemm began her food career working for Native Seeds/SEARCH, which at the time sold a mole mix. She recalls that no one knew how to use it, but she remembered her grandmother making moles for the family. It was several years later with people asking for mole mixes that Schwemm decided this was something she could do. She took business and accounting classes and rented kitchen space from a small bakery. Meanwhile, Schwemm was helping to clean out her great-aunt's household accumulation and found a small mano for a molcajete, worn smooth from years of spice grinding. Another family member passed along the molcajete that went with it. Seeing Schwemm's interest, the great-aunt confessed she had given away her mother's metate, but asked for it back. Thus the name of the new business was born: Mano y Metate.

Then began the task of trying to replicate the exact flavor of the authentic mole her great-grandmother had made according to her mother's memory. Schwemm made numerous passes until finally her mother agreed that she had hit on the perfect combination. That blend of four kinds of

Amy Valdés Schwemm carefully weighs the ingredients for her six distinctive mole mixes.

dark chile, raisins, dried bananas, ground almonds, and lots of sweetened Oaxacan chocolate became Schwemm's Mole Dulce mix, her most popular. It is what is used at EXO Roast coffeehouse in their delicious Mole Dulce Latte.

Next in development was the much spicier Mole Negro with more bitter notes from unsweetened cacao nibs, four kinds of nuts, and smoky chipotle chile. An herby Mole Verde followed with jalapeño, green chile, cilantro, parsley, and epazote.

As the business developed, Schwemm kept experimenting, adding Pipian Rojo, a mixture of Santa Cruz mild chile, pumpkin seeds, almonds, and herbs, followed by Pipian Picante, a spicier version of Rojo. The most recent addition is Adobo, with chiles, garlic, and lots of herbs, which works great as a dry rub before a steak goes on the grill.

All the mixes are packed in charming, highly reusable, made-in-America 2-ounce steel tins. Customers who are heavy users can save a little by buying the 4-ounce packs in not-as-charming plastic bags. Mano y Metate products are available in small specialty stores and independent food stores throughout Tucson and from Tubac, Arizona, to Seattle, Washington, and from Santa Ana, California, to Santa Fe, New Mexico.

Monsoon Chocolate

The bonbons look like precious baubles in the display case, each a different glowing color and shape. The names alone are enough to send any chocolate lover into a swoon. The selection rotates, but the day I visited my eye lingered on one described as blood orange dulce de leche with lemon curd, shortbread, and a dark chocolate ganache. Owner Adam Krantz opened the shop in a former tortilla factory in spring 2018 to an enthusiastic reception.

In addition to the bonbons, the shop also offers small single-origin chocolate bars that you could consume in two minutes or spread out tiny bite by delicious bite. The bars all range from 70 to 77 percent dark chocolate. Each variety is made from a single source of chocolate that is grown by small farmers who are paid a reasonable price for their product.

The best-selling bar, though, is the mesquite white chocolate presented in a turquoise wrapping that evokes Tucson. The ground mesquite pods come from San Xavier Co-op Farm.

Their Southwest-inspired chocolates won fourteen awards in the 2019 Americas Bean-to-Bar and Chocolatier Competition. Among the winners were

Monsoon Chocolate's award-winning bonbons gleam like polished semiprecious stones. (Maribel Alvarez)

their mesquite and blue corn atole white chocolate bars, mezcal and prickly pear chocolate-enrobed caramels, and a Whiskey del Bac Dorado bonbon.

SALSAS

Salsas can have as many variations as there are cooks. Most local Mexican restaurants make their own salsa and some of them package it up so customers can take it home. The "best" salsa is the one that tastes like you want it to.

Here are a few local salsa makers that have developed their salsa-making skills into a full-time business.

The young woman in the big sombrero has graced the labels of Tucson-made Poblano Hot Sauce since the 1940s.

Poblano Hot Sauce

The Poblano Hot Sauce label shows a young woman in a big sombrero holding a chile. Her image on the tall thin bottles has been a staple on Tucson home and restaurant tables for decades. The Segura family has run the Poblano Hot Sauce business since the 1940s. Nicolas Segura opened a restaurant in 1924 and, of course, made salsa for his customers. In the 1940s he closed the restaurant to concentrate on the hot sauce. He died only a few days after passing on his secret recipe to his son. Now the third generation is continuing the business.

Customers are loyal to their favorite sauce and the product mix has not varied with the same four varieties always available. There's green jalapeño sauce, red jalapeño sauce, salsa ranchera, and Mexican hot sauce.

Poblano Hot Sauce is available exclusively in Arizona. If out-of-state customers find they can't live without it, someone at the processing plant will ship it to them.

Poco Loco Specialty Salsa

"Cooking has always been in my blood," says Adela Dorazo as she artfully rearranges the containers of salsa in her Udall Park Farmers' Market booth. She had to rearrange them because customers were buying them so quickly.

The native Tucsonan used to take whatever salsa she had recently made as a hostess gift when she went out to dinner. People were disappointed when she turned up without the salsa. Then it dawned on her—maybe she had something there. One weekend in the mid-1980s she made a few batches of her fruit salsas, loaded them into an ice chest, set up at a farmers' market, and sold out in an hour.

Today, she still sells only at farmers' markets, at Udall Park, Oro Valley, and Rillito Park. She specializes in fruit salsas, and each comes in three levels of spiciness: mild, hot, and what she calls "stupid hot" with ten types of chiles.

Chilttepica Products

For beginners to the universe of chiles, there's no better introduction to chiltepins than Chilttepica fresh salsa made by husband-and-wife team Gloria and Huémac Badilla. The Badillas created three salsas, a mild red, a hot red, and a green, based on family recipes that Huémac grew up with in Caborca, Mexico.

After they had their salsa business established, they expanded to fresh chorizo. Theirs is a mix of beef and pork, garlic, chile, oregano, and salt. And, of course, chiltepins. Gloria Badilla says that because they include just enough fat in the meat, their chorizo does not release lots of grease when it is cooked.

The Badillas also sell dried chiltepins in 1-ounce bottles.

PUTTING THE DESERT INTO THE BEER

by Ford Burkhart

In the 1860s, Tucson beer pubs offered a welcome respite from the dry, dusty desert. There's no record of brewers adding prickly pears, creosote flowers, or mesquite flour to the lagers. Not yet.

Several brewers were Prussians, like Alexander Levin, a bearded gent who opened Pioneer Brewery on Camp Street, now Broadway Boulevard, near Stone Avenue. In the 1870s he ran a 3-acre beer garden called Levin's Park, with music and dancing.

Finding ideal water was a challenge where wells could be alkaline and results less than satisfying. "The less said about the quality the better," said Sergeant John Spring in 1866. Levin bought Wheat's Saloon and dug his own artesian well. The local paper said he even created a hop plantation with "2,000 hop sets." Lagers, sold at around a nickel a pint, used imported barley, hops, wheat, or rye, said Ed Sipos, author of *Brewing Arizona*.

More breweries followed—the City Brewery, the Park Brewery. The French Brewery sold beer at the French Saloon. The Excelsior Brewery's product was on tap at the Excelsior Saloon on Meyer Street. Some brewers crushed their own whole malt, making 50 to 200 gallons a week. The words "drunk" and "drunken" dotted George O. Hand's diary.

By 1879 Levin bragged that the brewery in his park contained rock cellars for malting and storing his lager. But the next year, 1880, the first railroad train arrived, and with it came industrial beer brands. This first era of craft brewing in the desert faded, until a resurgence in the last decades of the twentieth century.

Now a new craft beer era is rolling. Here are some of the players.

Borderlands Brewing Company, 119 East Toole Avenue

One of the earliest brewery sites in town was Toole Avenue, along the Southern Pacific tracks, and today on Toole, west of the original train station, the Borderlands Brewing Company has refurbished a red brick warehouse beside the tracks. Since 2011, the former produce depot has housed a classy pub and craft beer factory that's become a leading advocate of local ingredients.

Borderlands head brewer Ayla Kapahi checks the carbonation level of the beer in the brite tank. (Roger C. Wolf)

Ayla Kapahi and Cassidy Johnson use a hydrometer to assess the progress of the fermentation of a tank of beer. (Roger C. Wolf)

In 2016, the president of Borderlands, Michael Mallozzi, and his brewing colleagues—mainly from Ten55, Sentinel Peak, 1912, Barrio, Beast, Borderlands, Catalina, Dragoon, Iron John's, Pueblo Vida, The Address and Thunder Canyon—decided to test how their customers would react to local beer ingredients. They put together a year-long event called Baja Brews. Every other month, the breweries would all use a single local ingredient in a new small-batch variety.

Food writer John Washington wrote in *Edible Baja Arizona* magazine that the Baja Brews ingredients included cactus and tree fruits, cracked nuts, scavenged seeds, White Sonora wheat, and Sonoita-grown hops. The flavorings also included mesquite beans and, of course, all sorts of chiles, even chiltepin and the milder serrano, jalapeño, Hatch, and devil's tongue.

Those brewers were part of a regional committee of the Arizona Craft Brewers Guild, calling themselves the Baja Arizona Brewers. They and their fans met in various brew pubs, and proceeds went to Tucson nonprofits including the food-harvesting Iskashitaa Refugee Network and Desert Harvesters, a group that operates milling machines to turn mesquite pods into flour.

The experimental beers became favorites across the city.

A local orientation has driven Mallozzi from the start. "Craft breweries have a sense of place," he says. "They have authenticity to that place. And as part of that, there has been a motivation to use local ingredients, not only from a sustainability perspective but also to highlight the flavor, the culture of a region that we do business in."

Borderlands' Prickly Pear Wheat uses prickly pear juice from Cheri's Desert Harvest, based in Tucson. Its Noche Dulce, or Sweet Night, uses Mexican vanilla, from Mayanik, a company with a plant in Mérida, Yucatan, Mexico. Mayanik sends up a 55-gallon drum of vanilla twice a year or so.

But it's not always that easy.

"There's a challenge in using any local ingredient," Mallozzi says. "Often the local ingredients aren't commercialized, and they are not necessarily quality tested. We've spent a lot of time and effort in collaboration with Cheri's Desert Harvest to develop the prickly pear product to where we know it's going to behave and taste similar. That's always going to be the challenge."

One issue is that in any biota—the totality of plants and animals in any region—each plant or product is going to have its own microbiota, a collection of microscopic organisms. "Thus the product will be covered with bacteria that could infect the beer," Mallozzi said. "In the case of prickly pear juice, it is pasteurized at Cheri's Desert Harvest. But with other ingredients, it's harder," Mallozzi said. "There will not be the processes and knowledge base to develop those products so that the beer will be more or less sterile."

Iron John's Brewing Company, 222 East Congress Street

Ripe red saguaro fruits give the Saguaro Goat beer at Iron John's a vibrant purple pink, almost fuchsia, color. Tiny yellow creosote flowers added to the Saison de Juhki evoke the smell of rain in the desert. Using desert ingredients has been a lifetime passion for John Adkisson, Iron John's founder and head brewer.

Iron John's inner-city brewery produces 65 beers in a year, in two-barrel batches, about four kegs' worth, and releases something new almost every week. Adkisson keeps a list of his local ingredients, some from local vendors, some that they gather on friends' property around town, including prickly pear and saguaro fruits and creosote flowers. His eclectic list includes almonds and *bellotas* (acorns); figs; hibiscus flowers; sunflower and sesame seeds; pine nuts; pecans; green and red chiles from San Simon Chile Company in Safford; honey; green corn masa, which Adkisson uses in a Mexican lager; mesquite pod flour; peaches from Cochise County; and pumpkins from Robbs Family Farm in Willcox.

The bellotas come from Emory oak trees that grow in the woodland hills along the Mexican border. Iron John's leaches out the bitter tannins with baking soda and dries them in the sun. Next, they are toasted in an oven. In the beer, they taste like pecans or graham cracker crust.

When Adkisson first set out to harvest saguaro fruit, he needed long poles like the ones the Tohono O'odham have used for centuries. He used swimming pool extension poles to reach up 15 feet to collect the red-fleshed pods during the few weeks in summer when they are ripe. Adkisson gathers and dries the fruit in the sun, then freezes it until it's time to add to his gose wheat beer (a top-fermented style that originated in Goslar, Germany).

The Saguaro Goat beer is inoculated with a *Lactobacillus* culture of goat yogurt from a local producer, Fiore di Capra in Pomerene, Arizona. The lactic acid matches up well with the saguaro flavor, Adkisson says. The beer has a mildly fruity finish, not too sweet. "It just glows in the glass," Adkisson said, looking through his own glass at the morning sunlight.

After harvesting the creosote flowers, he dehydrates and freezes them. When it's time to brew the Saison de Juhki, the flowers go into a hot tea with orange peel and white sage, giving the French-style saison a local twist. "This beer has evoked tears from customers who grew up in Tucson and are reminded of that aroma of creosote when rain hits the desert floor," Adkisson says. "That is powerful."

In some beers, like the Mesquite Porter named to honor Petey Mesquitey, a local icon of desert culture, Adkisson adds a few pounds of mesquite flour produced by the mill in the La Madera neighborhood of Tucson. "The mesquite has sugars and adds to the fermentation," Adkisson says. "The flavor has almost a cinnamon character."

While the local ingredients may be just 2 to 5 percent of what goes into a beer, they are central, Adkisson says. "They reflect the classic terroir, the sense of place. These things are unique to where we live. The beers represent Tucson."

Pueblo Vida Brewing Company, 115 East Broadway Boulevard

The head brewer at Pueblo Vida, Landon Swanson, sat on a barstool in the morning sun and reflected about White Sonora wheat. The question was, "What is a true wheat beer character and texture?"

"A lot of wheat can have a nuttiness," Swanson says, "and come off with a peanut kind of character. White Sonora doesn't. It's subtle, tender, a true wheat kind of flavor."

Swanson, like many of Tucson's twenty or so head brewers of craft beer, gets White Sonora from BKW Farms. "It's an unmalted white wheat that we use in probably 80 percent of our beers. It's really a fantastic, tender grain."

Of the White Sonora, he says, "It's easy to work with, with its small kernels. It's a lot softer than some of the unmalted wheats that you can get up north."

Pueblo Vida's Sonoran Heritage line is based on a traditional farmhouse ale. "The style is big in Europe and elsewhere, but we wanted to make a sense-of-place beer for us here in the desert. We have some rules to be able to give it that designation: It has to have a local Tucson native ingredient, and it has to go into oak to be part of the Sonoran Heritage series. In Belgium or France, they would have saisons. Our designation for a saison is Sonoran Heritage."

On the day we visited, the Sonoran Heritage offering was the Aldea (or "village"). "It was the first in the new line," says Kyle Jefferson, one of Pueblo Vida's owners.

Their namesake product is Vida Beer, a lager using heritage Hotevilla Hopi pink corn sourced from Ramona Farms. The corn ranges in color from lavender to pomegranate, and is grown near the Grand Canyon. "The little corn cobs are just about this big," he says, holding up his fingers to indicate a few inches. "It's a very old corn," he adds.

Pueblo Vida's Brevedad is a tart ale in the Sonoran Heritage series, with White Sonora, orange peel, and coriander.

Once a year, a new seven-barrel batch of their Harvest beer appears, with 5 or 6 gallons of prickly pear nectar from Cheri's Desert Harvest for each batch.

Pueblo Vida is always experimenting with local ingredients. "Every day," Swanson says. "We call ourselves a little research and development brewery. We have the freedom because of our size to make whatever we want to."

Pueblo Vida works with Pivot Produce, which supplies citrus gathered by the Iskashitaa Refugee Network and fruit from farmers in Willcox. Peaches from the San Xavier Co-op Farm show up in a Sonoran Heritage beer called Desert Gold, one of about fifty beers produced each year.

Pueblo Vida, which opened in 2014, illustrates the market for craft beer that has quickly blossomed. "We like that sense of terroir in beer," Jefferson says. "Consumers like something that's unique with a sense of place. And the support that local farmers have gained has been a big bonus for us."

Corbett Brewery, 309 East 7th Street

October pumpkins caught the eye of Cody Sexson, the head brewer at Corbett Brewery, at the heart of a craft beer zone along North 4th Avenue. To celebrate the autumn season, he worked up a beer using pumpkins from Buckelew Farm west of Tucson. Uncle Buck's Pumpkin Ale has become one of his more popular items. Each fall he drives west to the Buckelew fields, gathers a load of the squash cultivar, and takes it back to be cooked down the block from 7th Street at O'Malley's Bar & Grill (Corbett's owner, Scott Cummings, also owns O'Malley's and two other pubs in town). The resulting beer is a rich, almost red, slightly sweet brew.

Sexson says the Tucson community of craft brewers is dedicated to providing local alternatives to the nation's megabrewers, for whom he has few good words to share. At Corbett's 18,000-square-foot quarters, old red brick walls speak of the long history of commerce north of the railroad tracks. Corbett plans an extensive expansion with pizza ovens and a fancy beer hall. In the future, Sexson plans to develop a new beer using saguaro fruit and is working with Tohono O'odham officials about arranging for deliveries to Corbett.

Catalina Brewing Company, 6918 North Camino Martin

To reach the north-side Catalina Brewing Company, you drive past the mesquites and palo verdes and creosote of the desert as you approach the Santa Catalina Mountains.

On the brewery shelves is mesquite flour in 50-pound boxes. In the freezer are prickly pears, hand-picked not far away, and the nectar of agaves from Mexico.

"As kids, we'd ride our bikes on trails through the desert," said Hank Rowe, the brewing partner. "You'd pick a couple of mesquite pods off a tree and chew them and suck on them. There's a very distinctive sweetness."

Hank Rowe, brewing partner at Catalina Brewing Company, incorporates flavors from his desert childhood into his beers. (Roger C. Wolf)

Patrons at Catalina Brewing Company can order a flight of beer to sample local flavors of mesquite, pecans, and prickly pear. (Roger C. Wolf)

That sweetness is in his best-selling beers, a light amber Mesquite Agave and a darker, coffee-colored Mesquite Porter. "The Mesquite Agave is smoother, so it lets more of the mesquite flavor come out," Rowe said. The darker Mesquite Porter is a robust brew, with a roasted malt taste, accented with the earthy sweetness of the mesquite flour. Number 9 on the beer billboard was his Pecan Dopplebock, with pecans from Santa Cruz Valley pecan growers, roasted and ground into flour for a nutty taste.

Beers with local ingredients were the first that Rowe crafted at home twenty years ago, in the town of Catalina. He gave the beer away to friends until he started his business in 2016. "I started off thinking, what kind of signature beers could I brew? The first step was to grind up some mesquite pods. I did a test batch with a lighter beer that became the Mesquite Agave. It took off like a firestorm."

Next came a round of prickly pear trials. He wanted a style that would match with the prickly pear. He chose a cream ale he called La Rosa, Spanish for pink or rose colored. "At our house in Catalina we couldn't see the sunset, but when the sun is setting, we could see the mountains turning pink," Rowe said. "The beer was almost the same rosy pink as the mountains at sunset."

Button Brew House, 6800 North Camino Martin

For Todd Button and his wife, Erika, owners of Button Brew House, their Chiltepin Red, a spicy red ale, is the essence of the Tucson region, synonymous with Sonoran culture. They brew their interpretation of a Sonoran-style spice beer in the summer, using fresh lime zest and lemon peel. "The chiltepin is native to our desert," Button says. "It's spicy and still it has a great flavor. It's one of our year-round classics."

Button Brew House uses White Sonora, from BKW Farms, almost a neighbor in Marana, in their seasonal El Jefe (The Boss), a German Hefeweizen–style beer brewed in spring and summer when Button figures demand is highest for that style of beer. Some White Sonora is used in their sour Berliner Weisse–style beers. "Actually, in every wheat beer, we use some of the local wheat," Button says. "And we are looking for ways to do more."

Button uses local mesquite honey in his Porter beer and adds orange blossom honey from suppliers in Mexico or the United States for his IPA.

Dragoon Brewing Company, 1859 West Grant Road

Eric Greene and his wife, Jana U'Ren, loved the Dragoon Mountains so much they named their brewery after them. "We used to climb there all the time. Used to. We got busy," says Greene, a founder of the Dragoon Brewing Company in 2012. Now, as Dragoon's head brewer, he says those mountains two hours east of Tucson are mostly a memory, living on through Dragoon's labels.

Dragoon's tall shiny fermentation tanks make thirty-five beers in a year. The entrance is tucked away in a rear corner of a funky industrial area west of I-10, but Dragoon's brand is well known for its support of local food events like those run by the Mission Garden and by Native Seeds/SEARCH. "We support those events because they attract people that care about the same things that we do," Greene said. "Local beer *is* local food."

Perhaps its best-known—and least expected—local ingredient is blue corn from New Mexico, added to Dragoon's Saison Blue. "It provides sort of a nuttiness and adds complexity to the flavor. It also lightens the body," Greene says. The blue corn combines with blue agave nectar from several suppliers in Mexico and small amounts of local White Sonora wheat.

"Saison is a French and Belgian historical style that was typically brewed on a farm using whatever ingredients were available, plus the malted barley," says Greene. "They were brewed with large portions of wheat or spelt, buckwheat, or sorghum, whatever was available on the farm. We took that idea and rather than brew a traditional interpretation, we used ingredients that are available locally such as the blue corn and White Sonora wheat and agave nectar.

"The Sonora White adds a pretty distinctive cereal taste, and it also contributes a little more haze—a cloudiness, which we like in certain styles," Greene says. He adds White Sonora to his Santa Cruz'r golden ale and Ojo Blanco (along with local lime and cumin from Maya Tea Company) and to the Whetstone Wheat (named for the Whetstone Mountains, about 16 miles south of Benson) and the Half Moon, a traditional German Dunkelweizen.

"The Sonoran Desert is pretty interesting," Greene says, "with a wide variety of regional elements for creating things."

1912 Brewing Company, 2045 North Forbes Boulevard

It takes thirteen chiltepin berries to flavor a six-barrel batch of craft beer. And no one knows such details more precisely than the president and head brewer at the west-side 1912 Brewing Company, Allan Conger. Since he opened in 2015, naming his brewery for the year of Arizona statehood, Conger has been experimenting with every possible regional ingredient. He concocts sixty-five beer types in a year, some seasonals, some one-offs. His ingredients range from citrus to White Sonora wheat to locally ground coffees from Presta Coffee Roasters in the Mercado San Agustín.

"We want to give each beer a unique flavor," Conger said. "Local wheat gives it a kind of mouth feel and body. The coffee gives flavors to the darker beers. And the chiltepins give a nice spice flavor—they put a kick in a couple of our beers."

His top-selling beer with local elements is the Naughty Naranja, with intense blood orange highlights and "a ton of BKW wheat." The blood oranges he gathers around town and from suppliers. "We make so much of that beer we have to get them wherever we can." It's citrusy, with a touch of salinity and coriander. The "naughty" part reflects its alcohol content: 8.5 percent. By comparison, some beers run 4 to 5 percent.

"We always try to use local ingredients to do cool things," Conger said. "That's the thing about craft. It's hyperlocal, a local focus. When you start a craft brewery, it's not a get-rich kind of business. It's more of an impactful business. It's more about community. It's about collaboration."

In early 2019, Conger began a partnership with Native Seeds/SEARCH, the Tucson-based conservation organization, to brew sour beers with fresh and dry lemon basil grown at the Native Seeds headquarters on River Road. That popular cultivar's formal name is "Mrs. Burns' Famous Lemon Basil," coined by Barney Burns, a co-founder of Native Seeds and son of the woman honored in the name.

Another of 1912's collaborations is with Barrio Bread, using its sourdough culture to brew a beer called Leaven Life. "And then Barrio takes a couple of buckets of our spent grain, the Red Fife and the White Sonora wheat, after we've used it in beer, and they bake bread with it," Conger said. "So it comes full circle."

LOCAL FLAVORS DOMINATE TUCSON-MADE SPIRITS

Hamilton Distillers, 2106 North Forbes Boulevard

Think back to a time you were sitting around a campfire with friends, gazing at a dark starry sky, savoring the distinct aroma of mesquite smoke. The folks at Hamilton Distillers have taken that fragrance, turned it into flavor, and put it into their Whiskey del Bac. It's a whiskey for whiskey lovers as well as desert folks who never drank whiskey previously (like myself), but love that smoky flavor.

Stephen Paul began as a maker of fine mesquite furniture in his Arroyo Design Company. That left him with lots of little mesquite chips. It was his wife's suggestion that they use those chips to

Stephen Paul (left), founder of Hamilton Distillers, and Nathan Thompson-Avelino sample their Whiskey del Bac surrounded by whiskey aging in American white oak barrels. (Tim Fuller)

Nathan Thompson-Avelino pulls dried two-row barley malt out of the germination tank after the completed malting process. (Tim Fuller)

smoke some barley and make their own Scotch. He bought a small 40-gallon copper still, and, after wrangling with the health department, began experimenting. He got his barley from Marana grain farmer Ron Wong's BKW Farms. Grain has to be malted (sprouted) to make the sugars available. At first, Paul did that simply by wetting it and spreading it out on tarps on the floor. Then he smoked it.

As the years passed, Paul kept experimenting and finally had a product that was so good it was time to grade up. He moved into an industrial building on Forbes Boulevard near I-10 and began accumulating equipment.

It was tricky to design and set up a tank in which to malt the barley, but those involved with the process really wanted to stay with local grain and that meant having their own equipment. Eventually it all worked out and they were able to devise a system that would let them malt 5,000 pounds of local BKW barley. The barley soaks for 24 hours while being gently agitated, then is transferred to the germination tank where it rests at a temperature between 70 and 90 degrees Fahrenheit. This is when the mesquite smoke is piped in. The grain is then ground, cooked, and fermented. Eventually the liquid ends up in American white oak barrels. When the barrels have served their purpose, they are sold to local beer brewers for their Porters. The spent grain goes to E & R Pork for feed.

Now Tucson is in love with Whiskey del Bac. The three basic styles each have their fans. Dorado is golden brown and mesquite-smoke aged. Bartenders like Mesquite Smoke Clear for making cocktails, while the Classic unsmoked has more of a spice and honey finish. Hamilton Distillers also makes custom flavors for private labels.

Organizations can schedule private tastings where someone from Hamilton will give you a tour and school you on what you should look for as you roll each whiskey over your tongue. At the back of the room is a long table with high stools where they conduct tastings. It's fun to look at all the kegs of whiskey stacked high along the walls, then just close your eyes and taste that campfire.

OUR SONORAN CULINARY HERITAGE—
IT'S A TUCSON THING!

M ANY OF THE ITEMS THAT appear frequently on Tucson dinner tables can be traced directly to our Sonoran-Mexican heritage. Tucson children are as likely to have a quesadilla for lunch as a grilled cheese sandwich.

As Carlotta Flores of El Charro Café says, "This was Sonora before the Gadsden Purchase. Just because they put a line through the desert didn't change who the residents were as a people." Or what they ate, she might have added.

Part of the tradition starts with the meat. Walk into a Mexican meat market and many of the offerings will be completely different from anything you'll see on the meat counter of a typical supermarket. There are cuts that are seldom used in American-style cooking and cuts that don't look anything like the steaks and roasts we usually see.

According to Filiberto Islas, who worked with three of his brothers at the American Meat Company for 30 years, that is because Mexican butchers and their customers are using the Spanish way of cutting meat with the grain. When Father Kino brought cattle to Sonora, and on to what is now Tucson, he brought vaqueros who taught the locals how to raise, skin, and butcher the animals as they did in Spain. And that tradition persisted. (American cuts are from the English tradition, across the grain.)

"Mexicans from Sonora will eat the cow from oxtail to tongue, inside and out," Islas said, as a preface to explaining the use of the unusual cuts.

You'll find items that will never land in a typical grocery store. For example, *tripas de leche* are small intestines that are grilled and eaten as a snack while waiting for the main course to be cooked. Pig snouts are displayed next to cow tails. Cuts have different names in Spanish as well. For example, the eye of round, a long muscle, is called a *guzano*, or "worm."

Although the American Meat Company is now closed, some members of the second generation of the Islas family have stayed in the business. Filiberto's nephew Jack works at the UA meat lab and Robert has opened Islas Meat Company on Irvington Road.

While the city government and visitors bureau tout "the best 23 miles of Mexican food in the U.S.," with a multitude of Mexican restaurants (including the two oldest continuously operating ones in the United States) within those 23 square miles of the urban area, another set of chefs has taken a fresh look at our heritage ingredients. They are offering their customers delicious and novel presentations of our local ingredients, mixing some wild foods with produce from local farmers. Sometimes you'll find both the traditional and the novel on the same menus as chefs satisfy customers with the expected while also exercising their creativity with local ingredients.

TUCSON'S SONORAN FOOD TRADITIONS

Here are some of the dishes that define our local Sonora-influenced cuisine as discussed by local chefs and home cooks.

Maria Murrietta, a Yaqui, makes wheat tortillas on a grill at Pascua Village in Tucson in 1976. (Arizona State Museum, University of Arizona, Helga Teiwes, photographer)

Wheat Flour Tortillas

An absolute basic for Tucson food is flour tortillas. Folklorist Jim Griffith, who usually has an amusing story about everything, gives up on tortillas. "There is no way of telling you the history of tortillas," he writes. "It's sort of like the history of toothpicks. There are things we write down and then there are things everybody just does, like tortillas."

We've discussed elsewhere in the book how the arrival of wheat in Sonora changed the eating habits of the population as wheat flour tortillas began to supplant the age-old corn version. According to Reuben Naranjo Jr., the Tohono O'odham used to make a kind of small and thick wheat-based tortilla called *wakial cecemait*, or cowboy tortillas. They were brown and thick and made by O'odham cowboys who would cook them at their campsites when rounding up cattle. Velvet

Button, whose parents run Ramona Farms and who has both Akimel and Tohono O'odham heritage, says these traditional tortillas were about the size of an outstretched hand and were easy to dip into stew.

Over the years, cooks on both sides of the border began using refined white flour, stretching the tortilla thinner and bigger, draping it over their arm like a napkin as they proceeded. A misunderstanding has arisen that pairs the arrival of White Sonora wheat and the invention of flour tortillas with the subsequent development of the huge tortillas. White Sonora wheat is low in gluten making it great for crackers and pastries but not ideal for bread or tortillas which need the stretchiness imparted by gluten.

Don Guerra, who is committed to using heritage grains in his Barrio Bread bakery, uses a combination of hard wheats with a little White Sonora for flavor. When expert tortilla makers were offered the opportunity to begin using White Sonora wheat flour, they quickly indicated they preferred the all-purpose flour available from Mexican and American grocery stores.

Bill Steen, who has done extensive research on the flour mills of Sonora, says, "You can't make those big tortillas with the White Sonora wheat. Impossible. The flour to make the large tortillas apparently did not come from any of the mills in Sonora in that they weren't sophisticated enough to produce flour that fine. Perhaps Ures. As far as the tortillas these days, they are all done with commercial flours from the store. None of it is homegrown."

Making these big tortillas is an art form and the best tortilla makers can stretch a tortilla until it is nearly two feet across and almost translucent. Tortillas this size are usually cooked outside over a specially made griddle. When they are wrapped around a filling such as meat, beans, or even scrambled eggs, they are called burros, or if smaller, burritos.

The late musician Lalo Guerrero, known as the "father of Chicano music," wrote this song about Tucson's beloved tortillas. Tucson-born Guerrero was officially declared a national folk treasure by the Smithsonian Institution in 1980 and was presented with the National Medal of Arts in 1996 by President Bill Clinton.

THERE'S NO TORTILLAS
By Lalo Guerrero

I love tortillas
And I love them dearly
You'll never know,
Just how sincerely.

I love the corn ones,
Y tambien de harina,
But when my wife
cries out from La cocina,

CHORUS
There's no tortillas.
There's only bread.
There's no tortillas,
And I feel so sad.
My grief, I cannot hide.
There's no tortillas for my refrieds.

Without tortillas,
there would be no burritos.
Without the corn ones,
There would be no Fritos.

I love to hold them,
Tenderly and fold them,
Oh how I dread to eat with bread,
Believe me.

Used with permission

Burros and Chimichangas

Take one of those extra-large flour tortillas, spread some beans across one edge, add some grated cheese and maybe some meat, roll it up, and you've got a burro. It is the simplest of food. Drop that burro into hot oil and you have elevated that modest burro to a chimichanga, prompting heated debates on the relative merits of one chef's version over another's.

A dunk into hot oil turns a lowly burrito into the flaky gastronomic delight we call a chimichanga. Dressing it up with salsa, sour cream, and guacamole makes it irresistible, and so Tucson. (Roger C. Wolf)

An oft-repeated story puts the genesis of the chimichanga in the kitchen of a Tucson restaurant when in the cook's haste a burro was dropped into a pan of oil. However, when Tucson food writer Rita Connelly traveled around Southern Arizona to scope out the chimichanga story, she found restaurants from the Gila River to the Mexican border claiming that it was actually in *their* kitchen that the chimichanga was born. There might have been something back in the 1920s that led to this synchronicity of dropping burros in oil, but it certainly originated in the Sonoran Desert because that's where we have wheat tortillas.

Beef strips dry in the open air in a specially constructed cage at El Charro Café. The dried beef, called *carne seca*, was the traditional method of preserving meat before widespread refrigeration. (Roger C. Wolf)

The perfect iteration of a chimichanga has a crisp golden outer shell with little blisters adding an airiness and flakiness, the thin interior layers are tender but have a slight chewiness, and inside is an ample filling of well-spiced meat, beans, vegetables, or all three. Order it "enchilada style" and it will come covered with red chile sauce with melted cheese on top.

Carne Seca

The history of El Charro Café is the history of the last hundred years of Tucson's culinary story. Reigning over El Charro today is Carlotta Flores, great-granddaughter of Jules Flin, a French master stonemason hired to create the facade for Tucson's St. Augustine Cathedral. He also built a stone house on Court Avenue where El Charro is located today. After operating in several other locations, in 1983 Monica Flin, Flores's great-aunt, moved her small restaurant to the house.

One of El Charro's Sonoran specialties is carne seca, dried beef, which harks back to the hundreds of years between when beef was introduced to the area by Father Kino and when Tucson received widespread refrigeration. When an animal was butchered, the meat that wasn't eaten immediately needed to be preserved.

"Carne seca cannot be made in Phoenix or California," Flores says. "It's too humid. The sun and the heat are perfect in Tucson." Originally, Monica Flin cut the beef into strips and hung them on a clothesline in a shed to dry. Today, Flores's husband, Ray, has built a metal mesh cage that is filled with meat and hoisted above El Charro's roof to take advantage of the breeze and free air flow.

"We start with a whole side of a cow and slice it up," Flores says. "The strips hang for 24 to 36 hours depending on the weather. If you start with 500 pounds of meat, it will shrink to half of that."

When the beef is sufficiently dried, it is shredded by hand and becomes almost fluffy. Then it is mixed with green chile and fresh chopped tomato and becomes reconstituted, almost back to its original weight. The flavor is intensely meaty and savory as if the sun and desert air were a seasoning on their own.

A few other Tucson Mexican restaurants that stress the traditional methods still make carne seca, but it is a time-consuming and vanishing art.

Tamales

Behind the counter at Perfecto's Mexican Restaurant on South 12th Avenue is a shelf with twelve crystal plates—awards Perfecto's tamales have won at the annual Casino del Sol Tamale Festival.

Perfecto Leon began making tamales in the mid-1980s, selling them in front of a south-side Safeway. Over 23 years he became such a fixture people called him "the tamale man." When his children were established in careers in 2009, they bought him a recently vacated restaurant and named it Perfecto's. Everything there is good, but people come for the tamales.

Traditional tamales can be made with nixtamalized corn, meat, and red chile or with green corn, cheese, and green chile. (Roger C. Wolf)

What is it about those tamales, why so many awards? "Everything has to be fresh," Leon says. "It can never be frozen."

Green corn tamales used to be a late-summer treat, but today vendors bring fresh corn up from southern Mexico where the climate allows growing corn year-round. Leon goes through 15 dozen ears (that's 180) a day. Everybody pitches in to strip the husks and silk off the fresh corn.

Asked if they have a device to cut the kernels, Leon holds up his strong brown hands. He tried several tools that supposedly make the cutting easier, but he felt that the mechanical devices changed the texture of the corn. He also includes a strip of green chile with a slab of yellow cheese in the center so that it can be seen. White cheese just melts into the masa.

The beef tamales, made with nixtamalized dried corn, receive the same care. He buys chuck steak by the boxful for the filling and fresh red chile sauce from Tania's on Drexel Road.

Before the crew gets ready to roll the tamales, they need to get all the ingredients set. Then Perfecto does his magic with the masa. His daughter, Judith de la Rosa, who works with her father, says only he knows what actually makes them taste so good. "My dad's in his mid-sixties," she says. "One of these days the rest of us are going to have to learn his secret."

Maria Carbajal, one of the authors of the Mexican cookbook ¡*Buen Provecho!*, gives the same advice on making tamales to those who come for her cooking classes. The detailed directions in her book warn that making green corn tamales is an all-day process and it is wise to assemble a team of helpers. But she adds, "All this is offset by the sharing of labor, laughter, and love of the tamal."

Tacos

Chef Maria Mazon of Boca Tacos wants to make sure Tucsonans understand real Sonoran food, not the Americanized version with melted yellow cheese and sour cream (which she agrees is delicious), but what was served in Sonora when she grew up there.

According to Mazon, an authentic Sonoran taco includes a corn or wheat tortilla, carne asada, cabbage, and guacamole. Maybe a sprinkle of white cotija cheese and a swizzle of crema. Salsa of course, maybe with nopalitos along with the tomatoes. And the beef needs to be grilled, not fried. "It needs the grilled flavor," Mazon says.

Sonoran-style tacos can start with a corn or wheat tortilla. Fillings on this plate are, from left, carne asada (grilled beef), fried fish, and carnitas (crispy pulled pork). Salsa on the side. (Roger C. Wolf)

Back when early Tucsonans led a less wasteful life, a cow or steer was a valuable commodity and when one was slaughtered, cooks used every part of the carcass. A traditional Sonoran dish is *tacos de cabeza*. Mazon puts an entire skinned cow head in a very large pot, boils it ("it smells very strong and meaty," she says), then picks off the meat. Another use-it-all taco ingredient is tripas de leche, the cleaned intestines, grilled and chopped for tacos.

"I try to respect and do justice to the cuisine I grew up eating," Mazon says. "The idea is to present real Mexican food with a few less piñatas hanging from the ceiling."

Mazon tries to be as traditional as possible within the constraints of running a restaurant. "We lost a certain art of cooking because we are always in a hurry," she says. "But good food takes time. And tradition. In Mexico, techniques are passed down. People say with pride, 'This pot was used by my great-grandpa.'"

There's another style of taco that Carlotta Flores calls "the Tucson taco" and that Mateo Ortero, owner-chef of Rollies Mexican Patio, calls "Nana's taco," after his grandmother. Others call it the "patty taco." A corn tortilla is spread with finely ground beef. Then using a broad knife, the cook starts on one edge and scrapes half of the beef, pushing it to the center line, making a small ridge of beef. The empty half is folded over the meat and everything is fried until the meat is done and the tortilla is crisp but still pliable enough to be pried open for other fillings.

Sonoran Flat Enchiladas

For a long time, the only place you could get this dish was wherever your mother or aunt made it for you. Today it occasionally appears on menus in Mexican restaurants. In the days when Roman Catholics were forbidden to eat meat on Fridays, these were often served for supper.

Sonoran flat enchiladas are a regional specialty that once formed the basis for meatless Friday meals for Roman Catholic families. (Roger C. Wolf)

Elders who have lived in Tucson and Magdalena, Sonora, for seventy and eighty years told folklorist Jim Griffith that this was the only kind of enchilada served in the bi-national Sonoran Desert through the 1930s. Sonoran flat enchiladas are now listed in the Slow Food Ark of Taste catalog.

My friend Elda Islas, mother of five grown sons, says one of her boys calls these "disappearing enchiladas" because they get eaten so fast. This is the recipe she and her sister-in-law Armida Islas made for me. Over the many years that my friends and I have compiled the *Savor the Southwest* recipe blog, this is consistently, week after week, the most searched for recipe.

Soups

Called *cocidos* or *caldos*, soups have long been a way to make use of the bones of the cow after the meat has been used elsewhere.

Cooks look for specific cuts for each soup. Oxtails with beans and hominy become *gallina pinta*. Beef feet, usually chopped into pieces, are combined with tripe (stomach lining) to form the basis for menudo, a popular hangover remedy. Pork neck bones cooked with hominy make posole.

Maria Mazon at Boca Tacos cooks a different soup each week. *Caldo de queso* is rich with melted cheese and potatoes. For *cazuela*, she adds corn and cabbage to the savory beef broth. *Sopa de albondigas* includes little meatballs in a rich beef broth. Tortilla soup, with pieces of tortilla chips in a chicken broth, is now available everywhere—although each cook seems to have a different take on it.

Sonoran Flat Enchiladas

Makes about 18 enchiladas

2 pounds of fresh masa
2 tablespoons soft lard
1 teaspoon baking powder
1 tablespoon salt
1 cup queso fresco, grated
Optional: some cooks also add mashed potatoes, cottage cheese, or a beaten egg
Oil for frying
3 cups of chile sauce

Condiments:
Chopped lettuce
Grated queso fresco
Chopped green olives
Chopped radishes
Chopped green onion
Lime quarters

In a deep bowl, combine the masa, soft lard, baking powder, and salt. Knead until combined. It should be creamy and damp but not sticky. Knead in the queso fresco and any optional items.

Heat 1½ inches of oil in a large frying pan to 350 degrees Fahrenheit. While the oil is heating, form the masa into patties ¼ to 3/8 inches thick and about 4 inches in diameter.

Slip as many patties as will fit into the oil and fry until golden on the underside, about 3 minutes. Turn and fry another 2 to 3 minutes. Line a rectangular dish with paper towels and drain the finished patties on the paper.

While the patties are frying, heat the chile sauce and keep warm.

To serve, dip each patty in the chile sauce, arrange two or three on a plate and pass the condiments.

Raspados

Raspados are sweet, creamy, fruity, sometimes a little salty, and always very cold. Perfect to cool you down from the inside out on a Tucson summer day.

The typical prep steps are simple, but they vary from shop to shop. In general, it is a layer of shaved ice, then fruit in syrup, then the layers are repeated. A topping of sweetened condensed milk trickles down. Sometimes vanilla ice cream is the final layer. Or the ice cream could be added halfway up. Typical fruits are fresh strawberries or peaches. Go tropical with mango, coconut, or pineapple. Then there can be nuts or chile in some form.

The fancier raspados called Macedonias include several fruits and more creaminess. Obviously, you'll have to explore for yourself. You'll find raspado shops all over Tucson, usually from Speedway south.

Sonoran Hot Dog

A more recent arrival to the local culinary scene is the Sonoran hot dog. You can get a Sonoran hot dog at any of dozens of vacant-lot food stands spread from the Rincons to the base of the Tucson Mountains. Heated discussions have transpired about who makes the best dog based on the most minor of adjustments.

But it was Mexican immigrant Daniel Contreras, owner of the famed El Güero Canelo restaurants, who in 2018 received the James Beard America's Classics Award. The award is given to locally owned restaurants that "have timeless appeal and are cherished for quality food that reflects the character of their community." Contreras learned about the multi-condiment hot dog in his native Hermosillo. Sensing opportunity, he started his own hot-dog cart in South Tucson in 1993 and reports he was soon selling 10,000 hot dogs a week.

When the temperature tops a hundred degrees, Tucsonans crave a raspado, a mixture of crushed ice, sweetened chopped fruit, ice cream, and condensed milk. (Roger C. Wolf)

Dozens of roadside food trucks can fix you a great Sonoran hot dog, but it was Daniel Contreras of El Güero Canelo who received the James Beard America's Classics Award in 2018 for his version. (Photo courtesy of El Güero Canelo)

El Güero Canelo's version starts with a wiener of pork, beef, and chicken, wrapped in bacon and grilled. It goes into a soft bun and is unerringly topped with a scattering of pinto beans, grilled or raw onions, plenty of chopped fresh tomatoes, one line of yellow mustard and another of green hot jalapeño sauce, and a final squiggle of mayonnaise.

Why did the Sonoran hot dog suddenly become so popular? Contreras, a beefy guy with a luxuriant head of light red hair and a beard to match, shrugs his shoulders. "It's incredible what happened," he says.

He credits his attention to detail. "Always fresh," he says. "I'm very picky on quality." To that end he bakes his own pillowy bolillo rolls in Hermosillo and grows his own onions and peppers on a 24-acre farm near Magdalena.

Contreras has a shelf of awards in his corporate office: TripAdvisor gave him a Travelers' Choice Award, Thrillist called El Güero Canelo one of the twenty-one best hot dog joints in America, and he consistently makes Tucson's "best of" lists. Raúl Grijalva, a member of Congress from Tucson, gave him a write-up in the *Congressional Record*, saying, "Contreras' story demonstrates the power of the American Dream and the persistent, entrepreneurial spirt of our immigrant community."

SONORAN BAKERIES

Tucson's Mexican bakeries, or panaderías, borrow traditional shapes and flavors from Sonora. Top row, from left: niño envuelto (wrapped-up baby), coyota, bandera, orejas (ears). Middle row: chamuco, concha (shell), elotito, thumbprint cookie, leo (leg). Bottom row: cochito (little piggy), empanada (the holes in the top signal the filling), turnover, galleta de boda. (Roger C. Wolf)

WHAT ABOUT FRYBREAD?

Frybread, those delicious puffs of deep-fried dough drenched in honey or piled with beef in red chile sauce served at most Native American gatherings, is not an aboriginal food. It was born from necessity in a truly awful period of American and Navajo history.

When white settlers began to take over traditional Navajo lands in 1863, the interactions between the two groups became violent.

The U.S. government, headed by President Abraham Lincoln, sent Kit Carson to remove the Navajos from their homeland. For good measure, Carson and the soldiers burned their fields and orchards, ruined their irrigation systems, and killed their livestock. After that, soldiers rounded up any Navajos they could find and marched them 300 miles to Bosque Redondo near Fort Sumner in New Mexico. The people were used to farming, but they had terrible luck in Bosque Redondo when their crops were eaten by insects and then were destroyed by flooding.

To keep the Navajos from starving, the U.S. government issued them rations of white flour, lard, salt, baking powder, and some sugar. They probably expected them to make biscuits, but somehow somebody decided to melt the lard and fry the dough instead of baking it.

Eventually the government under President Andrew Johnson let the Navajos return home, and they took their frybread tradition with them. Other native groups throughout the Southwest, including the Tohono O'odham, adopted the frybread tradition, adapting it in small ways to their own taste.

Containing nothing but white flour and lard with a little water, baking powder, and salt, the irresistible puffs are as unhealthy as a doughnut, even worse as they are four times the size of a doughnut. With diabetes at epidemic levels among many Native American groups, health advocates in tribal administrations have been striving to educate their people on the hazards of making frybread more than an occasional treat.

Despite its nutritional bad rap, we're pretty sure frybread will still be around for as long as the unmistakable aroma wafts over fairs and festivals and rodeos. Just keep in mind the phrase "an occasional treat."

NEW SOUTHWEST CUISINE: FRESH AND LOCAL

Around the early 1980s a new breed of chefs began moving to the Southwest. They were well trained and knew French techniques and how to layer flavors. They were intrigued by the fresh produce available year-round in Tucson, the bright desert essences of citrus and chile, and the wild, dusky flavor of prickly pear. The New Southwest cuisine that developed was "fusion" cooking, marrying Mexican, Native American, and mainstream ingredients and techniques.

Janos Wilder is the dean of Southwest cuisine in Tucson. In 1983 he opened his eponymous restaurant Janos in the historic 1865 Hiram Stevens House, now part of the Tucson Museum of Art campus. He had just come from a year of cooking in France and brought what he learned to Tucson.

"I advertised for gardeners before I looked for staff," Wilder recalls. "I wanted fresh herbs, baby vegetables, edible flowers. Then I began looking for things that had always grown here and became involved with Native Seeds/SEARCH."

Wilder's take on fresh ingredients from local farms, spiced with some heritage foods, was so innovative that within a year his new venture was listed as one of the top regional restaurants in the country by *Playboy* magazine. The James Beard Foundation named Wilder as the top chef in the Southwest in 2000.

Did his customers care that they were eating heritage foods? "My guests liked what I was doing," he says. "And the food tasted great. That's my sacred bond with my guests—it has to taste good. But that wasn't enough for me as a chef. I wanted to learn about new flavors as long as I didn't break that sacred bond. My guests allowed me to take my personal ride of discovery."

One example was a fresh take on chile rellenos. "They didn't need to be exactly like they are in Sonora," he says. He tried using lobster and brie, and then he wrote a whole cookbook on chile rellenos.

Wilder remains at the top of his game, but he has added a more international flavor to the food at his current restaurant Downtown Kitchen + Cocktails. In the summers he features foods from other UNESCO Cities of Gastronomy and in the winters he offers a special Sense of Place menu highlighting a food representative of the Southwest with his own spin. In the rest of the menu, he's as likely to use kimchi as tepary beans (or combine the two). Over the decades, he has taught and inspired other local chefs to dig deep into the local desert foods, mixing the traditional flavors with modern menu design.

Today, almost four decades after Wilder introduced Tucson to a new cuisine, the "New Southwest" mantle has grown to include not only use of the old standby ingredients in new ways, but also an emphasis on locally grown produce, as local as possible. And the trend stretches from food trucks to the largest award-winning resort kitchens. Creative chefs from the foothills to the south side want to bring the flavors of Tucson to their appreciative customers.

Many of the chefs are young; they've cycled through their first jobs in several restaurants, learning as they go. Now they're ready to share their version of the Tucson flavor with their customers. The movement stretches from a funky food truck to foothills resorts, each chef inspired through their own vision to provide their customers with a taste of Tucson.

This is just a snapshot of seven of Tucson's restaurants serving fabulous Southwest flavors. They are representative of the creativity flowing through the town. Several of the chefs mention Pivot Produce as their conduit to local produce. (You can read more about Pivot on page 131.)

Geronimo's Revenge

Jeronimo Madril, who goes by Mo, parks his food truck in the evenings outside 4th Avenue area bars. His customers know where to find him and know he'll always have something special for them. He says he's "taking good food back to the streets." That's why he was voted Best Food Truck by *Tucson Weekly* readers just a year after he opened in 2017.

Madril grew up in his dad's restaurant and is also a culinary school graduate, giving him the ability to imagine new dishes and the skill to execute them. His menu changes daily and reflects what's in season, but most things come with a Southwest twist. Mo calls it "Sonoran-inspired comfort food on the prowl." While you're likely to find a Cubano sandwich or mac and cheese, the "cheese" might be a vegan-friendly cashew cheese. On a creative day, he might come up with a house-made maize noo-

dle, covered in a creamy corn sauce topped with cotija cheese, cilantro, green onion, and Tajín, a blend of lime, mild chile peppers, and salt.

Madril is committed to using local sustainable ingredients, keeps chickens for the eggs he uses, sources local goat cheese from a friend, and recycles the leftover veggies in a compost pile. He even makes his own syrups for sodas, coming up with inspired versions like cilantro-lime, orange-ginger, lemon-vanilla, and jalapeño.

Welcome Diner

At Welcome Diner, a casual restaurant with serious food, head chef Ian Rosales incorporates local food into practically every dish. "When I first got to Tucson, I did a deep dive into the local ingredients," he

Jeronimo "Mo" Madril is making corn pasta that will become part of one of his nightly specials at his innovative Southwest-inspired food truck, Geronimo's Revenge. (Marty Smith)

says. "I'm very passionate about food. I'm always thinking about food. How I can manipulate food and try to solve little puzzles. I'm curious about my customers' palate and trying to turn what would taste good to them into regional cuisine. How can these local ingredients work together? Some puzzles are easier to solve than others. You become a student of the game. Constantly pushing to get the results you want."

What is going to resonate with customers isn't always clear. His deviled egg dish with pickled cholla buds didn't go over well. On the other hand, fried nopalitos, another cactus preparation, is one of the most popular dishes.

Welcome Diner's clients come for dishes that are healthy while also being creative and delicious. Thus, most of the dishes Rosales creates feature lots of vegetables. A breakfast dish called simply Roasted Vegetables starts with a local tortilla, braised mustard greens, and Mayo Kama squash topped with two eggs. It is finished with both tomatillo sauce and ranchero sauce and sprinkled with cotija cheese.

Tucson's heritage foods shine in two popular vegan dishes. Rosales uses brown teparies like a refried pinto in a burrito with corn and beans. The white teparies go into a tamale pie.

Welcome Diner is also known for its cocktails. A favorite uses fresh Arizona citrus and Whiskey del Bac from local Hamilton Distillers.

EXO Roast Company

EXO, just north of downtown, opened as a coffee shop featuring highly curated beans sourced from small family farms. It has since grown into a community hub serving breakfast and lunch—all with a local twist—as well as an extensive selection of mescals and cocktails.

In charge of the early-morning meals is Rusty Ramirez, a pastry chef formerly responsible for the outrageous desserts at the B Line and Café à la C'Art restaurants. She's a Southern Arizona native who grew up in Mammoth and spent time visiting her grandmother's cattle ranch in Aravaipa Canyon.

Ramirez is passionate about keeping the ingredients in the dishes she cooks as local as possible. Breakfast tacos are stuffed with nopalitos, green chiles, or San Xavier ha:l squash. Eggs come from Beck's Best Eggs in Cochise, 81 miles to the east, and oil is a blend from Queen Creek Olive Mill, 90 miles to the north.

Ramirez makes EXO's granola from scratch adding ironwood and ocotillo flowers when they're in season. She also gathers barrel cactus fruits for jam. The seeds she adds to the granola. When verdolagas (purslane) is plentiful in summer, she pickles it and tosses it atop the kimchi bowls. Also in the summer, Ramirez gathers mesquite pods, boils them, and incorporates the warm caramel flavor into a simple syrup used in one of the custom coffee drinks.

Ramirez hasn't left her pastry skills behind. They shine in an almond frangipane with a gluten-free crust made from acorn meal she sources from wild food expert and herbalist John Slattery. And those barrel cactus seeds sometimes show up on homemade croissants.

EXO Roast Barrel Cactus Marmalade

Use ripe cactus fruits that are bright yellow. Barrel cactus fruit are easy to use because they have no spines. Most homemade jams use about equal amounts of fruit and sugar. Chef Rusty Ramirez has formulated this marmalade to use less sugar. But you have to follow the recipe. Before you begin, sterilize a 1-quart jar or several jars that combined hold 4 cups.

Makes about 1 quart

25 to 30 ripe barrel cactus fruits
Water to cover
1½ cups sugar
2 tablespoons Pomona's Universal Pectin (jells
    with low amounts of sugar)
4 teaspoons calcium water (instructions on how
    to make it are included in the pectin box)
¼ cup lemon juice

Rinse the fruits, cut off the tops and bottoms, and chop roughly. Place the chopped fruits with the seeds into a heavy-bottomed 2-quart saucepan and add water to about an inch over the fruits. Bring the water to a hard boil, and then reduce the heat to a slow boil for 30 minutes.

Breakfast diners at EXO Roast can order barrel cactus jam made in house by Rusty Ramirez to top toast from Barrio Bread. (Roger C. Wolf)

While the fruit is boiling, whisk together the sugar and pectin in a bowl and set aside.

When the fruit is cooked, remove from the heat and place into a fine mesh strainer or cheesecloth in a sink. You should have about 3 cups. Rinse the fruit with cold water until there isn't much mucilage left in the fruits. They should be tender when you squeeze them. The seeds will collect at the bottom. You can add them to the marmalade or dry them in the oven to snack on later.

Transfer the cooked and rinsed barrel cactus fruits back into the saucepan with 4 teaspoons of calcium water and the 1/4 cup of lemon juice. Stir well with a heatproof spatula. Bring the fruit to a soft boil and add the sugar/pectin mixture to the pot slowly while continuously stirring the fruit so that the pectin doesn't clump. Before you remove the marmalade from the heat, make sure that all of the sugar/pectin mixture has dissolved. Put your sterilized jars on a heat-resistant surface. Carefully ladle the marmalade into the jars, filling to the neck and leaving about a half inch at the top.

Cover with the lids and let the marmalade cool completely. Store in the refrigerator for up to three months.

"I try to pull from what I learned growing up," Ramirez says. "People think there is nothing to eat on the desert, but there is an abundance just waiting to be used. My question is always, 'Is it sustainable?' If so, we can keep it on the menu."

La Cocina

As you enter La Cocina you step back into Tucson's history. This outdoor restaurant, located under shady trees and with twinkling lights at night, is situated downtown in what was once the northeast corner of the Presidio San Agustín, the area where they kept the stables. In 1782, Apaches attacked this part of the wall, possibly looking for some of those horses. After the Presidio declined, this block of land was purchased by Julius Goldbaum in the 1870s. Goldbaum lived there and also used it for his business of repackaging raw whiskey from Kentucky, tequila from Jalisco, and bacanora from Sonora. It is one of the longest continuously inhabited blocks in Tucson.

Owner Jo Schneider and cook/baker Nick Carson honor the history of the complex by putting together an eclectic menu that includes lots of local and heritage ingredients. Carson makes marmalade from Seville oranges and calamondins, and jam from barrel cactus. Local Mission figs appear in compote, bourbon bread pudding, and with chocolate in a mole sauce. Mesquite meal turns up in brownies and crackers. The most popular dessert is prickly pear cheesecake. Cocktails include prickly pear and local fruit juices.

Schneider says, "There's always lots of interest when we put something on the menu and say it is from the Sonoran Desert."

The shops surrounding the courtyard sell local artisan wares, jewelry, vintage goods, and alcohol.

Café Botanica

Café Botanica, nestled deep within the Tucson Botanical Gardens, has a menu that celebrates Southern Arizona food. Longtime Tucson caterer Kristine Jensen took over the café in the fall of 2013 and has made lunch there as lovely an experience as smelling the flowers and citrus blossoms that permeate the air in the spring.

Because Jensen is committed to using as much local produce and other products as possible, she designed her menu to be flexible to include what is fresh and available. In the winter her sopes and tortas are stuffed with cool-season greens such as kale and chard. In the summer it's more apt to be verdolagas (purslane).

"Most chefs have flavor profiles they work with a lot," Jensen says. "I'm Southwest born and bred. My comfort dishes are Southwest fare. I'm also committed to working with locally produced foods, so my menu is melded with the products that we are able to get. The menu flows with the seasons."

The Black-Eyed Peas and Pork Belly Stew from Café Botanica at Tucson Botanical Gardens includes heritage black-eyed peas from Ramona Farms and local produce, which varies depending on the season. (Roger C. Wolf)

Black-Eyed Peas and Pork Belly Stew

Black-eyed peas have been a staple of Sonoran cooking since the days of Father Kino. Kristine Jensen, chef at Café Botanica at Tucson Botanical Gardens, uses the original heritage bean from Ramona Farms in this recipe, but black-eyed peas are available at most grocers. To account for the soaking time, you need to start this recipe the day before you plan to serve it. Jensen advises that if you can't spend time cooking the beans, you can substitute canned beans for the black-eyed peas, but you will lose the flavor and feel of the true pea. The pork belly or bacon and the oil add hearty richness to the beans. Jensen uses the mixture to fill sopes, shallow cornmeal cups, but it works equally well as a filling for tortillas.

2 cups dried black-eyed peas
¼ cup oil (for example, rich olive or avocado oil)
1 large yellow onion, thinly sliced into crescents
2 to 3 large cloves garlic, puréed or minced
1 pound pork belly or thick-cut bacon, chopped into ⅛- to ¼-inch-square chunks
3 tablespoons chopped Mrs. Burns' Famous Lemon Basil or other flavorful basil
Salt, to taste

Soak the black-eyed peas overnight in a large pot with water to cover.

Next day, rinse and cover again with plenty of fresh water. In a heavy pot, simmer over low heat for 45 minutes to an hour until they are tender but still intact. Rinse and set aside.

Heat a large cast-iron or stainless-steel skillet for a few minutes on high heat.

Add the oil, wait about 30 seconds, and then add the onions and garlic. Stir briefly with a wooden spatula. Allow them to brown before stirring again.

When they are browned nicely, add the pork belly or bacon and stir.

Turn the heat down to medium and continue to cook the pork until it is done, stirring occasionally.

Stir in the beans and sprinkle with the basil. Add salt to taste. Stir gently. Use it to fill tortillas or sopes.

When Jensen first opened, she found it difficult to obtain the local produce she wanted. Now she is a grateful customer of Pivot Produce, which delivers local vegetables. "Now I'm using 90 percent local produce," she says. "It was the final piece for the café being farm to table."

Jensen is also committed to using sustainable foods like native corn, tepary beans, and prickly pear. She buys native dent corn from Ramona Farms, soaks it in lime, and grinds it wet to turn it into tamales, corn tortillas, and the crust for her quiche. She uses fresh prickly pear juice in tea and smokes nopales (prickly pear pads) before including them in salsas. Heritage beans that have been in Tucson since Father Kino came through, such as garbanzos and black-eyed peas, show up in her hearty salads.

In the spring, neighbors bring her bags of plump Meyer lemons and limequats that she turns into preserves to serve with her freshly made breads. She also makes preserved lemons to include in other foods.

One of the most popular items on the Café Botanica menu is a corn pudding from the Frida Kahlo cookbook. Jensen has modified it a bit since Frida was probably using field corn while today we have access to a sweeter variety of corn. Jensen serves it with a tomatillo crema made with tomatillos, reduced cream, poblano chiles, and onions.

"The corn pudding has followers from New York to Hawaii," Jensen says. "I'll never be able to take it off the menu. Some customers buy it by the loaf to take home."

Maynards Market & Kitchen

Brian Smith, executive chef at Maynards Market & Kitchen, has traveled to three continents (Italy, Brazil, and China) to represent Tucson at gatherings of UNESCO City of Gastronomy chefs. In Italy at a ten-course dinner for fifty people, he made a Sonoran wheat berry pudding and served it with dates, pecans, and a prickly pear foam.

"My main focus is to serve the best food possible and cook it very well," he says. "To do that I shop for quality. It's easy to call up a purveyor, but the local produce is better. The time and care the farmers put into the product translates into taste. The farmers are growing what they should at the right time. The organic food they are growing is sensitive to our climate and soil. The quality is getting better every year. They are doing more research into what grows well in the desert and they stick to it."

Smith pauses to mentally scan his menu. "This winter, we're getting 65 percent of our produce from local sources. We go through 60 pounds of Swiss chard a week—sometimes from several different growers. High Energy Agriculture has been sending us fabulous arugula that we use in salads. Quinces from Mission Garden become a vinegar."

Like other local chefs, Smith is a fan of Pivot Produce. "When I put together my winter menus, I first look at the list Erik from Pivot Produce sends to me so I know how much the farmers will be producing of each vegetable," Smith says. "The cost of local produce is almost double conventional vegetables. We can raise the menu prices a bit, but we need to stay competitive.

"When we use the local produce, we spend a lot more time with each vegetable. It puts a little spark in us not to waste any of it. We try to use each product to full capacity. It's nice to see the cooks' care with each tomato. Before we put anything in the compost, we ask, 'What can we do with this?' I fry up the sweet potato peels to make a garnish for the salads. We use the guts and seeds of the butternut squash in a mole. I spread the seeds on a sheet pan and put them under the broiler until they get black. That brings out the sweetness."

And what is that called? I ask.

"Butternut squash gut mole," Smith says with a laugh. Of course.

Smith honors Tucson's deep heritage with corn grits and tepary beans he sources from Ramona Farms.

In addition to vegetables from local farms, he also includes wild foods from the Sonoran Desert. "We use the native ingredients, but tweak 'em up a bit. The possibilities are endless; it's almost an untouched field."

Chiltepin chiles show up in a honey lime vinaigrette, cholla buds become part of a salsa, and a mesquite crumble tops a flourless chocolate cake. Prickly pear fruit he harvests himself shows up in sorbets, ice cream, and a homemade vinegar. He's even made miniature meringues shaped like barrel cactus that included barrel cactus seeds.

Brian Smith, executive chef at Maynards Market & Kitchen, designed a summer offering using Pima corn grits from Ramona Farms with locally grown collard greens, peaches, and corn topped with green goddess butter. (Jeaninne Kaufer)

Loews Ventana Canyon Resort

Loews Ventana Canyon Resort is nestled in the Catalina Foothills on a hundred pristine acres that is a virtual supermarket of desert foods. And executive chef Ken Harvey finds a way to put most of it on his menu. The resort's three gardeners and culinary team of fifty all participate in gathering the food.

Breakfast guests are served granola with mesquite flour, and pastry and lavash flecked with saguaro seeds. Barrel cactus fruit can show up in an upside-down cake. Prickly pear juice is added to lemonade or a margarita. The team dries cholla buds on the hotel roof, then cleans off the stickers with a blowtorch.

Harvey even attended a Tohono O'odham saguaro camp where he harvested 20 gallons of saguaro fruit, which, when boiled down, produced only a half gallon of syrup. Where there's just a limited supply of the wild-crafted foods, they are saved for special events or served to guests who are curious about them.

"If somebody is interested and wants to talk to us about our food, we have the story," Harvey says.

The hotel strives to use local vegetables and sources them from Pivot Produce. Vegetables at the hotel's Flying V Bar & Grill are 80 percent local.

Harvey is responsible for serving meals to 10,000 guests a week. Some of them come for conferences and don't have time to leave the hotel, yet they've heard about Tucson's honor as a UNESCO City of Gastronomy. Harvey is ready to give them a local experience through what he calls Flavor Partners. The products include Barrio Bread (Don Guerra sends up 30 loaves a week), tamales from Tucson Tamale, and beer from Dragoon Brewing.

The lettuce for the salad couldn't be more local. Through a partnership with the University of Arizona's Biosphere 2 and Chaz Shelton of Merchant's Garden, salad greens are grown hydroponically right on the grounds of the resort. Shelton will deliver live plants to the resort and they will grow there until the chefs need them. Bibb and Red Cherokee lettuces and three varieties of romaine provide 300 heads in each harvest.

Since the lettuce doesn't need to be refrigerated, it retains better flavor, color, and texture. "It will be live until it's ordered and the guest eats it freshly harvested," Harvey says.

Harvey cherishes the relationships he has with the local producers. "It's not the products, it's the partnerships," he says. "There are some really amazing people in Tucson who will bend over to help. Relationships are more powerful here than in other places. Those are the things money can't buy. That is why we are a UNESCO City."

But isn't all this expensive, I ask, since you are working on such a big scale? "We're looking for the right way, not the easy way," Harvey says. "We are trying to use a restaurant mindset in a large hotel."

Several other large resort hotels in Tucson use produce from their own gardens. For example, Westward Look Resort chefs grow a small garden and make jam from fruit they harvest from citrus trees that have been on the property for decades. The JW Marriott Starr Pass Resort grows herbs and produce in its own organic garden for the resort's Primo Italian restaurant, and the Ritz-Carlton in Marana has a large citrus orchard just outside one of their restaurants where guests can stroll to smell the blossoms and see where the juice in their cocktail originated.

The bartenders at Loews Ventana Canyon Resort give their prickly pear margaritas extra zip with jalapeño-infused tequila. (Roger C. Wolf)

FESTIVALS CELEBRATE TUCSON FOOD AND DRINK

Think of a festival as a ritual, a time when things shift their normal order—people transgress their comfort zones by eating different foods, dancing on the streets, talking to strangers, seeing what is familiar in a new light. In this way, we are able to imagine what a more democratic, equitable, and just world might look like.

— MARIBEL ALVAREZ, TUCSON MEET YOURSELF FESTIVAL CURATOR

Tucsonans love food and drink festivals and culinary events. The Tucson UNESCO City of Gastronomy organization has compiled a list of at least seventy annual food festivals—more than one a week. Think of a theme (maybe tacos?), hire a band, write a press release, and pin up a few posters, and you're bound to get a turnout. It helps if your event is going to support a good cause.

Here are some of the oldest and largest food events held in Tucson. Many other smaller food-themed events occur throughout the year.

TUCSON MEET YOURSELF. This is Tucson's oldest food festival, dating from 1974. The first couple of years of Tucson Meet Yourself, which is always held in early October, involved a few hundred folks, most of whom knew each other, sitting on a grassy hill behind the old county courthouse. Folklorist and musician "Big Jim" Griffith had pulled together musicians he knew, there were a few food stands, and everyone finished Saturday night two-stepping to a waila band (*waila* is the Tohono O'odham word for dance; sometimes also called "chicken scratch" because the happy dancing can kick up dust, just like chickens do when scratching around).

Over the subsequent decades, Tucson Meet Yourself has expanded in every way. Organizers now plan for at least 120,000 people over a three-day weekend for an expanded folklife festival. A hundred

Deon Harrison of Cee Dee Jamaican Kitchen works the grill in a booth at Tucson Meet Yourself.

acts perform onstage; about that many artists demonstrate their crafts. And people come to eat. Boy, do they eat. Dozens of vendors, many making money for their small organizations, will serve up food from just about everywhere. It's a regular United Nations of food with vendors from Somalia, Egypt, Jamaica, Greece, Peru, Mexico, Turkey, Thailand, and the Sonoran Desert itself.

People line up for takoyaki balls (octopus dumplings) from Japan, raspados (Sonoran sno-cones), cholla bud salsa from San Xavier Co-op Farm, grilled jerk chicken from Jamaica, and American corn on the cob.

Such a complicated festival doesn't just happen. Planning takes all year. More than two dozen sponsors step up to cover the $330,000 annual cost and make it free to anyone. It takes every bit of effort from 750 volunteers to pass out programs, empty the trash containers, and run the microphones and amplifiers. Ultimately, festival-goers pump $350,000 into the local economy.

Everybody has so much fun they can't wait to do it again next year.

AGAVE HERITAGE FESTIVAL. The Agave Heritage Festival, which began with one dinner and one night of mescal and tequila tasting, has evolved into more than a week of dinners with heritage foods, educational sessions, demonstrations, and tours of all things agave. That is in addition to the mescal and tequila imbibing, which remains a draw. The downtown Hotel Congress is the main sponsor and organizer, and many of the events take place there and in their expansive courtyard.

Mission Garden sponsors a guided tour of Hohokam agave fields on "A" Mountain. To demonstrate how the ancient inhabitants turned the spiny plants into food, ethnologist Jesús García of the Arizona-Sonora Desert Museum has dug a demonstration pit and roasts agave hearts à la AD 1500 with tastes for all. (Roasted agave is very fibrous, but it tastes sweet with a fruity edge.)

During the annual Agave Heritage Festival, Jesús García harvests and prepares an agave heart for roasting in the traditional earth oven. (Jeaninne Kaufer)

TUCSON GREEK FESTIVAL. Another very long-running and beloved festival is put on by St. Demetrios Greek Orthodox Church. It has expanded to four days to accommodate the 25,000 people hankering for some souvlaki. With a little imagination, Tucsonans can be transported to a Greek village for a few hours. Food prices are modest for everything from an appetizer plate with dolmades, hummus, and tzatziki to a complete roast leg of lamb dinner. Greek dancing and traditional music complete the atmosphere.

Southern Arizona Arts & Cultural Alliance Events

Six of the other largest food festivals are coordinated by the Southern Arizona Arts & Cultural Alliance (SAACA) with its well-organized staff and army of seasoned and competent volunteers. SAACA raises money to advance its mission: "The creation, preservation, and advancement of the arts."

The festivals are spaced through the year with the first in early February. Local restaurants send chefs in their sparkling white coats and set out thousands of samples of their best dishes.

SOUTHERN ARIZONA FOOD & WINE FESTIVAL. Booths at the Savor Southern Arizona Food and Wine Festival are set throughout the winding pathways in the lush 5-acre Tucson Botanical Gardens. Despite the early February date, days are usually pleasantly warm during the early-afternoon hours. The 1,300 attendees are a mix of tourists looking for some local flavor and locals, many of whom attend every year.

CARNIVAL. The date of the Mardi Gras and Carnival–themed festival held at the Rialto Theatre depends on when Easter falls. Guests dine on Cajun and Creole cuisine complete with authentic king cake, as well as dancing to live music. Attendees are encouraged to dress in the spirit of the celebration.

TUCSON 23 MEXICAN FOOD FESTIVAL. Most of the tourists have gone to cooler parts by mid-June, and it is time for Tucsonans to celebrate one of the things we love about our city: really great Mexican food. The highest concentration of these restaurants is found within a 23-mile area that includes the city of South Tucson, downtown, and lower midtown. Many of these terrific eateries are family owned and decades old. The Tucson 23 Mexican Food Festival takes place in the cool convention hall at the JW Marriott Starr Pass Resort.

WORLD MARGARITA CHAMPIONSHIP. When mid-August arrives, it is still hot, and Tucsonans are ready for some indoor fun. The Tucson Originals have joined SAACA to put on the World Margarita Championship at the Hilton El Conquistador Resort. Local chefs and bartenders battle to see who can produce the tastiest version of Tucson's favorite cocktail. Tucson Originals is an association of locally owned restaurants that have banded together to promote the value of Tucson's independent restaurants and support Tucson's culinary diversity.

SOUTHERN ARIZONA SALSA, TEQUILA, & TACO CHALLENGE. On Labor Day weekend in early September, two levels of the La Encantada shopping center are crowded with 1,200 ticket holders tasting food and drink at the Southern Arizona Salsa, Tequila, & Taco Challenge. Attendees vote for their favorites and compare their opinion with the local judges.

ARIZONA FARM & FOOD FESTIVAL. SAACA winds up its year by celebrating local and sustainable foods at the Arizona Farm & Food Festival at Casino del Sol. Southern Arizona beer and wine producers team up with local restaurants and caterers to offer tasty sips and bites that blend well together.

Only in Tucson

The events below celebrate wild and heritage foods found only in Southern Arizona.

SAN YSIDRO FESTIVAL. The San Ysidro Festival feast is held on the grounds of the Mission Garden and is celebrated in mid-May when the heritage White Sonora wheatfield is ready for harvest. The festival honors the patron saint of farmers. Mission volunteers, many of whose families have lived in the barrio surrounding the Garden for generations, cook up big pots of posole de trigo, a traditional stew with beef, vegetables, and wheat berries.

HA:SAN BAK SAGUARO FESTIVAL. The saguaro harvest marked the beginning of the year for the Tohono O'odham native people, who have lived on this desert for untold centuries. Since Colossal Cave Mountain Park includes a thick stand of saguaros, this is a perfect place to learn about the tradition. Tribal members tell of the significance of the harvest for their people, and guide harvesting and preparing of the saguaro fruit. It's hot in June so this event starts at sunrise.

Horses thresh the wheat in traditional fashion at Mission Garden's San Ysidro Festival in May. (Dena Cowan)

TUCSON HERITAGE FOOD & WINE FESTIVAL. This festival is held in the early fall on the grounds of the historic Hacienda del Sol Resort (it was formerly a boarding school for girls from the East). This event showcases local foods and includes a panel discussion on heritage foods and a farmers' market in addition to samples of Tucson's most interesting food, beer, and wine.

SONORAN HARVEST: TASTE THE DESERT. Head to the Arizona-Sonora Desert Museum in November for a harvest festival focused on foods found in the Sonoran Desert. Attendees can stand among the saguaros and taste creations from local chefs using prickly pear or mesquite in their offerings. It is a way for Tucsonans to really taste the desert.

TUCSON TAMAL & HERITAGE FESTIVAL. For more than 10,000 Tucsonans, this festival is part of the local holiday season, occurring between Thanksgiving and Christmas. And Tucson is all about tamales at this time of year. Held on the lawn at Casino del Sol, ticket holders can drift from booth to booth, sampling and comparing the finer points of pork over chicken and red chile over green chile. Local producers can present their creations to potential customers who might return for provisions for their holiday parties.

Beer-Themed Festivals

Tucson has an active craft brewing culture and these festivals are a way for attendees not only to have a good time and celebrate their favorite beverage but also to taste a variety of beers from many producers in one spot.

TUCSON CRAFT BEER CRAWL. Several of the breweries that produce craft beer are located downtown and many of the smaller local bars in that area have a number of local brews on tap. Revelers can walk among more than two dozen bars downtown and along 4th Avenue and 6th Street. The crawl is usually held in February.

BAJA BEER FESTIVAL. Members of the Arizona Craft Brewers Guild get together to showcase their creations on a balmy night in April in centrally located Armory Park. They invite chefs who are members of GUT (Gastronomical Union of Tucson) to produce beer-complementing food for purchase.

BORN & BREWED BEER BATTLE. Held in September in the Hotel Congress patio. Only local beers are poured,

Many thousands of tamales from dozens of cooks are consumed every year at the Tucson Tamal & Heritage Festival.

and both judges and partygoers get to vote for their favorites. The Cup Café provides beer-friendly food such as sausage on a pretzel bun and German potato salad.

OKTOBERFEST. It can still be plenty warm in the desert in the early fall, but folks looking for a more traditional autumn experience can drive up to Mount Lemmon Ski Valley for their Oktoberfest. The cooler air can encourage a taste for Bavarian bratwurst, German beer, and live German bands. Depending on the weather, some aspen leaves might be turning gold. The event runs from mid-September through mid-October.

Those not up for the drive can celebrate in early October at Trail Dust Town with local beers and polka music. Casino del Sol gets into the spirit in late October with jumbo German pretzels, and bratwurst from local butcher Forbes Meat Company to accompany the beer.

FOOD JUSTICE

Access to affordable, safe food that nourishes your body and your potential is a basic human right for all people.

— MICHAEL MCDONALD, CEO, COMMUNITY FOOD
BANK OF SOUTHERN ARIZONA

A CCORDING TO U.S. CENSUS DATA from 2015, Tucson is the fifth-poorest large city in America, a place where many don't have sufficient nutritious food. In fact, one in five Arizonans faced times in 2019 when they lacked enough money to buy food that they or their families needed. Although Tucson is a poor city, those citizens who are more fortunate are also generous and compassionate. Tucsonans and Tucson institutions are working together every day to address hunger in our community.

COMMUNITY FOOD BANK OF SOUTHERN ARIZONA SEEKS BROADER SOLUTION

It's an ordinary Tuesday morning at the headquarters of the Community Food Bank of Southern Arizona. Outside, a small farmers' market offers food produced by small growers who have taken the Food Bank's gardening classes and now have enough fruit and vegetables to sell to others. Carrots along with their tops, late melons, three varieties of chiles, and lush-leafed Swiss chard share table space with green onions and quinces.

In the Community Food Bank main building, what looks like a hundred people are lined up for a once-monthly emergency food bag or box. A similar line with different people is repeated every weekday. The emergency food boxes are designed to provide three days of food, but on this sunny though cool morning, clients leave with not just a box but a full grocery cart with bags of beans, macaroni, canned vegetables, breakfast cereal, and bread, all groceries the Food Bank has received from corporate donors. These extra offerings differ daily depending on what donations they have received. Supplementing the dried food today are dozens of ripe cherry tomatoes and a giant watermelon.

FOOD JUSTICE

The Community Food Bank of Southern Arizona relies on volunteers for many activities including loading the bags that hold the monthly food supplement. The community annually volunteers more than 200,000 hours to Food Bank programs.

Everyone is invited to come back on Monday morning, every Monday, for more free produce whether or not they have already received their monthly food box. Much of this produce comes from warehouses in Nogales, Arizona, the largest point of entry for Mexican-grown vegetables shipped to grocery stores throughout the United States. Unless the unsold tomatoes, squash, and oranges are rescued and distributed to hungry people, they are dumped to rot in a landfill to make way for the next day's shipment.

When the Community Food Bank was founded in 1975, it provided 10,000 food boxes a year. Today, that is closer to 200,000 each year. One reason for the increase is that the Food Bank has expanded its reach and now serves five counties in Southern Arizona: Cochise, Graham, Greenlee, Pima, and Santa Cruz. In total, that represents just over 23,000 square miles and over 1.2 million people.

At some point in the year, 15 to 17 percent of Tucson's population uses the Food Bank to provide enough healthy food for their family. There are many reasons the family food budget might take a hit. It might be loss of a job, or an illness causing lost time at work, or an unusual expense like a costly car repair. Another reason is that Tucson, with a low industrial base, doesn't have enough high-paying jobs to let people provide adequately for their families.

Sixty percent of people who visit the Food Bank for food assistance report they are employed—it's just that some weeks their paycheck doesn't stretch far enough. Many of those who are not employed are seniors or have a disability.

The dedicated folks at the Food Bank know that while passing out a box or bag of food might alleviate a family's hunger for a couple of nights, it does nothing in the long term to eliminate the systemic problem of hunger in Tucson and in Arizona's other southern counties.

And the long term is how they view their response to the chronic food insecurity of so many Tucson residents with their mission: "Feeding the hungry today, and building a healthy, hunger-free tomorrow."

Spend a few hours or days with any of the Food Bank's staff members or volunteers and you will recognize a place where compassion is paramount, and the goal is that nobody goes hungry.

"Access to affordable safe food that nourishes your body and your potential is a basic human right for all people. We have a moral obligation to assure that in our community all people have access to healthy food," says Michael McDonald, chief executive officer of the Community Food Bank. "Hypertension, poor mental health, obesity—all of that is related to diet, to nutritional options available to people. Fate is tied to ZIP code, where you live. Some people in our community don't have the same range of choices other people have. And, therefore, health is compromised, individual health, household health, and family health.

"We talk about some people living in a food desert, but some people live in a food swamp where the type of food being pushed is cheap and of poor nutritional value. Maybe they have poor or inadequate transportation and are unable to walk far to a store. And even if they did, they can't afford the higher price for produce at a farmers' market."

Although the major food distribution happens at the Food Bank warehouse on South Country Club Road, there are numerous other sites throughout Tucson and Southern Arizona where people can pick up food, making access easier for those without cars.

"We have eight locations where we do some level of distribution and work with about 350 partner agencies over five counties we serve," McDonald explains. "That can be large nonprofits like Primavera or the Salvation Army or they can be little church pantries in the middle of nowhere, or they can be in a park where we bring a truck. The reason for all those nodes is that poverty and food insecurity is everywhere and people's ability to get to a central location is compromised and may not work for their schedule. They may have multiple jobs, or kids in school, or they don't have a vehicle that works that well. That is why over many decades all these partnerships have developed. It's a web, a network of food-sharing partners."

In addition to getting a once-monthly food box, anyone who needs additional food can access it from pantries located in about sixteen churches and mosques and twelve schools. Some are open just once a month, others nearly every day. And these pantries are not limited to a few cans of food; often the Food Bank will deliver an entire pallet of fresh vegetables to be distributed.

"We think school pantries are really beneficial," McDonald says. "Families are showing up. It gives the school personnel and volunteers an opportunity to interact with the people that come in. One of the problems we are trying to solve is social isolation—this disconnectedness that modern America has. If a family needs food, they can quickly come in, access a food pantry, and interact with school personnel or a caring volunteer. That helps give the community a safety net."

McDonald describes one pantry that is working particularly well. "Lawrence Elementary School right outside Pascua Yaqui tribal land serves tribal members and has a very popular school pantry. There are counselors on-site. Other types of services have started to evolve because of relationships that have grown. It's not just 'Here's your food.' There's a relationship that is strengthened between a family and its school and the greater community."

McDonald sees community building as a key part of the process. "It's good to see some of our faith community partners who may be people of privilege be able to come to a low-income, high-stress school," he says. "It gives them the opportunity to cross a socioeconomic boundary and have a relationship with people they might not encounter otherwise."

Because 75 percent of the people who come to the Community Food Bank for assistance have a family member with diabetes or heart disease, many of the Food Bank programs focus on helping their clients have access to not just food, but healthy food and an understanding of what healthy food is. That led the staff to do an analysis of the food given in the food boxes. In some cases, they weren't happy with the results. In the short term, the food buyers switched to canned goods with lower sodium. For the long term, they are working with University of Arizona nutritionists and clients to develop a food box that will better address a therapeutic diet for people with health issues like uncontrolled diabetes.

Learning to shop wisely is another step toward preparing budget-conscious nutritious meals. Jessica Sheava, head of the Food Bank's health initiatives program, takes adult participants on a tour of a grocery store, teaching them how to read labels and make their SNAP food benefits go further. In some of the schools that maintain school pantries, the Food Bank staff have identified parents who can serve as education leaders for other parents at the school, demonstrating how to use the products and produce available.

Let's take a look at some of the additional programs under the Food Bank's umbrella.

Gaining Skills While Helping Others at Caridad Community Kitchen

The four students graduating from the Caridad Culinary Class Number 27 were emotional as they heard praise from their teachers and got ready to start new careers in the food industry. They joined a fraternity of 180 previous graduates of the program. After receiving their graduation gift of a chef's knife, they invited their friends and family for a feast they had prepared: steak and shrimp tacos, mini chimichangas, and small Beef Wellingtons wrapped in tender puff pastry. For dessert, chocolate mousse, arroz con leche (rice pudding), and tres leches cake. Each of the students had faced some life challenges and applied for the program looking for a fresh start. Now, armed with skills and confidence, they were on the verge of their next chapter.

Although the Community Food Bank of Southern Arizona accepts donations of many tons of canned, frozen, packaged, and fresh food each year, Caridad Community Kitchen is where some of that food gets turned into meals for people who otherwise might not eat. Or certainly not eat that well.

Located north of downtown on Main Avenue, the Caridad Kitchen's cooks, students, and volunteers are responsible for preparing 30,000 meals a month in a sparkling 2,800-square-foot kitchen (that's about two-thirds of a college basketball court). Nine walk-in refrigerators and freezers store the meat and vegetables, and the latest high-tech ovens and warmers line the walls. Two commercial tilt skillets hold 45 gallons each and can be used to fry, sauté, grill, simmer, or steam. They can make a savory beef stew, a dessert compote of golden peaches and ruby cherries, or a creamy soup rich with chicken and cheese, all in large batches.

The eleven cooks, half-dozen volunteers, and handful of culinary students who bustle about the kitchen every day need the space as they prepare five different meals for varying populations of vulnerable and hungry Southern Arizonans. Despite producing quantities that would overwhelm a non-professional, the cooks care deeply about the food they prepare, tasting to adjust the recipe, adding a bit of this or that to spike it up, make it richer, more flavorful.

Three times a year a class of students who could use a new start in life and think that it might be in food service complete a 10-week course that prepares them to work in a professional kitchen. They start with the basics: knife skills. One day they cut onions for hours, the next day it's potatoes. They fabricate (fancy word for cut up) chickens—30 of them—until they can do it quickly and correctly. At the end of the exhausting day, they go home with blisters because they are learning to hold a knife in a new way.

Then it is on to the five French mother sauces. None of what they make goes to waste because their teacher, Chef Ismael Ramón, has figured that ingredient into one of the meals he is responsible for overseeing that day.

While the students have varying dreams for their future, each of the students in the class has plans for entrepreneurship. Tina and a friend want to start a food trailer serving burgers and hand-cut fries; Sita and Marco, the lone man in this class, want to have food trucks; Jessica likes to bake and wants to rent out her house for weddings, providing both the food and the wedding cakes.

The students are tentative at first, but when I drop in two weeks into their class, they are well integrated into the running of the kitchen. Jessica is having fun using the professional-size mixer to bake 371 vanilla cupcakes for senior meals, and Tina is arranging chicken breasts produced during the day-long lesson on chicken. The students learn to use the large-scale equipment they might find in a casino or large resort kitchen, and they also practice on smaller professional stoves and with mixers similar to what are used in a restaurant.

Chef Ismael Ramón, Caridad Community Kitchen instructor, coaches student Sita on the proper and professional way to cut chicken breasts.

Caridad Community Kitchen student Jessica gets to work making cookies. She hopes to open her own wedding catering business.

Caridad Kitchen partners with Catholic Community Services and Lutheran Social Services to make food for the Meals on Wheels program for seniors and others unable to shop and cook for themselves. A registered dietitian oversees the menus for the program, which is partially funded by the government through the Pima Council on Aging. These meals are not made from donated food, but instead are prepared from ingredients delivered by Shamrock Foods four times a week.

Volunteers help portion the meals into the divided trays and send them through a device that attaches plastic film to the top. Laura Daniels, a spritely 81, shows up early four days a week to get things set up for the volunteers who arrive at noon. She is cheery, happy to be involved, and easily lifts the heavy trays.

Thirteen hundred meals are delivered to homes throughout Tucson and as far away as Coolidge, Eloy, Florence, and Green Valley. To cut down on delivery time, recipients receive one chilled and one frozen meal with the fresh salads packaged separately. Designing meals that can be heated in a microwave and still remain appetizing adds an extra challenge for those who plan the menus. Meals are also delivered in bulk to senior centers for people who can show up to enjoy the social interaction of eating their meal with others.

On the other end of the age scale are supper meals provided for kids at a Boys and Girls Clubs program, at a parks and recreation program, and at a youth or-

Caridad Community Kitchen student Marco works on a sauce for a chicken dish he is making.

ganization. The U.S. government pays for the food through the Child and Adult Care Food Program, but it falls to the Caridad staff to plan and prepare meals that not only are nutritionally complete but will also be acceptable to the children.

The chefs also need to get to work each day preparing the community meals, which are sent out to Tucson churches four days a week. Anyone can show up any late afternoon and have a hot meal, no questions asked. (See Gathering for a Community Meal below.)

Every day, Ramón is challenged to create a meal for about 125 people using food that has been donated to the general Food Bank warehouse. It might be meat donated by a food distributor or produce rescued from Nogales, Arizona, importers. His years of professional cooking and the hundreds of recipes he carries in his head guide him in developing a delicious meal with whatever is on hand. On a late November day, eighteen frozen turkeys, apparently unclaimed for Thanksgiving dinners, were delivered by a local grocery store and rested in one of the walk-in freezers until Ramón could devise a menu to use them.

Volunteers show up in the afternoon and are largely responsible for packing up about 250 sack lunches every day. Each lunch has a meat sandwich, a piece of fruit (soft because many clients have dental problems), and an extra or two such as a bag of chips or a cookie. There's also a bottle of water or Gatorade. The sack lunches can include donated products or food purchased from the general fund or grants. The brown bags are distributed at Sister Jose Women's Center, Saint Francis Men's Shelter, Holy Family and Life in Christ churches, and the Tucson Homeless Work Program. Anyone can also pick up a lunch at Caridad Community Kitchen between 3 and 4 pm any weekday.

The people at the Community Food Bank recognize that it is cold living on the street in the winter, even in Tucson. From November 1 to March 1 they add the Soup Patrol. The cooks produce 10 gallons of soup and 10 gallons of hot chocolate, which is passed out along with some bread. The warming food is delivered by volunteers from Most Holy Trinity Church to three sites where the homeless tend to congregate. On the first day of the Soup Patrol the cooks started off with a creamy chicken Alfredo soup; on another night they produced a tomato-vegetable version.

After their initial-learning weeks, the culinary students participate with the other cooks in preparing the meals that go to feed Tucson's hungry and vulnerable people. For some, the good feeling that comes with this work doesn't leave them. At the time of my visit, eight of the professional Caridad cooks were former students who had, after working in the community, returned to the big kitchen on Main Avenue putting together delicious meals for Tucsonans who cannot cook for themselves.

Gathering for a Community Meal

It's been a hot late-September Monday and at 5:30 pm about 45 men and women and several children are lined up in the shade outside the Northminster Presbyterian Church at Fort Lowell Road and Tucson Boulevard waiting for dinner. Some greet friends with hugs; others stand apart, shrouded in their aloneness. They have arrived by bus and bicycle. Those with cars bring friends.

Inside the church in the spacious commercial kitchen, Northminster parishioners are putting the finishing touches on the hot food just delivered by the Community Food Bank of Southern Arizona.

HUNGRY KIDS GET FED
EVEN IN SUMMER

When school's out for summer, the three-quarters of Tucson schoolchildren who receive some or most of their nutrition through free or reduced-cost meals at school don't stop needing food. School districts throughout the city open up school cafeterias where kids can get breakfast or lunch. Let's drop into one:

It's a hot, humid July morning and by 7 o'clock Ronnie Truit, a TUSD food service worker, is in the kitchen at John B. Wright Elementary School getting breakfast ready. In an hour, a couple of dozen hungry kids, participants in the KIDCO recreation program, will come in the door. Breakfast is also available to any child in the neighborhood who needs a breakfast. Truit likes to offer the children a choice, so he puts out plain and chocolate milk, small whole-grain bagels and cream cheese, breakfast bars, string cheese, and cups of applesauce or peaches and mangoes. He also heats up whole-grain pancakes and adds an envelope of syrup.

The kids clatter in. Most have been up for a couple of hours and they are ready to eat. Today Lily, 5, and Zane, 6, choose pancakes with their fruit, cheese, and milk. Tessa, 6, has a lighter appetite and makes do with milk, fruit, and cheese.

There is no payment line; it is free for any child age eighteen or under. The food cost is covered by the Summer Food Service Program for Children, a federally funded program operated by the U.S. Department of Agriculture. In addition to Tucson Unified, Amphitheater, Sunnyside, Flowing Wells, and Marana School Districts participate in the program. Meals are also available at some Tucson Parks and Recreation sites and Boys and Girls Clubs.

As soon as the children go off to their activities, Truit cleans up and begins thinking about lunch. He's about as far as you can get from the stern lunch lady associated with too many bad memories. With a background working as a chef in hospitals and nursing homes, he's avuncular and obviously cares

On a hot July afternoon, Melina and Leanna Lopez pick up a lunch provided by the Amphitheater Public Schools' Summer Lunch Program outside Woods Memorial Library.

about the kids, urging them to take the right combination of fruit, protein, and whole grains that the USDA recommends.

At noon, the KIDCO group is back for lunch. Today it is chicken tenders, mashed potatoes with gravy, applesauce, and milk. As soon as they are finished, Ronnie packs everything up and drives to Martha Cooper Library, a small branch that also serves as a community center.

There, Truit is prepared to serve lunch to as many as fifty children up to age eighteen. Martha Cooper Library is in a low-income neighborhood where 89 percent of the children qualify for free lunch during the school year so the summer program is essential. Without this meal, many would go hungry or have to fill up on nonnutritious food.

Felicia, who lives nearby, walks over at lunchtime every day with the six children she cares for: her two daughters, a niece, a nephew, and two great-nephews. After lunch they can stay to play board games or work on one of the computers.

So that takes care of Monday through Friday. If a child is afraid there will be nothing to eat at home over the weekend, they can request a bag of food at Martha Cooper's service desk. The bag holds a jar of peanut butter, four small bagels, a single serving of Cheerios, an orange, and three small cartons of milk that do not need refrigeration.

Students in the Food Bank's Caridad Community Kitchen culinary program cooked the meal earlier as part of their training.

Everyone is welcome to join in the dinner—the only requirement is to sign in before taking a place at one of the long tables in an activity room. The tables are set with tablecloths, pitchers of water and lemonade, and baskets of sliced bread. As soon as folks are seated, volunteers begin serving Styrofoam plates generously filled with the day's menu: a tasty ragu made from ground turkey, peas and carrots in a tomato sauce, mashed potatoes, and a romaine salad. Over the next 15 minutes, another 30 people drift in and fill in spots at the tables. Those who have finished are offered chocolate-chip cookies.

The kitchen volunteers, a rotating group of about ten each week, say that they generally expect to feed anywhere from 65 to 95 people every Monday. Sometimes in the winter, when the homeless population climbs, there might be up to 110 or 130. Numbers also tend to swell toward the end of the month when people's funds and SNAP benefits are depleted. If it appears that everyone has been fed and there is food left over, people are invited to line up for seconds. Food must be eaten at the church because of health concerns over improper storage if it is taken out.

UNIVERSITY CAMPUS PANTRY:
HELP FOR HUNGRY STUDENTS

The image of the carefree college life is not true for a high percentage of students who find the huge expense of getting through school an economic struggle. When all the other bills are paid, sometimes there isn't any money left for food. To address the need, a Campus Pantry was opened in 2012 in the Student Union at the University of Arizona. The operation has grown since then as the greater need has been identified.

In a campus survey, 20 percent of UA undergraduates reported skipping a meal because of lack of money and more than half of students reported that they often or always ate unhealthy meals because healthier options were too expensive.

The Campus Pantry is open two days a week. Students need to show campus identification and can take up to four items, sometimes more. There is always peanut butter and bread. Fresh items come from a garden on the rooftop of the Student Union. Arizona Department of Economic Security representatives can help eligible students sign up for SNAP benefits.

CASA MARIA: DECADES OF DISPENSING SOUP

It's in a tiny three-room house on a dusty lot south of 22nd Street, but since 1981, Casa Maria has been offering food to anyone who needs hot coffee, a doughnut, a cup of soup, and a sack lunch. Come to the door, you get a lunch, no questions asked.

Since 1983, Casa Maria has been run by Brian Flagg, who oversees a group of folks in the Catholic Worker Movement and a rotating group of community volunteers, some from the surrounding neighborhood, others from all over the Tucson basin. Flagg was a young guy back then; now his long curly hair has strands of gray. From the time my husband and I used to volunteer every Sunday morning in the late 1980s, not much has changed. There is now a large walk-in refrigerator to store the donations and a solar array on the roof to help offset the cost of running it. But the men outside all look the same, older, bearded, quiet.

The goal of the Catholic Workers is "to practice daily the works of mercy and works of justice." Flagg does the job willingly, year after year, but he doesn't think he should have to. "This is the most powerful, richest country on earth," he says. "People shouldn't have to get their food here."

Today, three women from Corpus Christi Catholic Church on Tucson's east side arrived at 6:45 am to start the huge pots of soup. They used what had been donated—several kinds of meat, lots of fresh vegetables, beans, and macaroni. By about 9 o'clock, they were ladling it into Styrofoam cups and handing it out along with sack lunches.

In the small back room, six volunteers stood around a long table making sandwiches and portioning cookies and chips into smaller bags. Meanwhile, I helped Vivian, a nurse working on her day off, to

Families in need can pick up a bag of fresh produce and donated baked goods from Casa Maria Soup Kitchen simply by asking.

It's only 7 am and already Luz Acosta has the soup on at Casa Maria Soup Kitchen.

transfer donated chopped fresh fruit from the plastic grocery store containers into smaller baggies to be added to the sack lunches. Each baggie contains about a cup of watermelon, honeydew, pineapple, blueberries, and strawberries. The fruit has been resting in the walk-in refrigerator and soon my hands are numb with cold.

Every day except Thanksgiving and Christmas (when Tucson puts on big community meals), about 500 sack lunches go out the door of Casa Maria. But because the need in the surrounding neighborhood is so great, volunteer Luz, who hails from Michoacán, stuffs 150 family bags with fresh vegetables. Many of the veggies come from Felicia's Farm, which donates most of its produce and 100 dozen eggs a year to Casa Maria. (Read more about Felicia's Farm on page 108.) The family bags usually have some donated treats as well such as cookies, day-old doughnuts, occasionally an entire cake. Today it was a bag of pumpkin-flavored marshmallows, apparently not a marketing success.

The work goes quickly. Brian stands at the door handing out the bags, greeting the regulars. Once the soup is all ladled out, someone starts preparing chicken to help tomorrow morning's soup makers. A donated 6.3-pound turkey breast needs to be shredded. It found no buyer at $62.94.

By 10:30 am the volunteers are sweeping and mopping the floor, wiping down the picnic tables, and getting the trash into the barrels. Tomorrow morning another group of volunteers will do the same. And another group of hungry folks will wait for coffee, soup, and a lunch to go.

ISKASHITAA REFUGEE NETWORK: MAKING FRIENDS, MAKING JAM

We were a collection of seventeen strangers—a mixture of Tucsonans and refugees from five countries—when we gathered in the Iskashitaa parking lot on a still-chilly morning. Shortly we would fan out to four homes where Iskashitaa had been invited to glean unwanted citrus. We ranged from those old enough to have gray hair to Pima Community College students.

At the first stop, we confronted a huge orange tree planted and tended for forty years by an elderly gentleman who took great pride in his small grove. The volunteers enthusiastically went after the ripe fruit with hooked pickers on sticks. The lower outer fruit came off easily, but then they began reaching for the oranges deeper inside the tree and those on the highest branches. Two refugees, Farshed from Iran and Xiukui from China, set up a friendly rivalry going after the most elusive specimens, while others carried away filled plastic bins. In just forty-five minutes of working together, the international and intergenerational group had become friends. Then it was back into the cars and on to the next house, the next trees.

Barbara Einsworth, who has worked in environmental science in both East and West Africa, founded Iskashitaa in 2003 as a way not only to help acclimate United Nations refugees who had been resettled in Tucson, but also to find a way to rescue and make use of some of the unharvested and

Iskashitaa has served refugees from thirty-two ethnic groups. Here women get together to make friends and make preserves from fruit they have gathered. (Steven Meckler)

unused fruit that goes to waste in Tucson. The first group Einsworth worked with was from Somalia. The warm camaraderie the women developed led to the name of the group. *Iskashitaa* means "working cooperatively together" in a Bantu language spoken in Somalia.

Each year 800 to 1,200 refugees from more than 20 countries are resettled in Tucson, all of them forced by conflict to start a new life in the United States. Many of them were farmers in their native land. They understand plants, and they also have heritage recipes for cooking and preserving desert foods, many of which grew in their homelands.

To reach out, Iskashitaa has flyers in Arabic, Kiswahili, Nepali, Tigrinya, and Spanish as well as English.

Einsworth says, "U.N. refugees are challenged to become part of the society. Working with our American volunteers, they get to practice their English, develop job skills, and begin to feel part of the community." It's not only work, it's a support network using the universal language of food. And it doesn't go just one way. The refugees teach the Americans new and delicious ways to cook familiar desert foods.

"When we work together, we are learning from the refugees how they use certain fruits and vegetables," Einsworth says. "One example is immature pumpkins and pumpkin leaves and shoots. They also have delicious and healthy ways to season food without lots of fat, salt, and sugar."

Each year the volunteers harvest a cumulative 100,000 pounds of vegetables and fruits including grapefruits, oranges, pomegranates, dates, mesquite pods, even desert berries—90 different food items—all of which would have been discarded without their attention. "And still, it's only the tip of the iceberg," Einsworth says.

For several years the refugees have helped Forever Yong Farm south of Tucson with their garlic harvest, pulling 2,500 pounds of garlic from the soil. After enjoying a farmer-style vegetarian buffet lunch, the volunteers each went home with 10 pounds of the fresh garlic for their own use.

In the fall of 2019, refugees and other volunteers drove up to Mt. Lemmon where at 8,000 feet they found two apple trees, one of which yielded 5,000 pounds of apples, the other more than 800 pounds. They even traveled north to harvest 5,000 pounds of dates from palms at a college campus in Tempe.

Frequently, as in the case of the dates and apples, there is more food harvested than the refugee gleaners can use themselves. The extra produce is donated to other refugee families, the Community Food Bank, schools, and soup kitchens. With so many Tucsonans suffering from food insecurity, the food always finds a welcome home.

Iskashitaa volunteers create a social event to clean dates. Some of the dates were processed into sweet-tart vinegar. (Bill Hatch)

Einsworth sees this as a double positive. "The work is an opportunity for refugees to give back to the people of Tucson while also providing for their families," she says. When there is adequate material to work with, the volunteers and refugees gather in the kitchen at Saint Francis in the Foothills Church to turn the fruit into products to sell. They make jams with exotic flavors you don't get at the grocery store, such as grapefruit-ginger marmalade, fruit powders, pickled garlic, and a delicious date vinegar, all of which they sell at farmers' markets and small events such as church fairs. Volunteers also got together in the professional kitchen at Mission Garden for a food preservation class during which they turned dates, apples, garlic, and pumpkins into a Harvest Chutney with almost exclusively locally harvested foods. On a winter day at the beginning of the citrus season, volunteers Trudy Duffy and Janet Griffitts were working in the church kitchen slicing rinds of Seville oranges to go into marmalade.

Duffy, who has been volunteering in both harvesting and cooking workshops, says her favorite part is the sharing. "When we work together the refugees learn to use the things that grow here in Tucson and we learn their ways of preparing food. We learned to make the date vinegar from a man from the Middle East."

Seville Orange Pound Cake

Every spring Tucson trees produce tons of Seville oranges. They are too bitter and sour to eat like navel or Valencia oranges, but they make wonderful marmalades and baked goods. Longtime Iskashitaa volunteer Janet Griffitts devised this recipe by modifying an existing recipe.

Cake
¾ cup butter
¾ cup sugar
3 large eggs
1 teaspoon almond or vanilla extract
5 tablespoons milk or buttermilk
Zest of 1 or 2 Seville oranges
¾ cup almond flour
¾ cup all-purpose flour
¾ teaspoon baking powder
¼ to ½ teaspoon salt

Syrup
½ cup orange juice
½ cup sugar

Preheat oven to 350 degrees Fahrenheit. Grease and flour 1 loaf pan, or a small bundt pan, or 2 or 3 smaller cake pans or, for ease of removal, first line with parchment paper and then grease and flour.

In a large bowl, cream butter and sugar, then add eggs and combine. Add the almond or vanilla extract, milk or buttermilk, and the orange zest and mix well.

In another bowl, mix together the almond flour and the all-purpose flour, the baking powder, and the salt. Add to the liquid ingredients and beat just until combined. If the batter seems too thick add a bit more water or milk or buttermilk a teaspoon at a time.

Transfer batter to prepared pans. Bake in preheated oven until a toothpick inserted in the middle comes out clean. One loaf pan takes about an hour; smaller pans will take less time.

While the loaves are baking, make the syrup. Extract the juice from the oranges you have zested to obtain ½ cup. Mix the ½ cup of sugar and ½ cup of Seville orange juice in a small saucepan. Bring to a simmer and cook for a minute or so until syrupy.

When the cake is done, place it in its pan on a rack, poke the top all over with a toothpick or skewer, and brush on the syrup. Then gently take it out of the pan and poke the sides and bottom, brush on syrup, and put back into the pan to let the syrup soak in at least overnight, in the fridge. Remove loaves, wrap, and return to fridge or freeze.

The smooth running of such a complex operation requires not only lots of labor, but also organization to make sure people are where they need to be and the perishable food that is harvested gets distributed and used. Einsworth has a small staff, but she also relies on local volunteers and interns. Volunteers come through volunteer sites such as United Way and Volunteer Match and from audiences who hear Einsworth's presentations to various civic groups.

College-age interns who are service minded—around twenty-five a year—come from all over the United States, some during summer break, some during other breaks during the year. They pay their own way and go home with lessons in sustainability, immigration issues, and compassion.

Interns are given substantial tasks—they help to weigh and distribute harvests, oversee making food products from fruits not consumed immediately, set up and oversee composting, and work on communication and community outreach. And everyone, from the newest intern to the executive director, are full-time fruit spies, looking for unharvested trees where fruit might be going to waste.

For many of the refugees, particularly the younger ones, the fruit harvesting is just an entrée to their new culture. They are on their way to becoming fully integrated Americans. In November 2018, some refugees gathered with local volunteers to celebrate Thanksgiving, an unfamiliar holiday for the newcomers. Four 20-year-old Somali women, all Pima Community College students, enjoyed paper plates of roast turkey, dressing, and mashed potatoes while sharing their dreams for the future. Fatima is planning a career in the dental field. Samay is studying to be a dietitian. Hima will become a registered nurse, and Haredo looks forward to making great discoveries in medical research.

They may not have time for fruit harvesting just now, but there are more refugees like these enterprising women arriving in Tucson every year. With a warm welcome from Iskashitaa, they will begin to make Tucson their home. Working throughout the year, in the chilly winter mornings and the very warm summer days, the refugees, volunteers, and interns glean not only foods but also a better idea of what it means to live in a community.

PRODUCE RESCUE ORGANIZATIONS:
ON THE TABLE, NOT IN THE LANDFILL

We line up in the Tucson High School parking lot on a sunny winter morning to pay our $12 fee and gather some empty boxes to collect our produce. The Borderlands volunteers have been here for hours unloading boxes of fruits and vegetables and setting up the distribution tables. As we push our boxes along the line, the volunteers tell us to take 12 Roma tomatoes, 3 boxes of cherry tomatoes, 15 zucchini, 4 yellow squash, 9 green peppers, 8 oranges, 3 honeydews, and 2 watermelons.

We end up with two heaping boxes plus the watermelons. It's more than a small family can use, but the idea is to share what you can't use with your neighbors.

This is one week's rescued produce during the fall-winter season in the Borderlands warehouse in Nogales. There are two other produce rescue warehouses in Nogales, Arizona, where food crosses the border from Mexico. The produce will be distributed through nonprofit agencies, then the warehouses will fill up again. (Brian Schutmaat)

Why so much cheap produce? That's because in the deep of winter when snow and ice cover gardens in Minnesota and Illinois, Americans still want fresh vegetables. Mexican farmers in warmer spots are happy to do the growing and they are very productive. Much of that produce—worth $4 billion a year—comes through the border at Nogales, just 60 miles south of Tucson. It goes into huge refrigerated warehouses before it is loaded into tractor-trailers headed for parts east.

Alas, some of those zucchinis and tomatoes and oranges don't make the trip east. They are perfectly nutritious, but they have a little spot, they are oddly shaped, or there are just too many of them. They can't languish because there is another load coming the next day that needs the room. For too many years, they were dumped to rot in the Nogales, Arizona, landfill. When the total reached 30 million pounds a year, it became unsustainable.

Finally, a couple of creative-thinking Nogales residents realized that all that food could feed many hungry Arizonans and two organizations were formed to distribute the food rather than sending it to the dump. Neither organization requires signing up or certification. Show up with the nominal fee and you can go home with armloads of whatever is on offer that week.

Yolanda Soto was involved with the Borderlands Food Bank in Nogales in the early 1990s. They gave out the traditional boxes of nonperishable food. Then in 1994, Soto realized that the macaroni and peanut butter could be augmented by fresh vegetables for little cost. The big distributors were happy to work with her; she saved them $40 plus gas every time they had to go to the landfill.

She calls the program P.O.W.W.O.W. (Produce On Wheels Without Waste).

Now Borderlands has two 13,000-square-foot warehouses to accept the unwanted vegetables. The warehouse is open on Mondays for organizations to pick up produce for their clients. Tuesdays through Fridays, Nogales residents may come by the warehouse for a load of vegetables. Soto also has a network of food banks in 23 states throughout the country that she notifies by email when she has produce that is fresh enough to withstand a road trip. They can send a truck to pick it up and pay a fee.

Produce at the peak of ripeness that needs to be consumed or processed quickly is sent to volunteer-run, pop-up open-air markets held Saturday mornings in parking lots and churchyards in Tucson, greater Phoenix, Chandler, and Casa Grande. Vegetables that are over the hill for human consumption are usually fine for animals and are offered to local farmers for feed or go to the Compost Cats at their facility at San Xavier Co-op Farm.

Soto estimates that as of 2020, Borderlands has been responsible for distributing 600 million pounds of 39 varieties of fruits and vegetables.

The Market on the Move wing of the 3000 Club shares the same goal. When the Nogales Food Bank lost a major donor in 2008, Nogales resident Lon Taylor figured if just 3,000 people gave just $100 each, they could cover the budget. Eventually the Community Food Bank of Southern Arizona took over the Nogales Food Bank, but the process had been started and the depth of the need only grew.

With an abundance of produce to be rescued, Market on the Move has expanded beyond Nogales to 50 distribution sites in Tucson, greater Phoenix, and Northern Arizona. The 3000 Club maintains permanent centers in both Tucson and Phoenix as well as pop-up locations in church parking lots. Tucsonans can pick up produce on Wednesdays and Saturdays but it's always wise to check the website.

Today both the Borderlands and Market on the Move organizations are independent of the Nogales Food Bank and operate under their own 501(c)(3) nonprofit designation.

EPILOGUE
IN THE CORONAVIRUS CRISIS

HOW TUCSON UNITED TO FEED THE CITY

I BEGAN WORKING ON THIS BOOK in 2016, shortly after Tucson gained the designation of a UNESCO City of Gastronomy. Since then, the book project has been funded, researched, written, edited, and photographed, and it was nearly complete in early 2020 when the deadly coronavirus reached the city. Restaurants began shutting down in March.

The response to COVID-19 from the food community in the country's first UNESCO City of Gastronomy became Tucson's biggest food story in the last hundred years. Oranges and grapefruits still ripened on trees, lettuce and chard and kale still flourished in the fields, but challenges abounded.

Suddenly the story wasn't about which chef could make the most original sauce from prickly pear juice or who could make the tastiest vegetarian enchiladas with local squash. Instead, it was about how Tucson was going to provide school lunches for children when there was no school, especially when the parents of those kids had lost their jobs. How were restaurant owners going to feed customers who couldn't come inside? How would they keep even a few employees on the payroll? And how were farmers going to sell all the crops that continued growing despite the pandemic, especially with restaurant sales way off?

Tucson stepped up. With ingenuity, love of community, and selflessness, Tucsonans cooperated to feed as many people as possible and to keep the heart of the restaurant business afloat until life returned to normal.

School districts made use of experience providing meals to at-home kids through summer breakfast and lunch programs. Those plans often involved delivering the meals to the children on school buses making their rounds and meeting children at the usual stops. In some rural areas, families were notified where the buses would be parked. Rules for who could get meals were relaxed. In most cases children didn't need to be enrolled in the free or reduced lunch program, and they didn't even need to go to a school in that district. If kids were hungry, they got a lunch, and often a breakfast for the next day.

The small farms that serve Tucson had to find a way to get their produce to customers. You might keep a carrot in the ground for an extra week, but when broccoli is ready it needs to be picked. The Community Food Bank of Southern Arizona helped by buying local produce for distribution. The Food Bank purchased food from the small farmers who sold at the Santa Cruz Farmers' Market and packaged it for drive-up sale, cutting down on close-contact interactions.

Merchant's Garden hydroponic frames typically produce fresh salad for restaurants and 500 pounds of lettuce each week for TUSD schools. With their regular markets disrupted, they switched to providing fresh mixed greens to the community in a drive-up model.

It was a challenge for farmers usually consumed with thoughts of seeds, water, and harvest to switch gears to a new marketing model. Organizers at the Southern Arizona Young Farmers and Ranchers Coalition helped their members with setting up systems for payment, designing websites, packing, labeling, and shipping.

When Tucson shoppers couldn't find what they needed in grocery stores, local food producers stepped up. Erik Stanford of Pivot Produce revised his business model, which usually provides a link between local farms and restaurants. With his commercial accounts using less produce, he began delivering directly to homes. Kristine Jensen, no longer serving guests at her Café Botánica inside the closed Tucson Botanical Gardens, concentrated on her Gallery of Food catering business and added the provision of groceries, including local vegetables from Pivot Produce. Maynards Market, part of the Hotel Congress complex, expanded their market offerings to include meat, produce, dairy products, staples, and even pre-mixed cocktails for twice-weekly pickup. The custom butcher Ben Forbes offered home delivery of locally raised meats.

Some local farmers' markets continued operating, spacing the vendors several yards apart and cautioning customers to use social distancing. Fruits and vegetables, usually piled high in photogenic lushness, were now shrouded in plastic bags to keep them sanitary and protected from a wayward sneeze.

Restaurants switched to an all-carryout model, offering discounts and hoping customers would be willing to pick up a sack packed with their favorite entrees and serve themselves at home. The *Arizona Daily Star* ran a list of more than 500 local restaurants still cooking food. Among them was Doug Levy of Feast who redeployed some servers into a delivery team to send food from his midtown restaurant as far north as Saddlebrook and Dove Mountain, south to Green Valley, and as far east as Vail. The James Beard–honored chef Janos Wilder stayed open for several weeks, hustling around his Downtown Kitchen parking lot in Bermuda shorts and a face mask, carrying brown paper shopping bags packed with salads and entrees to customers who had ordered ahead. Each bag came with a thank-you card and free cookies.

Several restaurants stepped up to take care of their own—the many cooks and servers who were idled and lost wages due to the virus. Jo Schneider of the downtown restaurant La Cocina served out-of-work restaurant employees, while head chef Ian Rosales at Welcome Diner put out multiple servings of the daily staff meal for laid-off restaurant workers and anyone else who needed a meal.

The hope was that those who could pay would give a little more to help cover costs. Ben Forbes, the butcher, teamed up with Jeronimo Madril of Geronimo's Revenge every Monday in April to put together a carnitas meal for laid-off restaurant workers. Sammy's Mexican Grill in Catalina offered free meals to anyone who had lost their job.

And restaurant owners, along with everyone else in the city, expressed gratitude to Tucson's first responders—police, firefighters, and medical personnel. Many local restaurants offered 50 percent off to health-care workers and first responders, teachers, and musicians with canceled gigs. Carlotta and Ray Flores Jr., owners of Flores Concepts and several local restaurants, provided a month's worth of dinner kits to more than twenty local fire stations to supply the groceries they needed. Vina Vietnamese Street Food offered free meals to hospital personnel and the elderly. Every day, chefs and kitchen staff turned donations from their regular customers into free meals they delivered to hospital workers all over town.

Several mobile meal providers added clients who usually could care for themselves but because of their age had been advised to stay at home. Community members immediately volunteered to do the extra driving required to get the meals to those doorsteps. Those who needed food, got it.

Throughout town, neighbors checked on each other, shopped for each other, and dropped off cookies on doorsteps. For a while, hundreds of thousands of people became one big neighborhood.

Tucson's food community rose to the challenge, and when life gets back to normal, we can all celebrate with a prickly pear margarita and a big bowl of chips and salsa.

Carolyn Niethammer
May 21, 2020

INDEX

References to photographs and other illustrations are noted in italics.

Abundant Harvest Co-op, 96, *127*, 128
Adkisson, John, 149
aflatoxin B1, 19
agave, 7, 13–14, 27, *27*, 29–30, 45; Agave Heritage Festival, 91, 180; use in beer, 151–154, 180, *181*
agriculture, earliest, vii–viii; prehistoric use of irrigation, vii, 3, 24–25, 27, *28*, 31
Aguilar, Lindsay, 123
Ahil, Juanita, 13, 139
Anello, 132
Anza, Juan Bautista de, 39, 44
Aravaipa Creekside Growers, 111
Arizona-Sonora Desert Museum, 180, 182

Badilla, Gloria and Huémac, 146–147
Baja Arizona Brewers, 148
barrel cactus, 12–13, *12*; marmalade, 173, *173*
Barrio Bread, 5, 135–137, *137*, 155, 159
beans, common, 23, 27. *See also* tepary beans
bees. *See* honeybees
Benton, Dave, 114
beer brewers in Tucson, 147–155, *148, 152*
Big Skye Bakers, 142
Binghamton, 52

BKW Farms, 5, 150, 154, 156
Boca Tacos, 163–165
Borderlands (produce rescue), 201–203
Borderlands Brewing Company, 147–149, *148*
bread baking, with wild yeast, 137
Breckenfeld Family Growers, 100–102
Breckenfeld, Donald and Cristina, 100–102, *101*
Brinton, Chris, 114
Burgess, Martha A., xii, 11, 13, 139
Burkhart, Ford, 147
burros, 160
Buseck, Paul, 94–96
butchering: prehistoric, 116; Spanish style, 157; University of Arizona meat lab, 117
Button Brew House, 153
Button, Ramona and Terry, 37
Button, Todd and Erika, 153
Button, Velvet, 158

Café Botanica, 174–176, *175*
Camp Lowell, 51
Carbajal, Maria, 163
Caridad Community Kitchen, 5, 188–192, *190–191*
Carlson, Nick, 174

carne seca, 161–162, *161*
Carr, Barbara, 140
Carrillo, Leopoldo, 59
Casa Maria Soup Kitchen, 108, 195–197, *196*
Catalina Brewing Company, 151–158, *152*
Cheri's Desert Harvest, 5, 136, *138*, 148–149
chile, 5, 11, 160
Chilttepica fresh salsa, 146–147
chimichangas, 160–161, *160*
Chinese presence, farmers, 50–51, 59–62; grocery stores, 58–60, 63; restaurants, 58.
cholla buds, 8, *9*, 106
Chona, Maria, 8
Community Food Bank of Southern Arizona, ix, 5, 68, 185–188, *186*; assistance to farmers, 121–123, farmers' markets run by, 126–127, *127*; gardening workshops, 68; Las Milpitas 68–71, *70*
Community Gardens of Tucson, 64–67
community meal, 5, 192, 194
Community Supported Agriculture (CSA), 94–95, 110
Conger, Alan, 154–155
Connelly, Rita, 161
Contreras, Daniel, 166

Corbett Brewery, 151

corn: early cultivation, 23–24, 26; and
    rise in violence, 26

Cowan, Dena, 84

criollo cattle, 43, 117, *118*, 120

culinary programs: Caridad Community
    Kitchen, 188–192; Pima Community
    College, 4

Cummings, Scott, 151

Cutler, Felicia Ann, 108

Desert Archaeology, 25–27, 62, 85–86

Desert Forager, 141

Desert Harvesters, 19–20

Desert Tortoise Botanicals, 141

Desert Treasures, 102–103

Diehly, Michael, 31

Dorazo, Adela, 146

Double Check Ranch, 120

Dragoon Brewing Company, 153–154

Dreamflower Garden, 96, *97*, 131

E&R Pork, 5, 120, 156

Eat Mesquite and More, 19

Einsworth, Barbara, 197–199

El Charro Café, 157, 161, *161*

El Fuerte, 51

El Güerro Canelo, 166–167

EXO Roast Company, 172–174

Farmers' Markets, 124–130; who shops
    at, 125–126.

Farm to Institution Value Chain Initia-
    tive, 121

Farm to School Program, 106, 110, 123

Felger, Richard, 18

Felicia's Farm, 108, *109*, 197

Ferguson, Reverend George W., 103

Ferin, Clara, 60–61

festivals, beer, 183

festivals, food: Agave Heritage, 180; Ar-
    izona Farm and Food, 182; Carnival,
    181; Greek, 181; Ha:san Bak Saguaro,
    182; Heritage Food and Wine, 182;
    Mexican Food, 181; Salsa, Tequila,
    & Taco Challenge, 181; San Ysidro,

182; Sonoran Harvest: Taste the
    Desert, 182; Southern Arizona Food
    and Wine, 181; Tamal and Heritage,
    182–183; Tucson, 23; Tucson Meet
    Yourself, 179

Fish, Paul, 28, 30

Fish, Suzanne, 27

Flor de Mayo Arts, 139–140

Flores, Carlotta, 157, 164

food manufacturing businesses, in Tuc-
    son, viii–ix; artisan food producers,
    135–147

foodshed, Tucson, viii, x, 13, 110, 132

food, traditional Sonoran: burros, 160–
    161; carne seca, 161, *161*; chimichangas,
    160–161, *160*; frybread, 169; raspados,
    166, *166*; Sonoran bakery goods, *168*;
    Sonoran flat enchiladas, 164–165, *164*;
    Sonoran hot dog, 166–167, *167*; soups,
    37, 87, 105, 139; 165; tacos, 163–164,
    163; tamales, 162–163, *162*, 182–183, *183*;
    wheat flour tortillas, 158, *158*

Forbes, Ben, 119

Forever Yong Farm, 110

Fourier-Montes, Sofia, 108

Fort Lowell Park, 7, 38; Hardy archaeo-
    logical site, 7; military reservation, 51

Friends of Tucson's Birthplace, 52, 86.
    See also Mission Garden

frybread, 169

Gadsden Purchase, 49, 51, 90, 157

García, Jesús, 88–89, 180, *180*

Garcia, Samuel, *117*

gardening, by refugees, 67–68; Com-
    munity Food Bank, 68–71, *70*; Com-
    munity Gardens of Tucson, 64–67,
    66; Las Milpitas, 68–70, *70*; Pima
    County Library seed library, 76–78,
    77; school gardens, 71–74, *72*, *73*;
    Tucson Village Farm, 74–76, *74*, *75*

gastronomy, definition, viii

gastrotourism, x

Geronimo's Revenge, 171, *171*

Girod, Scott, 132

Greene, Eric, 153

Griffith, Jim, 158, 165

Guerra, Don, 5, 135, 137, 159

Guerrero, Lalo, 159

hackberries, 13

Hall, Jennifer, 66

ha:l squash, 106

Hamilton Distillers, 155–156, *155–156*

Harvey, Ken, 177–178

Haury, Emil, 30

Hayden Flour Mills, 54, 56, 120

Helfer, Dana, 94–96, 128

Hernandez, Justine, 76, *76*

High Energy Agriculture, 103–104, *130*

Hodgson, Wendy, 13

Hohokam, 27–31, 51, 85

Honeybee Village, 38

Hood, W. D., 36–37

Hought, Joy, 54, 57

International Rescue Committee, 67–69

Iron John's Brewing Company, 149–150

irrigation canals: Chinese use of, 50, 60;
    Las Milpitas, 68–71; prehistoric use
    of, vii, 3, 24–25, 27, *28*, 31, 39, 85, 104;
    Presidio era, 46, 49

Iskashitaa Refugee Network, 197–201,
    198, *199*

Islas, Elda, 165

Islas, Filiberto, 157

Jefferson, Kyle, 150

Jensen, Kristine, 174–176, *175*

Johnson, Cassidy, 148

Julian Wash Archaeological Park, 38

Kapahi, Ayla, *148*

King, Monica, 115–116

Kino, Eusebio, 41, *42*; cattle introduc-
    tion, 116–118; foods introduced,
    41–44, 84

Kino Heritage Fruit Trees Project, 4, 88

Krause, Kegan, 93

La Cocina, 174

Lancaster, Brad, 19

Larry's Veggies, 106–107, *107*
Larsen, Pete, 102
Las Capas, 25, *25*
Las Milpitas, 68–70, *70*
Leon, Perfecto, 162–163
Life'Sweet Honey Farms, 114
Loew's Ventana Canyon Resort, 177–178
Loftfield, Ann, 103–104
Lorenzini, Jill, 20
Los Morteros Conservation Park, 39

Mabry, Jonathan, vii, 3, 23, 44
Madril, Jeronimo, 171, *171*
Madson, John, 30
Magrane, Eric, 21
Mallozzi, Michael, 148–149
Mano y Metate, 142–144, *143, 144*
Manuel, Molly, 17
Manzo Elementary School, 71–73, *71, 72*
Marana: archaeological sites in, 24, 30, 40; beehives in, 114; brewery in, 153; farms in 5, 57, 63, 99, 103, 106, *107,* 136, 156; freed slaves in, 90; Pima County-owned ranch, 121; Ritz-Carlton hotel, 178; summer meals for children, 193
Market on the Move, 203
Marston, Sally, 71
Maynards Market & Kitchen, 176–177, *177*
Mazon, Maria, 163–165
McDonald, Michael, 185, 187–188
McGoffin, Greg, 103
meat, 157; cattle raising 119–120; chickens, 108, 119; criollo cattle, 43–44, 46, 48, 118–119, *117;* eaten by Presidio residents, 48; hogs and pigs, 119–121; Hohokam, protein sources, 30; mammoths, 116; rabbits, 26, 30, 86, 116; sheep and lambs, 119. *See also* butchering
megafauna, 116
membrillo, 85
Merchant's Garden, 96–99, *98, 122*
mesquite, 11–12, 17–21, 45; in beer, 150, 153; poem about, 21; recipes, 20–21
Mexican bakery, 168

Miksicek, Charles, 30
Mirocha, Paul, 116
Mission Garden, 4, 84–91, *84, 88, 90*
Mission San Xavier del Bac, 17, 48, 84, 86; establishment by Father Eusebio Kino, 41, 43; Father Phillip Segesser at, 44–45
Monsoon Chocolate, 145, *145*
Moroney, Dennis and Deborah, 120
Morris, Susie, 76
Mount, David, 66
Mule Deer, 116

Nabhan, Gary Paul, 4, 81
Naranjo, Reuben, Jr., 158
Native Seeds/SEARCH, 80–83, *80, 81, 82,* 170; cooperation with other groups, 5, 78, 88; history of, 81; herbs in beer, 155; involvement with White Sonoran wheat, 57, 83; products distributed, 19, 33, 37, 65; products used by other manufacturers, 139, 143, 154
Navajo Churro sheep, *118,* 120
New Southwest cuisine, 170
1912 Brewing Company, 154–155
nopales, 11
Nuestra Tierra, 68

O'Conor, Lieutenant Colonel Hugo, 46
Olson, Rani, 71, 123
Omik, David, 19
Opuntia engelmannii, 12. *See also* prickly pear
Ortero, Mateo, 164
Ortiz, Elena, 69

Paleoindians, 7
palo verde trees, 11
Park, Larry, 106–107, *107*
Patterson, Noel, 115
Paul, Steven, 155–156
Peck, Linda, *80*
Perfecto's Mexican Restaurant, 162
Phaseolus acutifolius var. *latifolius. See* tepary beans
Pima Club Wheat, 55, 106, 141

Pima Community College, 4, 129, 197, 201
Pima County Food Alliance, 5
Pima County Public Library Seed Library, 64, 76–79, *77*
pit houses, 7, 24, 26; in Los Moteros, 39; in Mission Garden, 84–86; at Steam Pump Ranch, 129
Pivot Produce, 131–133, 151, 176
Poblano Hot Sauce, 146
Poco Loco Specialty Salsas, 146
poshol, 37, 105, *105*
posole de trigo, 87, *87,* 91, 182
Presidio de San Agustín de Tucson, economy of, 48–49, 90, 118; establishment of, 46–48; food served at, 46, 47, 49; Hohokam village beneath, 29; La Cocina restaurant in, 174.
prickly pear, 12; in beer, 148–149, 151, 153; how to prepare pads, 15, *15;* how to use fruits, 16; included in products, 140–141, 145
protein sources, early, 30
Pueblo Vida Brewing Company, 150–151
purslane, 12, 87, 172, 174

Quijada, Miguel and Maria, 99

rabbits, 26, 30, 86, 106, 116
Ramirez, Rusty, 172–174
Ramón, Ismael, 189, *190,* 192
Ramona Farms, 37, 57, 111, 150, 159, 175–177
ranches, owned by Pima County, 121
ranching, in Pima County, 118–119, 121
raspados, 166, *166*
Rattlebox Farm, 94–96, *128*
recipes: Best Garlic Dip, 101; Black-Eyed Peas and Pork Belly Stew, 175; Chinese-style Turkey Stuffing, 59; Cinnamon Mesquite Waffles, 21; Desert Dry Rub, 20; EXO Roast Barrel Cactus Marmalade, 173; Flakey Sonoran Pie Crust, 54; Honeybee Ice Cream, 115; How to Make Bread with Wild Yeast, 137; Mano y Metate Mole Dulce Brownies, 143;

recipes (*continued*)
    Membrillo, 85; Poshol, 37; Posole
    de Trigo, 87; Prickly Pear Pads,
    15; Prickly Pear Syrup, 16; Seville
    Orange Pound Cake, 200; Sonoran
    Flat Enchiladas, 165; Tabbouleh,
    97; Tepary beans, 34–35; Tom's
    Mix Bean Soup, 139; White Sonora
    Wheat-Berry Salad, 55
Reid, Gene, 103
Reid, Maurice, 102–103
Reichhardt, Karen, 81
Robins, Bodie, 142
Rockey, Emily, *90*
Rollie's Mexican Patio, 164
Romanoski, Cheri, 5, 136, 138, *138*
Rosales, Ian, 171
Rowe, Hank, 151–153, *152*

saguaro, *10*, 11–12
salsas, 145
San Agustín Mission, 84
San Xavier Co-op Farm, 3, 5, 104–106,
    140, 151
Santa Cruz River, vii, 3, 23; agricultural
    settlements near, 24–25, 29, 39, 41,
    46, 50, 84–86, 104; erosion of banks,
    50–51; farm fields bordering, *48*; Las
    Milpitas near, 69; Presidio uses of, 118
Schneider, Jo, 174
Schwemm, Amy Valdés, 142–144, *143*, *144*
Schwennesen, Paul, 120
Segesser, Philipp, 44–45
Sentinel Peak, vii, *28*, 56, 59, 84–85
Sexson, Cody, 151
Sheava, Jessica, 188
Shelton, Chaz, 98
Sheridan, Thomas, 48–49, 118
Slattery, John, 141
Sleeping Frog Farms, 110, *125*
Smith, Brian, 132, 176–177
Smith, Elizabeth, 66
SNAP benefits, 5, 69, 188, 194–195; at
    farmers' markets, 127
The Sonoran Desert: A Literary Field
    Guide, 21, 116

Sonoran Desert Conservation Plan, 118
Sonoran Harvest: Taste the Desert, 182
Sonoran hot dogs, 166–167, *166*
soups, 165; Casa Maria, 195–197, *196*;
    Poshol, 37; Posole de Trigo 87, *87*;
    tepary bean, 34; Tom's Mix Bean
    Soup, 139; Soup Patrol, 192
Southern Arizona Water Rights Settle-
    ment Act in 1982, 104
Southern Arizona Young Farmers and
    Ranchers Coalition (SAYFRC),
    93–94
Southwest Bee Supply, 113
SouthWinds Farm, 110
Squash Under the Bed, 78
Stanford, Erik, 5, 131–133, *132–133*. *See also*
    Pivot Produce
Steen, Bill, 159
summer lunch programs, 193
sunflowers, *81*
Swanson, Landon, 150

tacos, 163–164, *163*
tamales, 162–163, *162*, 183
Tang, Ester, 63
tepary beans, 27, 33–37, *33*, 177; how to
    cook, 34–35
Tersey, Lorien, 96–97, *97*, 131
There's No Tortillas, 159–160
Thiel, J. Homer, 26, 29, 36
Thompson-Avelino, Nathan, 156
Thompson, Moses, 71
Tohono O'odham: Allotment Act, 104;
    as cattle raisers, 43–44, *117*, 118–119;
    as farmers, 81, 86, 89, 104, contact
    with European missionaries, 41–45;
    contact with Presidio soldiers, 50,
    53–54, 56; descendants of Hohokam,
    31, 38; frybread, 169; Ha:san Bak
    Saguaro Festival, 182; use of tepary
    beans, 33–38; use of wild foods, 8,
    9, *10*, 11, 13, 17, 20, 45, 106, 141; wheat
    and wheat tortillas, 53–54, 56, 158–159
tortillas, 54, 58; Father Kino served, 44;
    in farmers' markets,124–30; wheat
    flour, 158–159, *158*, 161

Tucson Honey Company, 114
Tucson Unified School District
    (TUSD), 5, 121; Farm to School
    Program, 123
Tucson Village Farm, 6, 74–76
Tumamoc Hill, 30, 40

Underhill, Ruth, 8
University of Arizona, Community and
    School Garden Program 71–74;
    Campus Pantry, 195
UNESCO City of Gastronomy, viii–xi, 3
UNESCO Creative Cities Network, viii
U'Ren, Jana, 153
Urquides, Maria, 61

Valenzuela, Phyllis, 106
Velvet Mesquite: Prosopis velutina, 21
verdolaga. *See* purslane
Vista del Río Cultural Resource Park, 40

Warner's Mill, 56
We B' Jammin Farm, 140
Welcome Diner, 171
wheat. *See* White Sonoran heritage wheat
Whiskey del Bac, 5, 155–156, *155*, *156*
White, Monica, 113
White Sonoran heritage wheat: growers,
    111, 136, 141; introduction by Spanish,
    53–57; at Mission Garden, 84, *84*; in
    tortillas, 159; use by breweries, 5, 148,
    150, 154–155
Wild Child Garden, 94, 99–100, *99*
wild foods: annual cycle of, 7–13; barrel
    cactus, 12–13, *12*; cholla buds, 8, *9*;
    Emory acorns, 13; greens, 8, 12; mes-
    quite, 11,13; palo verde, 11; purslane,
    12; saguaro, *10*, 11, yucca, 13. *See also*
    entries for individual plants
Wilder, Janos, 170
Wong, Ron, 57, 156

Yucca baccata, 13

Zepeda, Ofelia, 78
Zimmerman, Jeff, 56

ABOUT THE AUTHOR

Carolyn Niethammer received her MA in 1980 at the University of Arizona in journalism and history. She learned to love and understand the West growing up in small-town Northern Arizona, and has spent her life writing about the foods and people of the Southwest in award-winning ethnobotanies, cookbooks, and biographies. This is her eleventh book. Some of her publications on local cuisines are *American Indian Cooking: Recipes from the Southwest* (University of Nebraska Press, 1999), *Tumbleweed Gourmet* (University of Arizona Press, 1987), *The Prickly Pear Cookbook* (Rio Nuevo Press, 2004), *The New Southwest Cookbook* (Rio Nuevo Press, 2005), and *Cooking the Wild Southwest: Delicious Recipes for Desert Plants* (University of Arizona Press, 2011).

Niethammer leads Tucson gastronomy tours covering everything from edible wild plants to the latest farm-to-table restaurant offerings with heritage ingredients.

Visit her website at www.cniethammer.com.

The Southwest Center Series

Joseph C. Wilder, Editor

Ignaz Pfefferkorn, *Sonora: A Description of the Province*

Carl Lumholtz, *New Trails in Mexico*

Buford Pickens, *The Missions of Northern Sonora: A 1935 Field Documentation*

Gary Paul Nabhan, editor, *Counting Sheep: Twenty Ways of Seeing Desert Bighorn*

Eileen Oktavec, *Answered Prayers: Miracles and Milagros Along the Border*

Curtis M. Hinsley and David R. Wilcox, editors, *Frank Hamilton Cushing and the Hemenway Southwestern Archaeological Expedition, 1886–1889*, volume 1: *The Southwest in the American Imagination: The Writings of Sylvester Baxter, 1881–1899*

Lawrence J. Taylor and Maeve Hickey, *The Road to Mexico*

Donna J. Guy and Thomas E. Sheridan, editors, *Contested Ground: Comparative Frontiers on the Northern and Southern Edges of the Spanish Empire*

Julian D. Hayden, *The Sierra Pinacate*

Paul S. Martin, David Yetman, Mark Fishbein, Phil Jenkins, Thomas R. Van Devender, and Rebecca K. Wilson, editors, *Gentry's Rio Mayo Plants: The Tropical Deciduous Forest and Environs of Northwest Mexico*

W. J. McGee, *Trails to Tiburón: The 1894 and 1895 Field Diaries of W J McGee*, transcribed by Hazel McFeely Fontana, annotated and with an introduction by Bernard L. Fontana

Richard Stephen Felger, *Flora of the Gran Desierto and Río Colorado of Northwestern Mexico*

Donald Bahr, editor, *O'odham Creation and Related Events: As Told to Ruth Benedict in 1927 in Prose, Oratory, and Song by the Pimas William Blackwater, Thomas Vanyiko, Clara Ahiel, William Stevens, Oliver Wellington, and Kisto*

Dan L. Fischer, *Early Southwest Ornithologists, 1528–1900*

Thomas Bowen, editor, *Backcountry Pilot: Flying Adventures with Ike Russell*

Federico José María Ronstadt, *Borderman: Memoirs of Federico José María Ronstadt*, edited by Edward F. Ronstadt

Curtis M. Hinsley and David R. Wilcox, editors, *Frank Hamilton Cushing and the Hemenway Southwestern Archaeological Expedition, 1886–1889*, volume 2: *The Lost Itinerary of Frank Hamilton Cushing*

Neil Goodwin, *Like a Brother: Grenville Goodwin's Apache Years, 1928–1939*

Katherine G. Morrissey and Kirsten Jensen, editors, *Picturing Arizona: The Photographic Record of the 1930s*

Bill Broyles and Michael Berman, *Sunshot: Peril and Wonder in the Gran Desierto*

David W. Lazaroff, Philip C. Rosen, and Charles H. Lowe, Jr., *Amphibians, Reptiles, and Their Habitats at Sabino Canyon*

David Yetman, *The Organ Pipe Cactus*

Gloria Fraser Giffords, *Sanctuaries of Earth, Stone, and Light: The Churches of Northern New Spain, 1530–1821*

David Yetman, *The Great Cacti: Ethnobotany and Biogeography*

John Messina, *Álamos, Sonora: Architecture and Urbanism in the Dry Tropics*

Laura L. Cummings, *Pachucas and Pachucos in Tucson: Situated Border Lives*

Bernard L. Fontana and Edward McCain, *A Gift of Angels: The Art of Mission San Xavier del Bac*

David A. Yetman, *The Ópatas: In Search of a Sonoran People*

Julian D. Hayden, *Field Man: The Life of a Desert Archaeologist*, edited by Bill Broyles and Diane Boyer

Bill Broyles, Gayle Harrison Hartmann, Thomas E. Sheridan, Gary Paul Nabhan, and Mary Charlotte Thurtle, *Last Water on the Devil's Highway: A Cultural and Natural History of Tinajas Altas*

Thomas E. Sheridan, *Arizona: A History, Revised Edition*

Richard S. Felger and Benjamin Theodore Wilder, *Plant Life of a Desert Archipelago: Flora of the Sonoran Islands in the Gulf of California*

David Burkhalter, *Baja California Missions: In the Footsteps of the Padres*

Guillermo Núñez Noriega, *Just Between Us: An Ethnography of Male Identity and Intimacy in Rural Communities of Northern Mexico*

Cathy Moser Marlett, *Shells on a Desert Shore: Mollusks in the Seri World*

Rebecca A. Carte, *Capturing the Landscapes of New Spain: Baltasar Obregón and the 1564 Ibarra Expedition*

Gary Paul Nabhan, editor, *Ethnobiology for the Future: Linking Cultural and Ecological Diversity*

James S. Griffith, *Saints, Statues, and Stories: A Folklorist Looks at the Religious Art of Sonora*

David Yetman, Alberto Búrquez, Kevin Hultine, and Michael Sanderson, with Frank S. Crosswhite, *The Saguaro Cactus: A Natural History*

Gary Paul Nabhan, editor, *The Nature of Desert Nature*

Carolyn Niethammer, *A Desert Feast: Celebrating Tucson's Culinary Heritage*

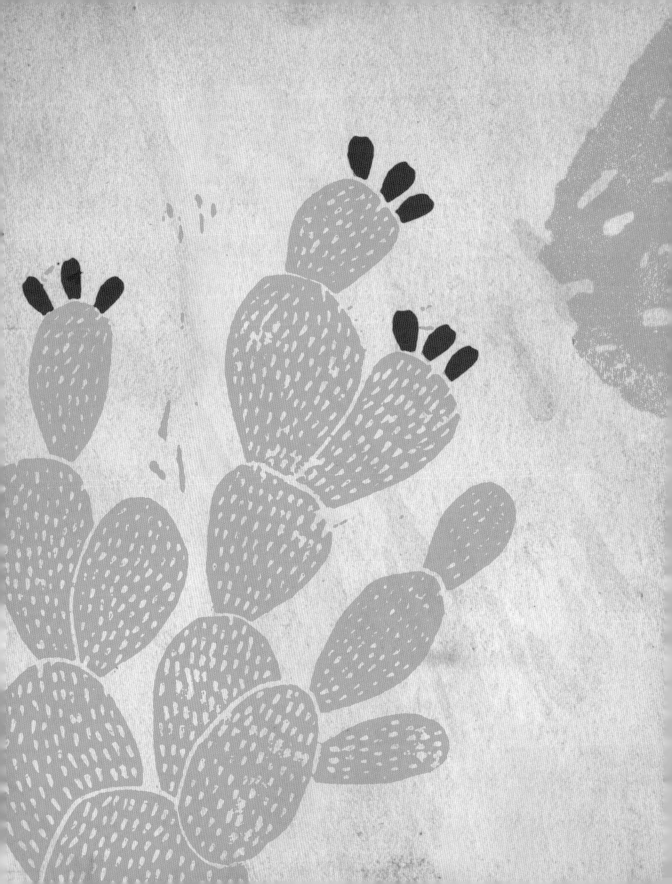

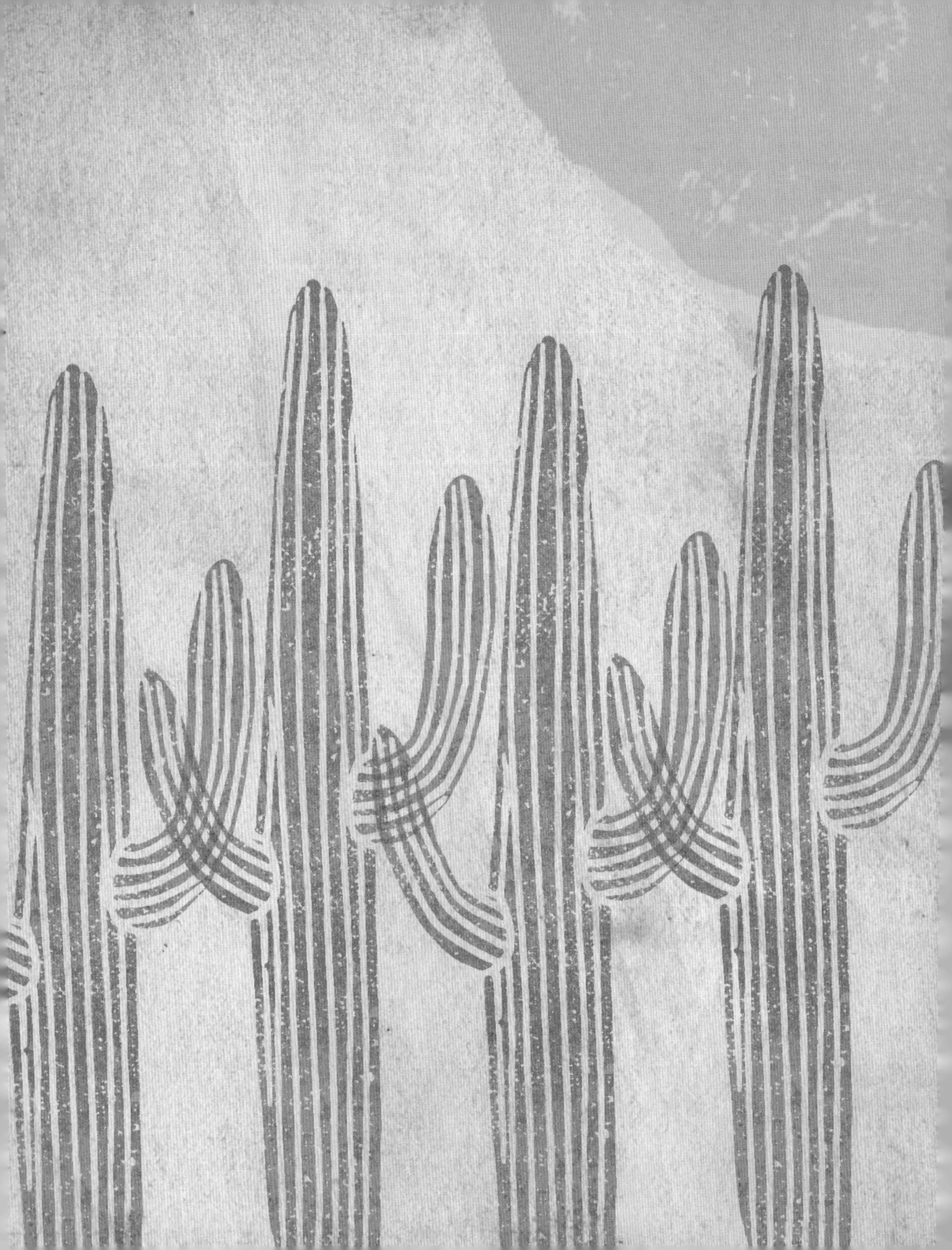

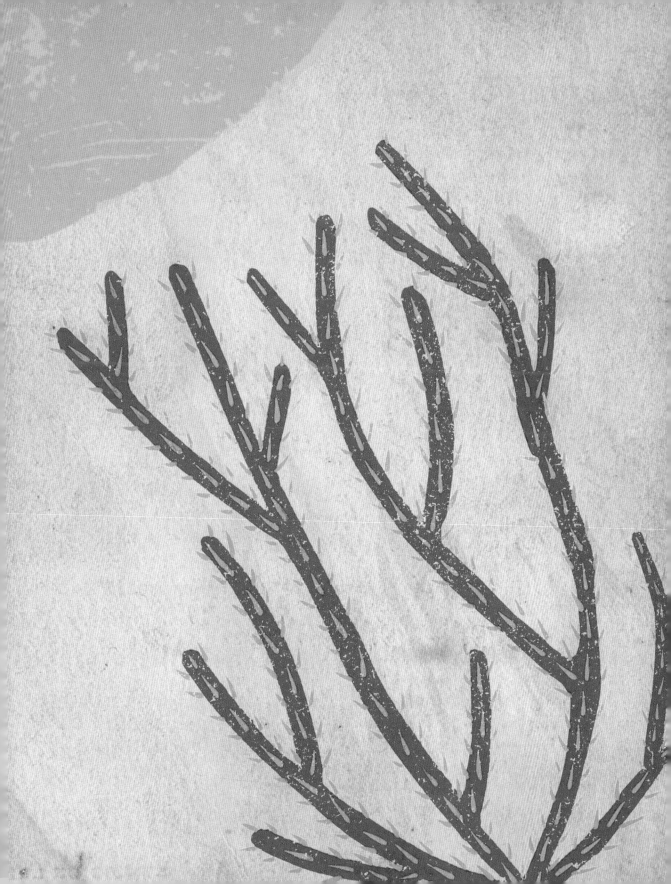